土建类高职高专创新型规划教材

建筑英语口语
Oral English of Architecture

主 编 张成国

副主编 张珂峰 冒 端

参 编 （以拼音为序）

蔡晶晶 郭峰池 韩恩娟
刘良林 唐艳芝 夏正兵
徐一欣 袁 方 张 文

东南大学出版社
·南京·

内 容 提 要

《建筑英语口语》一书遵循"实用为主,够用为度,以应用为目的"的指导原则,采用基于工作过程模块化的内容体系,涉及建筑专业和课程、建筑求职面试、建筑相关职业、建筑施工企业、建筑物类型、建筑材料等共 20 个模块。

本书可作为各类成教、大专、高职、中专的建筑类相关专业的英语口语教材使用,也可供涉外建筑施工和管理人员、从事建筑出国劳务、工程承包的各类人员自学使用。

图书在版编目(CIP)数据

建筑英语口语 / 张成国主编. —南京:东南大学出版社,2013.1(2021.3 重印)
土建类高职高专创新型规划教材
ISBN 978-7-5641-4062-5

Ⅰ.①建… Ⅱ.①张… Ⅲ.①建筑—英语—口语 Ⅳ.①H319.9

中国版本图书馆 CIP 数据核字(2012)第 318793 号

建筑英语口语

主　　编：	张成国
出版发行：	东南大学出版社
社　　址：	南京市四牌楼 2 号　邮编：210096
出 版 人：	江建中
责任编辑：	史建农　戴坚敏
网　　址：	http://www.seupress.com
电子邮箱：	press@seupress.com
经　　销：	全国各地新华书店
印　　刷：	苏州市古得堡数码印刷有限公司
开　　本：	787mm×1092mm　1/16
印　　张：	15.75
字　　数：	383 千字
版　　次：	2013 年 1 月第 1 版
印　　次：	2021 年 3 月第 5 次印刷
书　　号：	ISBN 978-7-5641-4062-5
印　　数：	7 001～7 800 册
定　　价：	35.00 元

本社图书若有印装质量问题,请直接与营销部联系。电话:025-83791830

高职高专土建系列规划教材编审委员会

顾　问	陈万年
主　任	成　虎
副主任	（以拼音为序）
	方达宪　胡朝斌　庞金昌　史建农
	汤　鸿　杨建华　余培明　张珂峰
秘书长	戴坚敏
委　员	（以拼音为序）
	党玲博　董丽君　付立彬　顾玉萍
	李红霞　李　芸　刘　颖　马　贻
	漆玲玲　王凤波　王宏俊　王　辉
	吴冰琪　吴龙生　吴志红　夏正兵
	项　林　徐士云　徐玉芬　于　丽
	张成国　张小娜　张晓岩　朱祥亮
	朱学佳　左　杰

序

　　东南大学出版社以国家 2010 年要制定、颁布和启动实施教育规划纲要为契机,联合国内部分高职高专院校于 2009 年 5 月在东南大学召开了高职高专土建类系列规划教材编写会议,并推荐产生教材编写委员会成员。会上,大家达成共识,认为高职高专教育最核心的使命是提高人才培养质量,而提高人才培养质量要从教师的质量和教材的质量两个角度着手。在教材建设上,大会认为高职高专的教材要与实际相结合,要把实践做好,把握好过程,不能通用性太强,专业性不够;要对人才的培养有清晰的认识;要弄清高职院校服务经济社会发展的特色类型与标准。这是我们这次会议讨论教材建设的逻辑起点。同时,对于高职高专院校而言,教材建设的目标定位就是要凸显技能,摒弃纯理论化,使高职高专培养的学生更加符合社会的需要。紧接着在 10 月份,编写委员会召开第二次会议,并规划出第一套突出实践性和技能性的实用型优质教材,在这次会议上大家对要编写的高职高专教材的要求达成了如下共识:

一、教材编写应突出"高职、高专"特色

　　高职高专培养的学生是应用型人才,因而教材的编写一定要注重培养学生的实践能力,对基础理论贯彻"实用为主,必需和够用为度"的教学原则,对基本知识采用广而不深、点到为止的教学方法,将基本技能贯穿教学的始终。在教材的编写中,文字叙述要力求简明扼要、通俗易懂,形式和文字等方面要符合高职教育教和学的需要。要针对高职高专学生抽象思维能力弱的特点,突出表现形式上的直观性和多样性,做到图文并茂,以激发学生的学习兴趣。

二、教材应具有前瞻性

　　教材中要以介绍成熟稳定的、在实践中广泛应用的技术和以国家标准为主,同时介绍新技术、新设备,并适当介绍科技发展的趋势,使学生能够适应未来技术进步的需要。要经常与对口企业保持联系,了解生产一线的第一手资料,随时更新教材中已经过时的内容,增加市场迫切需求的新知识,使学生在毕业时能够适合企业的要求。坚决防止出现脱离实际和知识陈旧的问题。在内容安排上,要考虑高职教育的特点。理论的阐述要限于学生掌握技能的需要,不要囿于理论上的推导,要运用形象化的语言使抽象的理论易于为学生认识和掌握。对于实践性内容,要突出操作步骤,要满足学生自学和参考的需要。在内容的选择上,要注意反映生产与社会实践中的实际问题,做到有前瞻性、针对性和科学性。

三、理论讲解要简单实用

　　将理论讲解简单化,注重讲解理论的来源、出处以及用处,以最通俗的语言告诉学生所学的理论从哪里来用到哪里去,而不是采用繁琐的推导。参与教材编写的人员都具有丰富的课堂教学经验和一定的现场实践经验,能够开展广泛的社会调查,能够做到理论联系实

际,并且强化案例教学。

四、教材重视实践与职业挂钩

教材的编写紧密结合职业要求,且站在专业的最前沿,紧密地与生产实际相连,与相关专业的市场接轨,同时,渗透职业素质的培养。在内容上注意与专业理论课衔接和照应,把握两者之间的内在联系,突出各自的侧重点。学完理论课后,辅助一定的实习实训,训练学生实践技能,并且教材的编写内容与职业技能证书考试所要求的有关知识配套,与劳动部门颁发的技能鉴定标准衔接。这样,在学校通过课程教学的同时,可以通过职业技能考试拿到相应专业的技能证书,为就业做准备,使学生的课程学习与技能证书的获得紧密相连,相互融合,学习更具目的性。

在教材编写过程中,由于编著者的水平和知识局限,可能存在一些缺陷,恳请各位读者给予批评斧正,以便我们教材编写委员会重新审定,再版的时候进一步提升教材质量。

本套教材适用于高职高专院校土建类专业,以及各院校成人教育和网络教育,也可作为行业自学的系列教材及相关专业用书。

高职高专土建系列规划教材编审委员会
2010 年 1 月于南京

前　言

　　中国加入 WTO，北京奥运会和上海世博会的成功举办，标志着中国更加开放，与外部世界的联系更加密切。建筑业是我国最早走出去的行业之一，建筑市场不断地在向国外拓展，国外公司也不断进入国内建筑市场，国际监理公司也因国际项目等原因介入国内工程项目的管理。建筑市场国际化离我们已不遥远。然而，我们却面临着巨大挑战：一方面，国外建筑企业进入国内市场，带来全新的管理模式，需要我们去适应；另一方面，国内建筑企业要进入国际市场，需要熟悉国外的管理方法、施工规范，需要懂外语的专业技术人员，但语言却成了相互沟通的最大障碍。语言与专业知识脱节十分突出，懂语言的不懂工程，懂工程的不懂语言，严重制约了建筑业的对外发展。为此，作者根据几年来的教学和工程实践精心编写了《建筑英语口语》这本教材，以期能有效提高建筑专业学生的英语口语水平，解决涉外建筑从业人员的语言障碍，为推进中国建筑行业的国际化进程作出贡献。

　　作为高职高专土建专业系列教材之一，《建筑英语口语》一书的编写遵循"实用为主，够用为度，以应用为目的"的指导原则，采用基于工作过程模块化的内容体系。全书共 20 个模块，内容涉及建筑专业和课程、建筑求职面试、建筑相关职业、建筑施工企业、建筑物类型、建筑材料、建筑机械、建筑图纸、建筑招投标、建筑合同、建筑法规、建筑试验、建筑测量、施工计划、施工检查、建筑安装、建筑装饰、建筑造价、工程索赔、工程验收等。每个模块又包括学习目标、专业词汇、情景对话、注释、必学句型、练习和补充材料 7 个部分。为方便读者学习和查阅，书后附有练习答案、情景对话问题答案及中文译文、词汇表和参考文献。

　　本书可作为各类成教、大专、高职、中专的建筑类相关专业的英语口语教材使用，也可供涉外建筑施工和管理人员、从事建筑出国劳务、工程承包的各类人员自学使用。

　　限于作者的语言水平和专业知识，加之时间仓促，书中不足乃至错误之处在所难免，恳请读者不吝指正，作者在此预致谢意。

FOREWORD

Marked by events of the entry of WTO, the successful holding of Beijing Olympic Games and Shanghai World Expo, China is contacting with the outside world more closely. As one of the first industries in China to go abroad, the construction industry continually develops the overseas market. Meanwhile, more and more foreign companies have been entering the domestic construction market; the international supervision companies begin to intervene domestic project management for some international projects. The internationalization of the construction market is not far away from us. However, we are faced with great challenges: on the one hand, by accessing into China's market, the foreign construction enterprises will bring about some new management modes, to which we have to adapt; on the other hand, to enter into the international market, the domestic construction enterprises need to be familiar with internationalized management methods and construction norms, need professional and technical personnel with a good command of foreign languages. In either of the above cases, the language is the greatest obstacle to communicate with each other. The gap of language and professional knowledge is very outstanding. People, who speaks the foreign language well, cannot understand the engineering project; and people, who understands the engineering project well, cannot speak the foreign language. Therefore, based on years of teaching and engineering practices, we have carefully authored the textbook *Oral English of Architecture*, with the purpose of improving the spoken English of architectural students, solving the language barriers of the foreign construction practioners, and making contributions to the internalization of China's construction industry.

As one of the series of higher vocational textbooks for architectural majors, the book is compiled under the guidance of practicality, and the content system is modularized on the basis of construction process. The whole book consists of 20 modules, involving architectural majors and courses, architectural job interview, architectural workers, construction enterprises, kinds of buildings, building materials, building machinery, architectural drawings, construction tendering, construction contract, construction laws and regulations, construction testing, construction surveys, construction plan, construction inspection, building installation, building decoration, building cost, claims and acceptance of construction works. In each of these modules, there are seven parts, which are learning objectives, special terms, situational conversations, notes, useful sentences, exercises and supplementary materials. To further facilitate the readers, appendixes of key to the exercises, answers to questions of the situational conversations, the Chinese translation of the situational conversations, glossary and references are attached in the end of the book.

The book can be used not only as the oral English textbooks for architectural students of various types of secondary and higher vocational as well as adult schools or colleges, but also as the self-study materials for constructors and managerial personnel in construction enterprises involving foreignness.

Due to the limits of the authors' language level and professional knowledge, as well as the lack of enough time, inadequacies and even errors can hardly be avoided in this book. Therefore, it is hoped that the readers will kindly point out our errors, and here we the authors express our thanks in anticipation.

目 录

MODULE 1　Architectural Majors and Courses　模块一　建筑专业和课程 ·············· 1
　　Learning Objectives 学习目标 ··· 1
　　Special Terms 专业词汇 ·· 1
　　Situational Conversations 情景对话 ··· 2
　　Notes 注释 ·· 3
　　Useful Sentences 必学句型 ··· 4
　　Exercises 练习 ·· 4
　　Supplementary Materials 补充材料 ·· 6

MODULE 2　Architectural Job Interview　模块二　建筑求职面试 ····················· 10
　　Learning Objectives 学习目标 ··· 10
　　Special Terms 专业词汇 ··· 10
　　Situational Conversations 情景对话 ·· 11
　　Notes 注释 ··· 12
　　Useful Sentences 必学句型 ·· 13
　　Exercises 练习 ··· 13
　　Supplementary Materials 补充材料 ··· 15

MODULE 3　Architectural Workers　模块三　建筑工程人员 ··························· 21
　　Learning Objectives 学习目标 ··· 21
　　Special Terms 专业词汇 ··· 21
　　Situational Conversations 情景对话 ·· 22
　　Notes 注释 ··· 24
　　Useful Sentences 必学句型 ·· 24
　　Exercises 练习 ··· 25
　　Supplementary Materials 补充材料 ··· 26

MODULE 4　Construction Enterprises　模块四　建筑施工企业 ························ 27
　　Learning Objectives 学习目标 ··· 27
　　Special Terms 专业词汇 ··· 27
　　Situational Conversations 情景对话 ·· 28
　　Notes 注释 ··· 29
　　Useful Sentences 必学句型 ·· 30
　　Exercises 练习 ··· 30
　　Supplementary Materials 补充材料 ··· 32

MODULE 5　Kinds of Buildings　模块五　建筑物类型 ································· 33
　　Learning Objectives 学习目标 ··· 33
　　Special Terms 专业词汇 ··· 33
　　Situational Conversations 情景对话 ·· 34
　　Notes 注释 ··· 35

Useful Sentences 必学句型	36
Exercises 练习	36
Supplementary Materials 补充材料	38

MODULE 6 Building Materials 模块六 建筑材料 39

Learning Objectives 学习目标	39
Special Terms 专业词汇	39
Situational Conversations 情景对话	40
Notes 注释	41
Useful Sentences 必学句型	42
Exercises 练习	43
Supplementary Materials 补充材料	44

MODULE 7 Building Machinery 模块七 建筑机械 46

Learning Objectives 学习目标	46
Special Terms 专业词汇	46
Situational Conversations 情景对话	47
Notes 注释	48
Useful Sentences 必学句型	49
Exercises 练习	49
Supplementary Materials 补充材料	51

MODULE 8 Architectural Drawings 模块八 建筑图纸 53

Learning Objectives 学习目标	53
Special Terms 专业词汇	53
Situational Conversations 情景对话	54
Notes 注释	55
Useful Sentences 必学句型	56
Exercises 练习	57
Supplementary Materials 补充材料	58

MODULE 9 Construction Tendering 模块九 建筑招投标 61

Learning Objectives 学习目标	61
Special Terms 专业词汇	61
Situational Conversations 情景对话	62
Notes 注释	63
Useful Sentences 必学句型	64
Exercises 练习	64
Supplementary Materials 补充材料	66

MODULE 10 Construction Contract 模块十 建筑合同 69

Learning Objectives 学习目标	69
Special Terms 专业词汇	69
Situational Conversations 情景对话	70
Notes 注释	72
Useful Sentences 必学句型	72
Exercises 练习	73
Supplementary Materials 补充材料	74

MODULE 11　Construction Laws and Regulations　模块十一　建筑法律法规 …………… 93
- Learning Objectives 学习目标 …………………………………………………… 93
- Special Terms 专业词汇 …………………………………………………………… 93
- Situational Conversations 情景对话 ……………………………………………… 94
- Notes 注释 ………………………………………………………………………… 95
- Useful Sentences 必学句型 ……………………………………………………… 96
- Exercises 练习 …………………………………………………………………… 97
- Supplementary Materials 补充材料 ……………………………………………… 98

MODULE 12　Construction Testing　模块十二　建筑试验 ……………………… 108
- Learning Objectives 学习目标 …………………………………………………… 108
- Special Terms 专业词汇 …………………………………………………………… 108
- Situational Conversations 情景对话 ……………………………………………… 109
- Notes 注释 ………………………………………………………………………… 110
- Useful Sentences 必学句型 ……………………………………………………… 111
- Exercises 练习 …………………………………………………………………… 112
- Supplementary Materials 补充材料 ……………………………………………… 113

MODULE 13　Construction Surveying　模块十三　建筑测量 …………………… 115
- Learning Objectives 学习目标 …………………………………………………… 115
- Special Terms 专业词汇 …………………………………………………………… 115
- Situational Conversations 情景对话 ……………………………………………… 116
- Notes 注释 ………………………………………………………………………… 117
- Useful Sentences 必学句型 ……………………………………………………… 118
- Exercises 练习 …………………………………………………………………… 119
- Supplementary Materials 补充材料 ……………………………………………… 120

MODULE 14　Construction Plan　模块十四　施工计划 …………………………… 127
- Learning Objectives 学习目标 …………………………………………………… 127
- Special Terms 专业词汇 …………………………………………………………… 127
- Situational Conversations 情景对话 ……………………………………………… 128
- Notes 注释 ………………………………………………………………………… 129
- Useful Sentences 必学句型 ……………………………………………………… 130
- Exercises 练习 …………………………………………………………………… 130
- Supplementary Materials 补充材料 ……………………………………………… 133

MODULE 15　Construction Inspection　模块十五　施工检查 …………………… 134
- Learning Objectives 学习目标 …………………………………………………… 134
- Special Terms 专业词汇 …………………………………………………………… 134
- Situational Conversations 情景对话 ……………………………………………… 135
- Notes 注释 ………………………………………………………………………… 136
- Useful Sentences 必学句型 ……………………………………………………… 137
- Exercises 练习 …………………………………………………………………… 138
- Supplementary Materials 补充材料 ……………………………………………… 139

MODULE 16　Building Installation　模块十六　建筑安装 ………………………… 140
- Learning Objectives 学习目标 …………………………………………………… 140
- Special Terms 专业词汇 …………………………………………………………… 140

  Situational Conversations 情景对话 …………………………………………………… 141
  Notes 注释 ………………………………………………………………………… 142
  Useful Sentences 必学句型 ……………………………………………………… 143
  Exercises 练习 …………………………………………………………………… 143
  Supplementary Materials 补充材料 ……………………………………………… 145
MODULE 17 Building Decoration 模块十七 建筑装饰 ……………………… 150
  Learning Objectives 学习目标 …………………………………………………… 150
  Special Terms 专业词汇 ………………………………………………………… 150
  Situational Conversations 情景对话 …………………………………………… 151
  Notes 注释 ………………………………………………………………………… 152
  Useful Sentences 必学句型 ……………………………………………………… 153
  Exercises 练习 …………………………………………………………………… 153
  Supplementary Materials 补充材料 ……………………………………………… 155
MODULE 18 Building Cost 模块十八 建筑造价 ………………………………… 157
  Learning Objectives 学习目标 …………………………………………………… 157
  Special Terms 专业词汇 ………………………………………………………… 157
  Situational Conversations 情景对话 …………………………………………… 158
  Notes 注释 ………………………………………………………………………… 159
  Useful Sentences 必学句型 ……………………………………………………… 160
  Exercises 练习 …………………………………………………………………… 161
  Supplementary Materials 补充材料 ……………………………………………… 162
MODULE 19 Claims of Construction Works 模块十九 工程索赔 …………… 164
  Learning Objectives 学习目标 …………………………………………………… 164
  Special Terms 专业词汇 ………………………………………………………… 164
  Situational Conversations 情景对话 …………………………………………… 165
  Notes 注释 ………………………………………………………………………… 166
  Useful Sentences 必学句型 ……………………………………………………… 167
  Exercises 练习 …………………………………………………………………… 168
  Supplementary Materials 补充材料 ……………………………………………… 169
MODULE 20 Acceptance of Construction Works 模块二十 工程验收 ……… 170
  Learning Objectives 学习目标 …………………………………………………… 170
  Special Terms 专业词汇 ………………………………………………………… 170
  Situational Conversations 情景对话 …………………………………………… 171
  Notes 注释 ………………………………………………………………………… 172
  Useful Sentences 必学句型 ……………………………………………………… 173
  Exercises 练习 …………………………………………………………………… 173
  Supplementary Materials 补充材料 ……………………………………………… 175
APPENDIX Ⅰ Answers to Questions of SC 附录 1 情景对话问题答案 ……… 177
APPENDIX Ⅱ Key to the Exercises 附录 2 练习答案 ………………………… 182
APPENDIX Ⅲ Chinese Translation of SC 附录 3 情景对话中文译文 ………… 199
APPENDIX Ⅳ Glossary 附录 4 词汇表 ………………………………………… 215
APPENDIX Ⅴ References 附录 5 参考书目 …………………………………… 237

MODULE 1　Architectural Majors and Courses
模块一　建筑专业和课程

Learning Objectives 学习目标

In this module, learners should:
- know the Chinese and English names of architectural majors and courses.
- be capable of making simple English conversations on the topic of architectural major and courses.

在本模块内，学习者应该能：
- 了解建筑相关专业及主干课程的中英文名称。
- 就建筑专业和课程这一话题进行简单的英语会话。

Special Terms 专业词汇

architectural engineering　建筑工程
architectural design　建筑设计
basic architectural design　建筑设计基础
architectural mechanics　建筑力学
history of architecture　建筑史
structural lectotype　结构体系与选型
mechanics of materials　材料力学
building mechanics　建筑力学
building construction　建筑构造
surveying　测量学
engineering mathematics　工程数学
civil engineering　土木工程
engineering machinery　工程机械
construction technique　施工技术
construction organization　施工组织
electricalinstallation　电气安装
heating and ventilation　供暖与通风

architectural economics　建筑经济学
conspectus of architecture　建筑学概论
architectural graphing　建筑制图
theory of architectural design　建筑设计原理
architectural psychology　建筑心理学
structural mechanics　结构力学
engineering mechanics　工程力学
building physics　建筑物理
building structure　建筑结构
building equipment　建筑设备
engineering cost　工程造价
hydraulic engineering　水利工程
municipal engineering　市政工程
construction overview　施工概论
construction budget　施工预算
water supply and sewerage　给水排水
electrical engineering of architecture　建筑电工

building 和 architecture 是两个常见词汇。building 的解释是：Any human-made structure or the act of construction. 人们建造的任何结构或建造的行为。architecture 的解释是：The process and product of planning, designing and construction. 人们规划、设计与施工的过程和产物。分析两个词的区别，building 应该可以翻译为建筑物，而 architecture 可以称为建筑学。

Situational Conversations 情景对话

Helen: You're a student, aren't you?

Xiaoli: Yes, but how did you know?

Helen: I saw it from your words and appearance, as you look very polite and elegant with a pair of glasses.

Xiaoli: You've good eyesight to know what I do.

Helen: Is it so? Can you tell me what major you are studying?

Xiaoli: Civil and industrial architecture.

Helen: How do you think of your major?

Xiaoli: Wonderful, I think. I like it very much.

Helen: Why so, young man?

Xiaoli: As you know, all the buildings are set up by hard-working and bright builders from ancient times to the present. They are really great. So I'm determined to study architecture, and after graduation I am going to be a builder and to build up high buildings and large mansions with my own hands.

Helen: Your dream of building millions of apartments for the country and the people must be realized, young man. I know you enjoy your major, and I believe you must be a top student in your college, and hope you will be a builder of benefiting people.

Xiaoli: Thank you for your encouragement. I am sure to treasure the good chance and to study hard to realize my dream.

Helen: I'm glad to hear that. Can you tell me how many courses there are in your major?

Xiaoli: More than ten, I suppose. Construction materials, architecture of houses, construction technique, construction organizations and mechanics, etc., are required courses; while English and political economics, etc., belong to basic courses.

Helen: So many! How do the teachers teach you?

Xiaoli: They seriously clarify the book knowledge from the shallower to the deeper and from the easier to the more advanced, and explain profound theories in simple languages.

Helen: I think it is the so-called programmed instruction. By the way, what about the teaching facilities?

Xiaoli: Very good. The basic theoretical knowledge of architecture is taught mainly in the classroom, while the operational skills are trained and practised in the modernized architectural labs as well as on the cooperated construction worksites.

Helen: For vocational colleges, it is effective and practical to integrate theory with practice and to do practice geared to the needs of the job. Is your college large?

Xiaoli: Not very large.

Helen: Oh, I know. Would you please show me around your campus?

Xiaoli: It's my pleasure. This way, please!

Helen: Thank you very much.

Questions

1. What major is Xiaoli studying?
2. Why is Xiaoli determined to be a builder?

Notes 注释

1. "... as you look very polite and elegant with a pair of glasses". 因为你戴着一副眼镜，温文尔雅。此句中的 as 表原因。
2. Your dream of building millions of apartments for the country and the people must be realized. 你建成广厦千万栋、兴邦立国为人民的理想一定能实现。must 在此表推测，意为"准是"、"一定是"。注意：(1)通常只用于肯定句，在否定句或疑问句中用 can 代之。如：It must be true. 那一定是真的。Can it be true? 那可能是真的吗？It can't be true. 那不可能是真的。(2)表示对现在情况的推测后接动词原形，该动词通常为状态动词(如 be, have, know 等)，若为动作动词，通常要转换其他说法。

如：He must be wrong. 他一定错了。如要表示"他一定会赢"，通常不说 He must win，可说 He is sure to win。(3) 其后可接进行式或完成进行式，用以谈论一个正在进行的动作。如：He must be writing a letter to his girlfriend. 他一定在给他女朋友写信。(4) 后接完成式，用来谈论已发生的情况。如：He must have arrived already. 他一定已经到了。

3. "required courses"为必修课，"basic courses"为基础课。
4. "... from the shallower to the deeper and from the easier to the more advanced." 意思是"由浅入深，由易到难"。
5. "... it is the so-called programmed instruction." 意思是"这就是所谓的循序渐进教学"。
6. "... the operational skills are trained and practised in the modernized architectural labs as well as on the cooperated construction worksites." 操作技能在现代化的建筑实验室以及拥有合作关系的建筑工地得以训练和实践。
7. "... to integrate theory with practice..." 意思为"理论联系实际"。
8. "... to do practice geared to the needs of the job" 意思为"对口实习"，"be geared to" 意思是"适应……的需要；面向"。此处"geared to..."为过去分词短语作定语修饰"practice"。

Useful Sentences 必学句型

1. Can you tell me what major you are studying? 你能告诉我你现在学什么专业吗？
2. How do you think of/about your major? 你认为你的专业怎么样？
3. I am sure to treasure the good chance and to study hard to realize my dream. 我一定珍惜机会刻苦学习，以实现我的梦想。
4. I am glad to hear that. 我很高兴听到你这么说。
5. By the way, what about the teaching facilities? 顺便问一下，你们学校的教学设施怎样？
6. For vocational colleges, it is effective and practical to integrate theory with practice and to do practice geared to the needs of the job. 对于职业院校，理论联系实际和对口实习是有效和实用的。
7. Would you please show me around your campus? 你愿意带我参观一下你的校园吗？

Exercises 练习

1. **Complete the following dialogue in English.**

   (A：*a Chinese student majoring in engineering cost*；B：*an American visiting scholar*)

B: How do you do?
A: _____? （您好）
B: May I ask you some questions?
A: _____! （当然可以!）
B: What do you do?
A: _____. （我是这个学校的一名学生。）
B: Can you tell me what major you are studying?
A: _____. （工程造价专业。）
B: How do you think of this major?
A: _____. （前景广阔，我喜欢。）
B: How many courses are there in this major?
A: _____.
（十多门课程，他们主要是专业必修课和基础课。）
B: Which course do you like best? And why?
A: _____.
（建筑施工技术，因为老师讲课由浅入深，由易到难，并能理论联系实际。）
B: Thank you very much.
A: _____. （不客气。）

2. Read and interpret the following passage.

Mathematics

In the university, mathematics is heavily emphasized throughout the engineering curriculum. Today, it includes courses in statistics, which deals with gathering, classifying and using numerical data or pieces of information. An important aspect of statistical mathematics is probability, which deals with what may happen when there are different factors or variables that can change the results of a problem. Before the construction of a bridge is undertaken, for example, a statistical study is made of the amount of traffic the bridge will be expected to handle. In the design of the bridge, variables such as water pressure on the foundation, impact, the effects of different wind forces and many other factors must be considered.

3. Pair work.

Suppose you are a student studying the Engineering Cost（工程造价）in an university of architectural engineering. Try to introduce yourself to the others including your major, subjects and others.

Supplementary Materials 补充材料

A Comparison of Architectural Majors in Higher Vocational and General Undergraduate Colleges or Universities
（高职高专与普通本科土建类专业目录对照表）

高职高专(Higher Vocational)		普通本科(General Undergraduate)	
专业代码(CM)	专业名称(Name of Majors)	专业代码(CM)	专业名称(Name of Majors)
560000	**土建大类 (Civil Engineering)**	**080000**	**工学/管理学 (Engineering/ Management)**
560100	**建筑设计类 (Architectural Design)**	**080700**	**土建类 (Civil Engineering)**
560101	建筑设计技术 (Architectural Design Technology)	080701	建筑学 (Architecture)
560102	建筑装饰工程技术 (Architectural Decoration Engineering Technology)	080701	建筑学 (Architecture)
560103	中国古建筑工程技术 (Chinese Ancient Architectural Engineering Technology)	080701	建筑学 (Architecture)
560104	室内设计技术 (Interior Design Technology)	080708	景观建筑设计 (Landscape Architecture Design)
560105	环境艺术设计 (Environmental Art Design)	080708	景观建筑设计 (Landscape Architecture Design)
560106	园林工程技术 (Garden Engineering Technology)	080708	景观建筑设计 (Landscape Architecture Design)
560199	建筑设计类新专业 (New Majors of Architectural Design)	080799	土建类新专业 (New Majors of Civil Engineering)
560200	**城镇规划与管理类 (Town Planning and Management)**	**080700**	**土建类 (Civil Engineering)**
560201	城镇规划 (Town Planning)	080702	城市规划 (Urban Planning)
560202	城市管理与监察 (City Management and Supervision)	080702	城市规划 (Urban Planning)
560203	城镇建设 (Town Construction)	080702	城市规划 (Urban Planning)
560299	城镇规划与管理类新专业 (New Majors of TPM)	080799	土建类新专业 (New Majors of Civil Engineering)
560300	**土建施工类 (Civil Construction)**	**080700**	**土建类 (Civil Engineering)**
560301	建筑工程技术 (Building Construction Technology)	080703	土木工程 (Civil Engineering)

续表

高职高专(Higher Vocational)		普通本科(General Undergraduate)	
专业代码(CM)	专业名称(Name of Majors)	专业代码(CM)	专业名称(Name of Majors)
560302	地下工程与隧道工程技术(Underground and Tunnel Engineering Technology)	080703	土木工程(Civil Engineering)
560303	基础工程技术(Foundation Engineering Technology)	080703	土木工程(Civil Engineering)
560399	土建施工类新专业(New Majors of Civil Construction)	080799	土建类新专业(New Majors of Civil Engineering)
560400	**建筑设备类(Building Equipment)**	**080700**	**土建类(Civil Engineering)**
560401	建筑设备工程技术(Building Equipment Engineering Technology)	080704	建筑环境与设备工程(Architectural Environment and Equipment Engineering)
560402	供热通风与空调工程技术(Heating Ventilation and Air-conditioning Engineering Technology)	080704	建筑环境与设备工程(Architectural Environment and Equipment Engineering)
560403	建筑电气工程技术(Building Electrical Engineering Technology)	080704	建筑环境与设备工程(Architectural Environment and Equipment Engineering)
560404	楼宇智能化工程技术(Building Intellectualization Engineering Technology)	080704	建筑环境与设备工程(Architectural Environment and Equipment Engineering)
560405	工业设备安装工程技术(Industrial Equipment Installation Engineering Technology)	080704	建筑环境与设备工程(Architectural Environment and Equipment Engineering)
560406	供热通风与卫生工程技术(Heating Ventilation and Sanitary Engineering Technology)	080704	建筑环境与设备工程(Architectural Environment and Equipment Engineering)
560411	机电安装工程(Mechanical and Electrical Installation Engineering)	080704	建筑环境与设备工程(Architectural Environment and Equipment Engineering)
560499	建筑设备类新专业(New Majors of Building Equipment)	080799	土建类新专业(New Majors of Civil Engineering)
560500	**工程管理类(Engineering Management)**	**110100**	**管理科学与工程类(Management Science and Engineering)**
560501	建筑工程管理(Architectural Engineering Management)	110104	工程管理(Engineering Management)

续表

高职高专(Higher Vocational)		普通本科(General Undergraduate)	
专业代码(CM)	专业名称(Name of Majors)	专业代码(CM)	专业名称(Name of Majors)
560502	工程造价 (Engineering Cost)	110105	工程造价 (Engineering Cost)
560503	建筑经济管理 (Architectural Economics and Management)	110104	工程管理 (Engineering Management)
560504	工程监理 (Project Supervision)	110104	工程管理 (Engineering Management)
560505	电力工程管理 (Power Engineering Management)	110104	工程管理 (Engineering Management)
560506	工程质量监督与管理 (Engineering Quality Supervision and Management)	110104	工程管理 (Engineering Management)
560507	建筑工程项目管理 (Construction Project Management)	110104	工程管理 (Engineering Management)
560599	工程管理类新专业 (New Majors of Engineering Management)	110199	管理科学与工程类新专业 (New Majors of Management Science and Engineering)
560600	**市政工程类 (Municipal Engineering)**	**080700**	**土建类 (Civil Engineering)**
560601	市政工程技术 (Municipal Engineering Technology)	080704	建筑环境与设备工程 (Architectural Environment and Equipment Engineering)
560602	城市燃气工程技术 (City Gas Engineering Technology)	080704	建筑环境与设备工程 (Architectural Environment and Equipment Engineering)
560603	给排水工程技术 (Water Supply and Sewerage Engineering Technology)	080705	给水排水工程 (Water Supply and Sewerage Engineering)
560604	水工业技术 (Water Industry Technology)	080704	建筑环境与设备工程 (Architectural Environment and Equipment Engineering)
560605	消防工程技术 (Fire-fighting Engineering Technology)	080704	建筑环境与设备工程 (Architectural Environment and Equipment Engineering)
560606	建筑水电技术 (Building Hydropower Technology)	080704	建筑环境与设备工程 (Architectural Environment and Equipment Engineering)
560699	市政工程类新专业 (New Majors of Municipal Engineering)	080799	土建类新专业 (New Majors of Civil Engineering)

续表

高职高专(Higher Vocational)		普通本科(General Undergraduate)	
专业代码(CM)	专业名称(Name of Majors)	专业代码(CM)	专业名称(Name of Majors)
560700	**房地产类 (Real Estate)**	**110200**	**工商管理类 (Business Administration)**
560701	房地产经营与估价 (Real Estate Operation and Valuation)	110201	工商管理 (Business Administration)
560702	物业管理 (Estate Management)	110212	物业管理 (Estate Management)
560703	物业设施管理 (Estate Facility Management)	110201	工商管理 (Business Administration)
560799	房地产类新专业 (New Majors of Real Estate)	110299	工商管理类新专业 (New Majors of Business Administration)

MODULE 2 Architectural Job Interview
模块二 建筑求职面试

Learning Objectives 学习目标

In this module, learners should:
- know the Chinese and English names of architectural schools and institutes.
- master skills of architectural job interview.

在本模块内,学习者应该能:
- 了解建筑院校及研究机构的中英文名称。
- 掌握建筑求职面试的技巧。

Special Terms 专业词汇

Institute of Architectural Engineering	建筑工程学院
Institute of Civil Engineering	土木工程学院
Vocational College of Architectural Engineering	建筑工程职业学院
Technical College of Construction	建筑技术学院
Workers and Staff College of Construction	建筑职工大学
Secondary Construction School for Workers and Staff	建筑职工中专
School of Architectural Engineering	建筑工程学校
Technical School of Building Installation	建筑安装技工学校
School of Urban and Rural Construction	城乡建设学校
Architectural University of Science & Technology	建筑科技大学
Academy of Building Research	建筑科学研究院
Architectural Design and Research Institute	建筑设计研究院
Institute of Architectural Designing	建筑设计院
National Institute of Building Science	国家建筑科学研究所
Research Institute of Housing Construction	房屋建筑研究所
Research Institute of Ecological Buildings	生态建筑研究院
Research Institute of Energy-saving Buildings	节能建筑研究院
Research Institute of Intelligent Buildings	智能建筑研究院

college 多指大学内的学院(part of a university)或分科学院(a school or an institution providing specialized courses); university 主要指综合大学(comprehensive),可授予学位(having authority to award bachelors' and higher degrees),通常配有研究设施(usually having research facilities); academy 指研究专门学术的学校(a school for training in a particular skill or profession)。

Situational Conversations 情景对话

Manager: Good morning! Please sit down!

Zhang Jie: Good morning, sir. Thank you.

Manager: First, I'd like to enquire about your architectural qualifications. Can you tell me something about that?

Zhang Jie: OK. As a five-year vocational student majoring in Civil Engineering, I am due to graduate in July from the City Vocational College of Jiangsu. In a span of five years, I have gained a lot. In terms of English level, I got certificates of PRETCO-A, PETS-3, and CET-4. Besides, I have obtained vocational certificates of cost engineer, construction engineer.

Manager: Pretty good. Will you please show them to me now?

Zhang Jie: Certainly. That is just what I think. Here you are.

Manager: Let me read it. Our group-corporation is one of China's top 100 and the world's top 500 construction companies. The current growth and expansion of business in both domestic and international markets requires us to enlarge the team of engineering and technical personnel. What would you like to take up as career in the posts?

Zhang Jie: A civil engineer.

Manager: Why do you apply for the post in our company?

Zhang Jie: First, the civil engineer is my ideal job, and it makes what I have learnt in college useful. Second, your company is located very near my home, so it would be very convenient for me to work here.

Manager: Er, I see. Among the qualities we are looking for are the technical abilities and practical skills. A lot of university graduates have paper qualifications — but can they deliver? What would you say to that?

Zhang Jie: Well, as engineering students of higher vocational colleges, in the first three years, we have been working mainly on theoretical aspects so that we can have a firm foundation. But in the last two years, the focus of study is shifting from theory to practice. And in each semester of the last two years, we have been asked to work on a practical project of some kind or other.

Manager: Can you give me an example?

Zhang Jie: Yes. During the last semester, I did some technical drawings of many modern buildings. And at the end of the semester I did a very excellent presentation for the best drawing I had made.

Manager: I see. It sounds a bit ambitious. That's all. I'll let you know soon what we decide.

Zhang Jie: Thank you, sir. I am looking forward to the good news from you.

Questions

1. What was Zhang Jie's ideal job? Why?
2. How did Zhang Jie say about his technical ability and practical skills?

Notes 注释

1. "As a five-year vocational student majoring in Civil Engineering, …"中"a five-year student"指五年制学生,五年制高职是我国高等职业教育的一种形式,目前有两种说法:(1)中高职三二分段制(三二连读制);(2)五年一贯制高职。"majoring in Civil Engineering"为现在分词短语(the present participle)作定语(attributive)修饰"a five-year student"。

2. "… I am due to graduate in July from the City Vocational College of Jiangsu." 我预期于7月从江苏城市职业学院毕业。此处"be due to"意思为"预期",如"His book is due to be published in October."他的书预定十月份出版。The City Vocational College of Jiangsu 江苏城市职业学院。

3. PRETCO-A(Practical English Test for Colleges-Band A),高等学校英语应用能力考试 A 级;PETS-3(Public English Test System-Band 3),全国英语等级考试3级;CET-4(College English Test-Band 4),全国大学英语等级考试4级。

4. cost engineer 造价工程师；construction engineer 建造师。
5. engineering and technical personnel 工程技术人员。
6. Among the qualities we are looking for are the technical abilities and practical skills. 此次招聘我们寻求的是技术能力和实操技能。将表语和地点状语（多为介词短语）置于句首加以强调时，其后通常用倒装语序，如"Around the lake are some tall trees."湖的四周有些高树。
7. "… but can they deliver?"意思是"如何把书本知识转化为实际能力"。
8. "… the focus of study is shifting from theory to practice"学习的焦点正从理论转向实践。"shift from A to B"由 A 转向 B，如"Graduation is the shift from thinking to being."毕业是由思考生命转变为活出真实的生命。

Useful Sentences 必学句型

1. I'd like to enquire about your architectural qualifications. 我想询问/了解一些你建筑方面的资格条件。
2. As a five-year vocational student majoring in Civil Engineering, I am due to graduate in July from the City Vocational College of Jiangsu. 作为土木工程专业的五年制学生，我将于今年7月从江苏城市职业学院毕业。
3. Will you please show them to me now? 现在你可以把你的证书拿给我看看吗？
4. What would you like to take up as career in the posts? 你想从事这一职业的哪一岗位？
5. It would be very convenient for me to work here. 对我来说，在这里工作将非常方便。
6. What would you say to that? 对此你想说些什么？
7. I am looking forward to the good news from you. 静候佳音。

Exercises 练习

1. Complete the following dialogue in English.
   (A: *a job seeker/hunter*; B: *a manager in charge of personnel*)
   B: Which school are you attending?
   A: _____.（我在江苏建筑职业技术学院上学。）
   B: When will you graduate?
   A: _____.（今年七月。）
   B: What do you do?
   A: _____.（我是这个学校的一名学生。）
   B: What is your major?

A：_____.（工业与民用建筑专业。）

B：How have you been getting on with your study?

A：_____.（我学得不错，是班里最优秀的学生之一。）

B：Have you obtained any certificate of technical qualifications?

A：_____.

（我拿到了大学英语四级证书、造价员资格证书和驾照。）

B：What special skills do you have, can you tell me?

A：_____.

（我有电脑操作经验，熟悉微软 Windows，Word 和 Excel。）

B：Why do you think you might like to work for our company?

A：_____.

（我的背景和经验非常适合这个工作，而且对这个工作也非常感兴趣，况且贵公司又是这个领域的佼佼者。）

B：What makes you think you would be a success in this position?

A：_____.

（我在学校所受的训练，加上实习工作经验，应该使我适合做这份工作。我相信我会成功的。）

B：How do you know about this company?

A：_____.

（贵公司在本市很有名，我听到很多对贵公司的好评。）

B：Thank you for your interest in our company.

A：_____.

（谢谢你，先生。我期待着能尽快得到您的消息。）

B：_____?

（你出去的时候能通知下一个应聘者进来吗?）

A：All right. Goodbye.

2. **Read and interpret the following passage.**

Dear Sir or Madam：

　　In answering to your want ad. in today's *Xinhua Daily* for Building Engineering and Technical Personnel, I beg to offer myself as a candidate for the post. My qualifications are as follows：

　　Place of birth：Shanghai, China

　　Age：22

　　Salary wanted：￥5 000 per month

　　Education：Graduated from Shanghai TV University majoring in civil & industrial architecture.

　　Work experience：With two years' architectural experience with Nantong No. 3 Construction Company.

　　If these meet your requirements, please grant me an interview. I am free for interview any afternoon between 3 and 5 o'clock, if you can give me one's week's notice.

Thank you in advance for your early reply.

Yours sincerely,
Li Hua

3. Pair work.

A acts as an interviewer, and B acts as an interviewee who wants to know what kind of engineering and technical personnel A's company requires and what qualifications A enquires about. Make up a conversation according to the above.

Supplementary Materials 补充材料

Sentence Patterns in Job Interview
(求职面试常用句型)

1. Prolusion (开场白)

(1) May I come in?
我可以进来吗?
(2) How are you doing, Mrs. Smith?
最近怎样, 史密斯女士?
(3) Miss Wu, will you come in please? Take a seat.
吴小姐, 请进, 坐下吧。
(4) I am coming for an interview by appointment. Nice to meet you.
我是应约来面试的, 见到你非常高兴。
(5) Did you have any difficulty finding our company?
找到我们公司有困难吗?
(6) How do you think of the weather today?
你认为今天的天气如何?

2. Personal Information (个人信息)

(1) What is your name, please?
请问你叫什么名字?
(2) Can you tell me what your full name is, please?
能把你的全名告诉我吗?
(3) How do you spell your full name?
你的全名怎么拼写?
(4) I was born on June 22, 1980.
我生于 1980 年 6 月 22 日。
(5) You look very young. How old are you?
你看上去很年轻。你多大了?
(6) I am just over twenty-two.
我刚过 22 岁。
(7) Where are you from?
你是哪里人?
(8) Where is your native place?
你的籍贯是哪里?

续表

(9) Where do you live now?
你现在住哪里?
(10) Can you tell me something about your family?
能介绍一下你的家庭情况吗?
(11) Are you married?
你结婚了吗?
(12) How long have you been married?
你结婚多长时间了?

3. Personality and Hobby(性格与爱好)

(1) What kind of character do you think you have?
你认为自己是什么性格的人?
(2) Are you introverted or extroverted?
你内向还是外向?
(3) What kind of person would you like to work with?
你喜欢和什么样的人一起工作呢?
(4) Do you have any particular strengths and weaknesses?
你有什么特别的优点和缺点吗?
(5) What basic principles do you apply to your life?
你生活中的基本原则是什么?
(6) How do you spend your spare time?
你的业余时间怎么度过?
(7) What kind of sports do you like most?
你最喜欢什么运动?
(8) What are your hobbies?
你的业余爱好是什么?
(9) I have an interest in traveling.
我对旅游非常感兴趣。

4. Educational Background（教育背景）

(1) What degree will you receive?
你将拿到什么学位?
(2) I will receive a bachelor's degree.
我将获得学士学位。
(3) How about your academic records at college?
你大学的成绩如何?
(4) I have been doing quite well at college.
我在大学时学习很好。
(5) My specialization at the university is just in line with the areas your institute deals with.
我在大学所学的专业和你们研究所所涉及的范围刚好对口。
(6) I was one of the top students in the class.
我是班里最优秀的学生之一。
(7) Which course did you like best?
你最喜欢哪门课程?

5. Personal Skills（个人技能）

(1) How do you think of your English?
你认为你的英语水平如何?

续表

(2) How do you think of your proficiency in written and spoken English?
你认为你的书面英语和口语熟练程度如何?
(3) I think my English is good enough to communicate with English speaking people.
我认为我能用英语和说英语国家的人很好的交流。
(4) What other foreign language do you speak?
你还能说什么其他外语吗?
(5) I have a good command of ...
我精通……
(6) Have you obtained any certificate of technical qualifications?
你获得过什么技术证书吗?
(7) What special skills do you have, can you tell me?
你能告诉我你有什么特殊技能吗?
(8) Have you gotten any special training in ...?
你接受过……方面的特殊培训吗?

6. Reasons for Quitting and Applying (离职和应聘原因)

(1) Why do you want to leave your present job and join us?
你为什么要辞去现在的工作来我们这里?
(2) Why do you want to apply for a position in our company?
你为什么想申请来我们公司?
(3) Your operations are global, so I can gain the most by working in this kind of environment.
你们公司的运作是全球化的,因此在这样一个环境中工作我会收获最多。
(4) Because I think my major is suitable for this position.
因为我认为我的专业适合这个职位。
(5) Because I'm very interested in the training program of your company.
因为我对你们公司的培训计划很感兴趣。
(6) Please tell me a little bit about your present job.
请告诉我你目前这个工作的一些情况。
(7) Why do you think you are qualified for this position?
你为什么认为你能胜任这个工作?
(8) My major and working experience make me qualified for this position.
我的专业和工作经验使我能胜任这个职位。
(9) How do you know our company?
你是怎么知道我们公司的?
(10) Your company is very reputed in this city; I heard much praise for your company.
贵公司在这个城市名声很好,我听了很多对贵公司的好评。
(11) The job is out of my major.
这份工作不属于我的专业范围。
(12) I want to do a job that can offer me the opportunity for advancement.
我想找一个能给我带来提升机会的工作。
(13) I am looking for a more challenging opportunity.
我想找一个更具挑战性的工作。
(14) My former company has been bankrupt.
我原先那个公司已经破产了。
(15) Your company has a great future and is conducive to the further development of my abilities.
贵公司前途光明,有助于我个人能力的发展。
(16) Working in this company can give me the chance to exert all my strengths.
在贵公司工作能发挥我最大的能力。
(17) Because that company didn't have a good future, I needed to consider my future.
因为那家公司没有什么前途,所以我必须考虑我的未来。

续表

7. Working Experience（工作经验）

(1) Do you have any work experience in this field?
你有这个行业的工作经验吗？
(2) What kind of jobs have you had?
你做过哪些工作？
(3) What is your responsibility at your present work unit?
在现在这个单位你负责什么工作？
(4) I am responsible for product distribution.
我负责产品销售。
(5) I have 4 years experience in staff management.
我有四年管理员工的经验。
(6) I have experience as a receptionist.
我做过接待员。
(7) What have you learned from the jobs you have had?
你从过去的工作中学到了什么？
(8) Would you like to tell me something about your outstanding achievements?
谈谈你的工作业绩好吗？
(9) How would you evaluate the company you are working with?
你将如何评价你现在的公司？

8. Working Objectives（工作目标）

(1) Are you a goal-oriented person?
你是一个目标明确的人吗？
(2) Tell me about some of your recent goals and what you do to achieve them.
告诉我你最近的一些目标以及如何实现它们。
(3) What are your short-term goals?
你的近期目标是什么？
(4) What is your long-range objective?
你的长远目标是什么？
(5) Where do you want your career to be in 5 years from now on?
五年内你的事业想达到什么水平？
(6) How long would you stay with us?
你能在我们这里呆多长时间？
(7) That obviously depends on how things go — whether I am suited to the firm and the firm to me.
这显然要依事情的发展而定，得看我和公司之间是否互相适合。
(8) How long I will stay with the company depends on whether the company and I are satisfied with each other.
我在贵公司会留多久完全依公司和我是否互相满意而定。
(9) I do believe this industry will be developed rapidly in 5 years' time.
我坚信五年内这个行业会飞速发展。

9. Salary Expectation（薪金期望）

(1) What are your salary expectations?
你期望的薪水是多少？
(2) I expect to be paid according to my abilities.
我希望能根据我的能力支付薪资。
(3) With my experience, I would like to start at RMB 4 000 per month.
以我的经验，我希望起薪是每月 4 000 元人民币。

续表

(4) What is your salary now?
你现在的薪水是多少?
(5) What is your expected salary?
你期望的薪水是多少?
(6) How long is my probation?
我的试用期多长?
(7) I think salary is closely related to the responsibilities of the job.
我觉得工资是与工作的责任紧密相关的。

10. Ending of the Interview (面试结束)

(1) Do you have any questions you want to ask?
你有问题要问吗?
(2) When will I know your decision?
我何时能知道你们的决定?
(3) How can we get in touch with you?
我们怎样才能和你取得联系呢?
(4) I can be reached at my office during work hours and at home in the evening.
工作时间我在办公室,晚上我在家,你们都能找到我。
(5) Thank you for your interest in our company.
谢谢你来参加我们公司的面试。
(6) I'm looking forward to hearing from you.
我期待着你的消息。
(7) Well, that's all for the interview.
好了,面试到此结束。
(8) And do I need the second interview?
我还需要第二次面试吗?

11. Express Thanks after the Interview (面试后道谢)

(1) I am calling to thank you for the interview yesterday.
我打电话是为了感谢你昨天为我安排的面试。
(2) It's thoughtful of you to call me again.
你能再次打电话过来,想得真周到。
(3) I am just calling to say thanks for the interview.
我打电话是为上次的面试向您表示谢意。
(4) We have narrowed it down to you and two other candidates.
我们已经把范围缩小到你和另外两个应聘者了。
(5) Do you have any questions we didn't cover in the interview?
上次我们面试时有没有未被提及到的问题要问?

12. Enquire the Interview Results (询问面试结果)

(1) I am just calling to follow up on the status of the position.
我打电话只是想问一下这个职位的招聘情况。
(2) We haven't made any decision yet.
我们还没有做任何决定。
(3) Do you have any idea when you might arrive at a decision?
你知道你们什么时候会做出决定吗?

13. Decline the Job (谢绝职务)

(1) I'd like to tell you that you can come to work for us.
我想通知你你可以来我们公司工作了。

续表

(2) I am sorry, but I just accepted another offer that I feel is more suitable to my needs.
很抱歉，我刚接受了一个我认为更符合我需要的工作。
(3) I really appreciate your offer, but I must decline it.
非常感谢贵公司的录用，但我不得不拒绝这份工作。
(4) Frankly speaking, I have been thinking that the position is not right for me after the interview.
坦白地说，面试后我一直认为这个职位不适合我。
(5) I really think that position doesn't suit my education background.
我真的觉得那个职位不适合我的教育背景。

MODULE 3　Architectural Workers
模块三　建筑工程人员

Learning Objectives 学习目标

In this module, learners should:
- know the Chinese and English names of architectural workers.
- be capable of discussing the work of different architectural workers in English.

在本模块内，学习者应该能：
- 掌握建筑类工程人员的中英文名称。
- 能用英语讨论不同建筑工种的工作内容。

Special Terms 专业词汇

civil construction worker　建筑工人
bricklayer　瓦工
carpenter　木工
concrete worker　混凝土工
scaffolder　架子工
plumber　水暖工
fitter　安装钳工
riveter　铆工
turner　车工
joiner　细木工
painter　油漆工
warehouse keeper　料工/库管员
crane operator　吊车司机
scraper operator　铲土机手
loader operator　装载机手
air-compressor operator　空压机工
cost estimator/engineer　造价员/师
safety supervisor　安全员

hoister　起重机司机
road builder　筑路工
steel fixer　钢筋工
stone mason　石工
building installer　建筑安装工
electrician　电工
welder　焊工
ventilator　通风工
assembler　装配工
plasterer　粉刷工
glazier　玻璃安装工
surveyor　测量工
bulldozer operator　推土机手
excavator operator　挖土机手
pneumatic drill operator　风钻工
building decorator　建筑装饰工
construction supervisor　监理员
contract administrator　合同员

construction crew　施工员
engineering documenter　工程资料员
quality inspector　质检员
construction material administrator　材料员

"-er"后缀多数情况下表示的人物社会地位较低，或从历史上看较低，如 driver 司机，worker 工人；"-or"后缀多数情况下表示的人物社会地位较高，或从历史上看较高，如 doctor 博士或医生，tutor（大学）指导教师，director 主任。

Situational Conversations　情景对话

Mr. White: Hello, young man, you work on this worksite, don't you?

Lin Qiang: Yes, sir. I graduated from a construction technical college.

Mr. White: Would you mind telling me what you are doing on the worksite?

Lin Qiang: Certainly not. I'm an electrician in charge of electric installation on the site.

Mr. White: Oh, an electrician, pretty good. Your job concerns electric safety of innumerable households or families, so no negligence is allowed, even the slightest. Am I right?

Lin Qiang: Yes. Responsibility is weightier than Mount Tai.

Mr. White: Who is the girl over there, I'd like to know?

Lin Qiang: She is a welder and technician in our company.

Mr. White: I see. Her skill must be great, right?

Lin Qiang: Yes, that is unquestionable. She is a top-notch welder, and nobody can compare with her. Last year, she was awarded the National March-Eighth Red-Banner Pacesetter.

Mr. White: It is really magnificent for such a young girl! That group of boys and girls are your workmates, aren't they?

Lin Qiang: Yes. They are recently engaged installers, including pipers, fitters, riveters, ventilators and so on.

Mr. White: They are all very young and energetic. Who's the elder man in front of them?

Lin Qiang: He is our site director, Mr. Wang.

Mr. White: What is he doing over there?

Lin Qiang: He is giving them a safety lecture. Need I introduce him to you, sir?

Mr. White: Yes, of course. Thank you!

Mr. Wang: How do you do, sir?

Mr. White: How do you do, director?

Mr. Wang: Please tell me which aspect you like to know, sir?

Mr. White: I am very interested in your recruiting and using workers here. You know, as a super worksite, the construction is intense but in regular order, and news of victory keeps pouring in. I wonder how many constructors there are on your worksite.

Mr. Wang: Over thousand. Almost 10% are engineering technicians and administrative staff.

Mr. White: What kinds of tradesmen are there now?

Mr. Wang: There are bricklayers, carpenters and plasterers. The main structures are going to be finished, so some civil construction workers are leaving here while installers and decorators are coming soon.

Mr. White: I see. Maybe you have enough skilled workers to accomplish your construction task. But why don't you consider to train some local people?

Mr. Wang: Good idea. We will employ several hundred local people during the construction peak period.

Mr. White: Employing local people to take part in your construction not only solves their employment problems but also picks up your construction speed.

Mr. Wang: It really satisfies both sides.

Mr. White: It's a fine thing, but how do you make sure that construction quality won't be affected?

Mr. Wang: According to requirements of different construction stages, we will class and train some local employees to get working skills as early as possible and to improve their awareness of quality and safety.

Mr. White: Excellent, thus they will improve your working efficiency a lot and guarantee that the construction tasks could be accomplished on schedule.

Mr. Wang: You are right.

Questions

1. What kinds of tradesmen are there on Mr. Wang's worksite?
2. What are the advantages of employing some local people?

Notes 注释

1. "... in charge of electric installation on the site." 负责工地的电气安装工作。这里的"in charge of"意思是"掌管,负责",如"The teacher is in charge of the class." 这位教师负责这个班。
2. "innumerable"意思是"无数的",相当于"numerous"。
3. Responsibility is weightier than Mount Tai. 责任重于泰山。
4. a welder and technician 焊工兼技师。
5. "top-notch welder"意思是"一流的焊工"。
6. the National March-Eighth Red-Banner Pacesetter 全国三八红旗手。
7. the elder man 年长者。elder 作名词时是"年长者,老人"的意思;也可作形容词,意思是"年长的"。
8. "... news of victory keeps pouring in." 意思是"捷报频传"。
9. the construction peak period 施工高峰期。
10. Employing local people to take part in your construction not only solves their employment problems but also picks up your construction speed. 雇佣当地人参与建设不仅解决了他们的就业问题,而且加快了建设速度。此句的主语为动名词短语(gerundial phrase),其构成为"doing+名词/代词",又如"Going to public concerts is often free of charge" 欣赏公开的演奏会通常是免费的。
11. "... awareness of quality and safety" 意思是"质量和安全意识"。
12. "on schedule" 意思是"按计划,准时",如"Given plenty of labor, the job will be completed on schedule." 假定有充足的劳动力,这项工作将准时完成。

Useful Sentences 必学句型

1. Would you mind telling me what you are doing on the worksite? 你介意做……吗?
2. Last year, she was awarded the National March-Eighth Red-Banner Pacesetter. 去年,她获得了"全国三八红旗手"称号。
3. It is really magnificent for such a young girl! 对于这样一个年轻的女孩来说,这真了不起!
4. I am very interested in your recruiting and using workers here. 我对你们这里的招聘及用工很感兴趣。
5. I wonder how many constructors there are on your worksite. 我想知道你们工地上有多少建筑工人。
6. But why don't you consider to train some local people? 但是,你为什么不考虑培训一部分当地人呢?

Exercises 练习

1. Complete the following dialogue in English.

Jack: Hi Peter. Can you tell me a little bit about your current job?

Peter: _____?（当然可以啊，你想了解什么呢?）

Jack: First of all, what do you work as?

Peter: _____.（我是一位驻地工程师，也是主管这个工地的工地主任。）

Jack: What are you responsible for?

Peter: _____.
（全权负责工地的安全施工，具体来讲，主要对施工项目进行安全监督与指导。）

Jack: How many constructors are there on your worksite?

Peter: _____.（目前，有1 000多人。）

Jack: Are their work different?

Peter: _____.
（是的，目前工地上有大约10％的工程技术和管理人员，其他主要是如瓦工、木工、粉刷工等土建工人。）

Jack: Are there some local people among the workers on the worksite?

Peter: _____.（有的，我们在施工高峰期会招聘几百名本地工人的。）

Jack: Can you give me some reasons for employing local people to take part in your construction?

Peter: _____.
（其一，这样能解决本地人的就业问题；其二，最大限度地加快我们的施工进度。）

Jack: How do you make sure that your construction quality will not be affected?

Peter: _____.（我们会及时地对新招聘来的本地工人进行培训的。）

Jack: So, what you did really satisfied both sides.

Peter: You are right.

2. Read and interpret the following passage.

Types of Work in Construction Production

There are four main types of work in building production. They are civil construction workers, building installers, building mechanics and building decorators. Of course, each of these includes more than eight types. For example, building installers can be divided into plumber, electrician, welder, hoister, ventilating worker, riveter, fitter and so on. The tradesmen of each types need to work in close cooperation, not a single one of them can be dispensed with. Each tradesman plays an important part in construction.

3. Pair work.

Imagine that you have been invited to a party. Discuss with your partner how to give your introduction each other including your major, job, company, worksite, and so on.

Supplementary Materials 补充材料

Professional Certificates of Architecture
（建筑职业资格证书）

证书名称 (Name of Certificates)	签发部门 (Approved & Authorized by)	报考信息 (More Information)
注册一级建造师 (Certified Constructor)	中国人力资源和社会保障部 (Ministry of Human Resources & Social Security of P. R. C.) 中华人民共和国住房和城乡建设部 (Ministry of Housing and Urban-Rural Development of P. R. C.)	http://www.cpta.com.cn
注册二级建造师 (Certified Associate Constructor)		
注册造价工程师 (Certified Cost Engineer)		
房地产经纪人 (Real Estate Agent)		
注册咨询工程师 (Registered Consulting Engineer)		
监理工程师(Supervising Engineer)		
注册建筑师 (Registered Architect)		
投资建设项目管理师 (Investment Construction Project Engineer)		
房地产估价师 (Real Estate Appraiser)		

MODULE 4 Construction Enterprises
模块四 建筑施工企业

Learning Objectives 学习目标

In this module, learners should:
- know the Chinese and English names of various types of construction enterprises.
- be capable of making introductions to the construction enterprises in English.

在本模块内,学习者应该能:
- 掌握各类建筑施工企业的中英文名称。
- 能用英语进行建筑施工企业的概况介绍。

Special Terms 专业词汇

CSCEC (China State Construction Engineering Corporation) 中国建筑工程总公司
CCEC (Civil Construction Engineering Corporation) 土木建筑工程总公司
CIEC (Construction Installation Engineering Corporation) 建筑安装工程总公司
RBECC (Road & Bridge Engineering Corporation of China) 中国路桥工程总公司
No. 1 Construction Engineering Company 第一建筑工程公司
Construction Decoration Company 建筑装饰公司
Construction and Installation Engineering Co., Ltd 建筑安装工程有限公司
Giant Building Machinery Inc. 巨人建筑机械公司
Construction Materials Supplying Company 建筑材料供应公司
Construction Transportation Company 建筑运输公司
Construction Engineering Branch 建筑工程分公司
Construction Engineering Brigade 建筑工程施工队
Construction Engineering Stock Company 建筑工程股份公司
Construction Engineering Limited Company 建筑工程有限公司
Jiangsu Nantong No. 3 Construction Group Co., Ltd 江苏南通三建集团有限公司
Nantong Construction Project Central Contracting Co., Ltd 南通建筑工程总承包有限公司
Nantong Construction Group Joint-Stock Co., Ltd 南通建工集团股份有限公司
Jiangsu Suzhong Construction Group Co., Ltd 江苏省苏中建设集团股份有限公司

company 泛指公司，指生产、出售产品的商行、公司，经营服务项目的公司或者从事公益事业的公司，常省略为 co.；corporation 指股份有限公司、集团公司、法人等，常用于一个或多个合伙人所拥有的商行、公司，以股份投资形式合股开办，也可独资开办，同时有法人的意思，常省略为 corp.；incorporation 有限公司，有限责任公司，常见于美加企业，常省略为 inc.

Situational Conversations 情景对话

Mr. Brown: Could you give me a brief introduction to CCEC, sir?

Zhang Yin: As the general manager of CCEC, I am glad to do that.

Mr. Brown: Is CCEC state-owned or private?

Zhang Yin: It is a state-owned enterprise with a history of more than 20 years, mainly contracting various kinds of civil and industrial construction works and providing labor service.

Mr. Brown: It is time-honoured and well-known both at home and abroad. And how much registered funds does it have at present?

Zhang Yin: 500 million dollars with the overseas business.

Mr. Brown: Oh, with very abundant capital funds, CCEC is indeed a large and powerful company.

Zhang Yin: That is indubitable, sir.

Mr. Brown: How many staff and workers are there in CCEC?

Zhang Yin: Over 600 000.

Mr. Brown: What about the composed structure?

Zhang Yin: Quite well. Among them are over 1 000 senior engineers, economists and experts, 5 000 engineers, economists and other related administrative talents.

Mr. Brown: And your skilled workers?

Zhang Yin: We've all kinds of skilled workers in fields of civil construction, installation, machinery, decoration, testing, surveying and maintenance.

Mr. Brown: Do they all have higher construction abilities?
Zhang Yin: Yes. The majority have had a good grasp of the Chinese traditional as well as the world-class construction techniques.
Mr. Brown: With so many dab hands and galaxy talents, I bet your corporation must be very competitive in the world.
Zhang Yin: Right. That is indisputable.
Mr. Brown: How many construction companies and technical service units are there in CCEC?
Zhang Yin: There are 40 construction companies and 16 technical service units, taking part in international tendering and contracting completed projects.
Mr. Brown: Wonderful! CCEC must have undertaken a variety of construction works in many parts of the world, is that right?
Zhang Yin: Yes, of course. These picture books have recorded all sorts of buildings built by us in recent years.
Mr. Brown: Let me have a look.
Zhang Yin: What do you think of them? Are they beautiful?
Mr. Brown: Oh, wonderful! Beautiful! CCEC had indeed lived up to its reputation!

Questions

1. What is CCEC mainly concerned about?
2. Does CCEC have a high competition in the world? Why?

Notes 注释

1. CCEC (Civil Construction Engineering Corporation)土木建筑工程总公司。
2. state-owned 国有的，private 私有的。
3. "… mainly contracting various kinds of civil and industrial construction works and providing labor service."主要承包各种工业与民用建筑工程施工并提供劳务。
4. time-honoured 历史悠久的，如"It is a time-honoured custom for the people to enjoy family reunion on Spring Festival."中国人在春节时合家欢聚是一项有悠久历史的习俗。
5. at home and abroad 意思是"国内外"，如"Our products command a good market both at home and abroad."我们的产品在国内外都有很好的市场。

6. registered funds 意思是"注册资金"。
7. indubitable 意思是"不容置疑的"。
8. composed structure 意思是"配置结构"。
9. have a good grasp of 对……有较好的掌握，如"My daughter had a good grasp/command of mental abacus after the special training."经过专业的培训后，我女儿对珠心算有了较好的掌握。
10. "With so many dab hands and galaxy talents, I bet..." "dab hands"意思是"能工巧匠"。"I bet"我敢打赌……（后面接某件事情，肯定的语气比较强烈），如"I bet you know this."我打赌，你肯定知道这事。
11. "... taking part in international tendering and contracting completed projects". "international tendering"国际投标，bid 招标。"contracting completed projects"意思是"承包成套工程"。
12. "live up to" 达到高标准，不辜负，履行。如"We must never fail to live up to the expectations of our parents and teachers."我们一定不要辜负父母和老师的期望。

Useful Sentences 必学句型

1. Could you give me a brief introduction to CCEC, sir? 你能给我简单地介绍一下土木建筑工程总公司吗？
2. It is time-honoured and well-known both at home and abroad. 这家公司历史悠久，驰名中外。
3. The majority have had a good grasp of the Chinese traditional as well as the world-class construction techniques. 大部分技术工人已经较好地掌握了中国传统的以及世界一流的施工技术。
4. With so many dab hands and galaxy talents, I bet your corporation must be very competitive in the world. 有这么多能工巧匠和优秀人才，我敢打赌，贵公司在世界上一定很有竞争力。
5. CCEC had indeed lived up to its reputation. 土木建筑工程总公司确实名不虚传。

Exercises 练习

1. Complete the following dialogue in English.

   A: Could you give me an introduction to your company, sir?
   B: _____. （当然可以。）
   A: Where is your company headquartered?
   B: _____. （位于素有"建筑之乡"美誉的江苏省南通市。）

A: Is it state-owned?

B: _____. (不，它是一个始建于1952年的自主经营、自负盈亏、自我发展、自我约束的民营经济实体。)

A: How much registered funds does it have?

B: _____.
(公司现有注册资本3.6亿元，总资产17亿元。)

A: Very abundant! Can you tell me the present scale of your company?

B: _____.
(公司下辖29个土建和专业子公司，分布于华北、华东、华南、西北、东北和海外六大区域市场，成员企业34家，从业员工2万多人，年经营规模近百亿元。)

A: What about the composed structure of your staff and workers?

B: _____.
(公司目前拥有各类经济技术管理人员近2 000人，具备中高级专业技术职称及执业资格人员数百名，其中研究员级高工7名、高职人员48名、中职人员109名、网上注册的一级建造师117名、二级建筑造师154名、其他注册类人员18名。)

A: Can you list some classical works of your company?

B: _____.
(太多了，比如国内的"天安门广场建筑群"、"首都民族文化宫"、"南京长江大桥"等；国外如科威特皇宫地下室、巴巴多斯国家体育馆、莫桑比克国家教育部等。)

A: What do you think of the competitive power of your company in China and even in the world?

B: _____.
(应该说竞争力还是很强的，我公司连续六年入选"中国承包商60强"、"江苏省建筑业综合实力30强"、"江苏省建筑外经10强"，四次荣登"ENR全球最大承包商225强"和"ENR全球最大国际承包商225强"排行榜，三度入围"中国民营企业500强"。)

A: What are your future development strategies?

B: _____!
(今后一段时间，我公司将倾力打造"研发、设计、施工、服务"一体化运营新模式，努力变知名的"建筑承包商"为卓越的"建筑服务商"，向着组织体系科学化、市场结构多元化、生产经营集约化、企业管理现代化的跨地区、跨行业、跨国经营的中国一流建筑强企的目标阔步迈进！)

A: Now I have already had a more clear picture of your company's past, present and future. Thank you very much!

B: You are welcome.

2. Read and interpret the following passage.

Corporation

A corporation is a legal entity, having an existence separate and distinct from that of its owners. The assets of corporation belong to the corporation itself, not to the stockholders. The owners of a corporation are called stockholders and their ownership is evidenced by transferable shares of capital stock. The corporation is responsible for its own debts, and must pay income taxes on its earnings. As a "separate legal entity", a corporation may enter into contracts and sue and be sued as if it were a person in count.

3. Pair work.

  A acts as a manager of a Construction Corporation, B acts as a guest who wants to know something about the corporation. Use the following expressions:

  A: *Can I help you, sir?*
  B: *Yes, I'd like to ...*
  A: *But what information do you ... ?*
  B: *It's ...*

Supplementary Materials 补充材料

Composed Structure of ×××Construction Corporation
(×××建筑公司机构配置)

Board of Directors (董事会)	
President Office (总经理办公室)	
Management & Operation Dept. (经营管理部)	Labor & Personnel Dept. (劳动人事部)
Planning Division (综合计划处)	Financial Affairs Division (财务处)
1st Business Dept. (业务一部)	Science & Technology Division (科技处)
2nd Business Dept. (业务二部)	Quality Supervision Division (质量监督处)
Overseas Company (海外公司)	Design & Consulting Company (设计咨询公司)
Asia Division (亚洲处)	Material Supply Division (物资供应处)
Europe-America-Pacific Regional Division (欧美太处)	Equipment Division (动力设备处)
Representative in Paris (驻巴黎代表处)	Construction Administration Division (施工管理处)
Hong Kong Office(驻香港办事处)	Factory Administration Division (工厂管理处)
Africa Division (非洲处)	Building Science Research Institute (建筑科研所)
Branch (分公司)	Construction Staff & Workers Hospital (建筑职工医院)

MODULE 5　Kinds of Buildings
模块五　建筑物类型

Learning Objectives 学习目标

In this module, learners should:
- know the Chinese and English names of various kinds of buildings.
- be capable of discussing different kinds of buildings in English.

在本模块内，学习者应该能：
- 掌握各类建筑物的中英文名称。
- 能用英语谈论不同类型的建筑物。

Special Terms 专业词汇

modern architecture　现代建筑
industrial architecture　工业建筑
residential architecture　住宅建筑
public architecture　公共建筑
pseudo-classic architecture　仿古建筑
ecological architecture　生态建筑
western style architecture　西式建筑
European-style architecture　欧式建筑
the English residence　英式住宅
office building　办公大楼
business building　营业大楼
apartment/flats　公寓
hotel-style apartments　酒店式公寓
box buildings　盒子房
skyscraper　摩天大楼
multi-storey building　多层建筑
lower-rise building　低层建筑
brick-and-timber building　砖木结构建筑
brick-and-concrete building　砖混结构建筑

ancient buildings　古代建筑
civil architecture　民用建筑
commercial architecture　商业建筑
agricultural architecture　农业建筑
energy-saving architecture　节能建筑
vernacular building　乡土建筑
Chinese style architecture　中式建筑
Spanish-style architecture　西班牙式建筑
the American residence　美式住宅
teaching building　教学大楼
married quarters　家属楼
mansion　豪华宅邸/大厦
low-rent house　廉租房
tube-shaped apartment　筒子楼
villa　别墅
high-rise building　高层建筑
bungalow　平房
steel building　钢结构建筑
reinforced concrete building　钢混结构建筑

flat 是英式英语(the British English)，是"公寓"的意思，通常指处于一个大建筑里面的若干间相似的小居所；而 apartment 则一般见于美式英语(the American English)，意思同上；house 则是泛指各种形式大小各异的房屋的总和。

Situational Conversations 情景对话

Peter: Excuse me, can you tell me what you are going to build here?

Li Ya: A multi-storey building.

Peter: A multi-storey building? How many storeys does this building have?

Li Ya: It has 5 storeys or so.

Peter: What do you mean by a multi-storey building? And what is the difference between high-rise building and low-rise one?

Li Ya: According to the Code for Design of Civil Buildings GB 50352-2005, buildings of more than 10 storeys are high-rise, of 7~9 are medium-high, of 4~6 are multi-storeys, and of less than 4 storeys are low-rise.

Peter: Oh, I know it. The classification is only fit for dwellings. How about public buildings?

Li Ya: For public buildings, the single-storey/multi-storey ones are less than 24 meters high, the high-rise more than 24 meters, and the super high over 100 meters.

Peter: I see. What is the predicted height of the building under construction?

Li Ya: Maybe more than twenty meters, but less than twenty four meters.

Peter: What is the building mainly used for?

Li Ya: Some storeys are for business and the rest for living.

Peter: Which storeys are for department stores or shops?

Li Ya: The lower part, that is to say, the ground and the first floor.

Peter: Can you tell me why?

Li Ya: Because there aren't any partitions in these two storeys. The big rooms are usually for offices and department stores or shops.

Peter: What about rooms in other storeys?

Li Ya: There're many partitions in rooms of the other storeys, so they are mainly used as bedrooms, sitting rooms and bathrooms.

Peter: Right. Is the building Chinese or western style?

Li Ya: I think it belongs to the western style. Buildings with overhanging roofs are usually of the Chinese-style, or belong to ancient architecture.

Peter: So the difference between ancient and modern architecture lies in whether there is an overhanging roof, right?

Li Ya: I think so. But there are many other differences in aspects of materials, structures, etc.

Peter: I am not quite clear. Please give me some examples of ancient architecture?

Li Ya: OK. The Forbidden City (also called Imperial Palaces) in Beijing and the Bell Tower and the Drum Tower in Xi'an, etc., are all glaring examples of ancient architecture.

Peter: And examples of modern architecture?

Li Ya: Too numerous to mention, such as the People's Hall in Beijing and Orient Pearl in Shanghai.

Peter: I see. Thank you for your detailed explanation.

Li Ya: It is my pleasure.

Questions

1. What does high-rise building mean?
2. What are the differences between ancient and modern architecture?

Notes 注释

1. the Code for Design of Civil Buildings GB 50352-2005，中国《民用建筑设计通则》(GB 50352-2005)，这一通则将住宅建筑依层数划分为：一层至三层为低层住宅，四层至六层为多层住宅，七层至九层为中高层住宅，十层及十层以上为高层住宅。除住宅建筑之外的民用建筑高度不大于 24 m 者为单层和多层建筑，大于 24 m 者为高层建筑（不包括建筑高度大于 24 m 的单层公共建筑）；建筑高度大于 100 m 的民用建筑为超高层建筑。
2. "… is only fit for …"中"fit for"意思为"适于，适合"，后面接名词，如"He turned out to be fit for the position."结果证明他是胜任这一职务的。"fit to"意思为"(使)与……相配[相称]，相对应"，后面接动词原形，如"The weather is not fit to go out in."这种天气不宜外出。
3. public building 意思为"公共建筑"，包含办公建筑（包括写字楼、政府部门办公室等)，商业建筑(如商场、金融建筑等)，旅游建筑(如酒店、娱乐场所等)，科教文卫建筑(包括文化、教育、科研、医疗、卫生、体育建筑等)，通信建筑(如邮电、通讯、广播用房)以及交通运输类建筑(如机场、高速公路、铁路、桥梁等)。公共建筑和居住建筑都属民用建筑。民用建筑和工业建筑合称建筑。

4. the predicted height 预期高度。
5. be used for/as 被用作；be used to doing 习惯于；used to do 过去常常做。
6. the ground and the first floor，英式英语中是"第一层和第二层"。
7. "So the difference between ancient and modern architecture lies in whether there is an overhanging roof, right?" 中 "lie in" 的意思是"在于"，如 "The foundations of good heath lie in love, laughter and self-confidence." 健康的基础在于爱，笑声和自信。"whether" 连词(表示选择或怀疑)是否，是不是，如 "It is unclear whether the meeting will go ahead as planned." 会议是否会如期举行还不清楚。overhanging roof 大屋顶。
8. the Forbidden City (Imperial Palaces) 紫禁城或故宫。
9. Bell Tower and Drum Tower 钟楼和鼓楼。
10. the People's Hall 人民大会堂；Orient Pearl 东方明珠。

Useful Sentences 必学句型

1. <u>What do you mean by</u> a multi-storey building? 多层建筑指的是什么意思?
2. What is the difference between high-rise building <u>and</u> low-rise one? 高层建筑和低层建筑之间的区别是什么?
3. The classification is <u>only fit for</u> dwellings. 这种分类仅适用于住宅建筑。
4. What is the <u>predicted height</u> of the building under construction? 在建的这幢楼的预期高度是多少?
5. What is the building <u>mainly used for</u>? 这幢建筑的主要用途是什么?
6. <u>I think it belongs to</u> the western style. 我认为这属于西式风格的建筑。
7. The difference between ancient and modern architecture <u>lies in whether</u> there is an overhanging roof. 古代建筑和现代建筑的区别在于是否有大屋顶。
8. <u>Too numerous to</u> mention. 举不胜举。

Exercises 练习

1. Complete the following dialogue in English.

    A：Can you tell me how to classify the buildings according to usage?
    B：_____.

(一般来说，建筑物按照使用情况可分为三大类，即民用建筑、工业建筑和农业建筑。)

A: What are civil buildings?
B: _____. (民用建筑包括居住建筑和公共建筑。)
A: Can you list some examples of public buildings?
B: _____.
(举不胜举。比如说写字楼、酒店、商场、学校、机场、车站等都属于公共建筑。)
A: I see. Can I say the National Stadium is one of the most glaring examples of public buildings?
B: _____.
(当然可以，国家体育馆不仅壮观，而且坚固，其主体结构设计使用年限达 100 年。)
A: Is there anything special in the design of its main structure?
B: _____.
(是的，由于大跨度空间的需要，屋顶采用钢结构，其他主要承重构件采用钢筋混凝土。)
A: Is the National Stadium a high-rise building?
B: _____.
(是的，对于公共建筑而言，建筑物两层以上高度 24 m 以上即为高层建筑。)
A: What about the high-rise for residential buildings?
B: _____.
(10 层以上的住宅建筑才算得上是高层。)
A: Oh, I see.

2. Read and interpret the following passage.

Dwelling House

There are many different kinds of houses in the world. They can be large or small, ancient or modern, Chinese style or Western style. Many houses are square and a few are round. Some houses have only one floor, and others have two or more, even there are lots of multi-storey buildings, too.

Many houses are designed similarly, with two or three bedrooms and bathroom upstairs, a dining room, kitchen and living room downstairs, and a small garden at the back or in front of them.

Most of houses are made of concrete, steel bar, wood, stone or bricks.

3. Pair work.

Suppose your partner lives in a small village and comes to a big modern city, and you are walking along the street and try to talk about the houses on both sides of the streets.

Supplementary Materials 补充材料

House Structures and Matching Facilities
房屋结构和配套设施

Structure （结构）	Reinforced concrete framework, pressure and quake resistance, fireproof. （钢筋混凝土框架，抗压、抗震、防火性能）
Roof （屋顶）	Waterproof fittings and covering slabs of heat insulation. （防水装置和隔热层）
External Wall （外墙）	Stone foundation and high-class wall bricks. （石头基础，高级墙砖）
Internal Wall （内墙）	Building bricks, coat with eco-paint. （建筑砖，环保油漆）
Elevator （电梯）	Famous brand elevator. （名牌电梯）
Stair （楼梯）	Public staircase with hard wooden rails and antiskid tiled landings and steps. （公共楼梯使用实木扶手，防滑地砖和台阶）
Floor （地板）	Marble tiles and solid wooden compound floor. （大理石地砖和实木复合地板）
Door & Window （门窗）	Color aluminum alloy windows of two kinds of opening type with double paned glass; Unit main door with fire prevention & security function. （彩色铝合金双层玻璃，双层开关式窗户；单元门有防火、防盗功能）
Master Bath （主卫）	Marble wall & floor, sanitary ware with faucets. （大理石墙面和地面，卫生设施，龙头）
Kitchen （厨房）	Unit cupboard and water heater. （整体橱柜和热水器）
Air-conditioner （空调）	Central air-conditioning system. （中央空调系统）
Power Supply （供电）	An independent electric meter, 20 kW/standard unit, 30 kW/house （独立电表，20 kW/标准单元，30 kW/套房）
Gas Supply （供气）	Pipe natural gas(2.5 m^3) 管道天然气(2.5 立方气表)
Telephone （电话）	3 ADSL lines per household. （每家 3 条 ADSL 线路）
CATV （有线电视）	Equipped with satellite and public antenna receiver. （配备卫星和公共天线接收器）
Security System （安全系统）	With intellectual door management, visiting confirmation by video intercom and monitoring cameras. （配备中央监控室，每户装备门禁智能管理系统，通过对讲机和监视器确定来访客人）

MODULE 6　Building Materials
模块六　建筑材料

Learning Objectives 学习目标

In this module, learners should:
- know the Chinese and English names of various types of building materials.
- be capable of inquiring, quoting and purchasing building materials in English.

在本模块内，学习者应该能：
- 掌握各类建筑材料的中英文名称。
- 能用英语对建筑材料进行询价、报价与订购。

Special Terms 专业词汇

installation materials　安装材料	decorative materials　装饰材料
foreign materials　外来材料	artificial materials　人造材料
additional materials　附加材料	defective materials　残次材料
explosive materials　爆破材料	insulating materials　绝缘材料
fire-proof materials　耐火材料	cementing materials　粘结材料
substitute materials　代用材料	roofing materials　屋面材料
rust-resisting materials　防锈材料	road materials　筑路材料
plastic materials　塑性材料	structural materials　结构材料
aluminum alloy factory　铝合金厂	steel tubing plant　钢管厂
enamel plant　搪瓷制品厂	plywood factory　胶合板厂
glass works　玻璃厂	ceramic factory　陶瓷厂
plastics factory　塑料厂	felt roofing factory　油毡厂
brick & tile works　砖瓦厂	cement plant　水泥厂
crushing stone mill　碎石厂	paint factory　油漆厂
asbestos tile works　石棉瓦厂	construction materials company　建材公司
fiber-board plant　纤维板厂	steel window factory　钢窗厂
glass-fiber factory　玻璃纤维厂	metal products plant　五金厂
metal-structure works　金属结构厂	electric bulbs factory　电灯泡厂
timber processing plant　木材加工厂	concrete parts factory　混凝土构件厂

factory 泛指一般意义的"工厂",是最普通、用得最广泛的一个词;works 多指与军事工程或市政公共事业有关的工厂;plant 指重工业工厂,尤其是重工业中的机器制造或电机制造业工厂;mill 原意是"磨坊",现主要指与(碾、碎、磨、压、组)等工序有关的工厂或与纺织有关的轻工业方面的工厂。注:受到约定俗成的影响,有些工厂表示的方法也有相互混用现象。

Situational Conversations 情景对话

Mark: We haven't seen each other for a long time, Mrs. Li. What can I do for you?

Li Lu: Long time no see! I am here to buy some building materials.

Mark: What materials do you want to buy?

Li Lu: Mainly common materials, such as cement, steel bar, timber and so on. Can you tell me their current market prices?

Mark: Oh, let me have a look. Cement is 1 dollar per kilogram, steel bar 500 dollars per ton, and timber 650 dollars per cubic meter...

Li Lu: Will you show me the price catalogue?

Mark: OK, here it is. The materials here are not expensive, but of the best quality. You can rest assured.

Li Lu: Honestly speaking, the prices are much higher than they were one year ago. Do you have any specials for frequent buyers like me?

Mark: To tell you the truth, the prices of the building materials have been rocketing up recently, which make it very difficult to return good profits. But for frequent buyers like you, we can offer varying degree of discounts, depending on the amount of your purchase.

Li Lu: I want to know the most favorable price you can offer for 200 tons of cement, 1,000 tons of steel bars and 1,000 cubic meters of timber.

Mark: In consideration of the quantity of the three building materials you intend to purchase, we can offer you 10% discount.

Li Lu: 10%? That's too low a rate. Could you see your way to increase it to 20%?

Mark: What? You want to drive me bankrupt? You can't expect us to make such a large reduction.

Li Lu: Oh, with such a large order on hand, you needn't worry anymore. Please think it over, my old friend.

Mark: Considering the long-standing business relationship between us, we shall grant you a special discount of 10%. As you know, we do business on the basis of equality and mutual benefit. Besides, the price of the building materials tends to go up and there is a heavy market demand for them.

Li Lu: Yes, I know the present market situations. Anyhow, let's meet each other halfway, how about 15%?

Mark: You are a real businesswoman! All right, I agree to give you a 15% discount.

Li Lu: Deal! But keep your words and deliver the materials in time!

Mark: Make yourself easy. We will go all-out to supply you with the materials and deliver them to your site without any delays.

Li Lu: Thank you!

Questions

1. What and how much building materials did Li Lu want to buy?
2. What is the total cost for the three building materials bought by Li Lu?

Notes 注释

1. common materials 大众材料。
2. current market prices 当前市价。
3. Honestly speaking, the prices are much higher than they were one year ago. 坦诚地说，这些建材的价格比1年前要高得多。"honestly speaking" 坦诚地说，类似的表达还有 "frankly speaking"，"generally speaking" 等。"much higher" 意思为"高得多"，比较级前用 a little, a bit, slightly, a great deal, a lot, many, much 等词语表示不定量，far, completely, still 表示程度或更进一步。
4. "To tell you the truth, ... which make it very difficult to return good profits." 中 "to tell you the truth" 为插入语，意思为"老实说，说实话"。"rocket up" 意思为"飞涨，升高"，如 "The budget will rocket up from $60 million to $340 million a year." 预算从6 000万美元飞涨至一年3.4亿美元。"which make it very difficult to return good profits" 是非限制性定语从句，意思为"使得我们很难有好的利润"。
5. But for frequent buyers like you, we can offer varying degree of discounts, depending on the amount of your purchase. 但是，像您这样的老客户，我们能根据购货

量的大小提供不同程度的折扣。

6. drive me bankrupt 逼我破产。"with such a large order on hand" 眼下这样大的一个订单。"on hand"在手边，在附近，在场，手头，如 "He has too much work on hand to go picnicking with us." 他手头的工作太多了，不能跟我们去野餐。

7. Considering the long-standing business relationship between us, we shall grant you a special discount of 10%. 考虑到我们长期的贸易关系，我们才给你百分之十的特别折扣。

8. meet each other halfway 互让，折中。

9. You are a real businesswoman! 你真是个了不起的女商人！

10. Deal! 成交！

11. Make yourself easy. 请放心。

Useful Sentences 必学句型

1. We haven't seen each other for a long time. 好久不见。

2. What can I do for you? 我能为你做些什么？类似的说法还有 "Is there anything I can do for you?", "Can I help you find anything?", "May I help you?"

3. Will you show me the price catalogue? 你能让我看一下价目单吗？

4. The materials here are not expensive, but of the best quality. 这里的建材不贵，但质量上乘。

5. You may rest assured that we shall do everything possible to cooperate with you in this matter. 请放心我方会尽力在这方面与你合作。

6. Do you have any specials for frequent buyers like me? 对于像我这样的老主顾，价格上有什么优惠吗？

7. The prices of the building materials have been rocketing up recently. 最近建筑材料的价格一直在飞涨。

8. In consideration of the quantity of the three building materials you intend to purchase, we can offer you 10% discount. 考虑到你所购买的三种建材的量，我们可以给你10%的折扣。

9. Could you see your way to increase it to 20%? 你能想办法把折扣提到20%吗？

10. As you know, we do business on the basis of equality and mutual benefit. 你知道，我们是在平等互利的基础上做交易的。

11. I agree to give you a 15% discount. 我同意给你15%的折扣。

12. We will go all-out to supply you with the materials and deliver them to your site without any delays. 我们将全力以赴备好建材，并运送到工地，不会误事的。

Exercises 练习

1. Complete the following dialogue in English.

A: Are you being served, sir?
B: _____. (是的,我打算从你这里订购一批石材。)
A: For what purpose?
B: _____. (主要用于家装。)
A: All the samples of stone materials are here. What do you want to buy?
B: _____.
(我对你这里的大理石很满意。如果价格合适,我现在就想订货。)
A: I'm very glad to hear that.
B: _____. (这种纯白色大理石最低价是多少?)
A: 700 *yuan* per square meter.
B: I think the price is too high. Can't you reduce it?
A: _____.
(恐怕不行,700元是我们的底价。更何况这是纯天然的,每一块都具有独一无二的图案和色彩。)
B: But there are some beautiful marbles in the market priced at 120~180 *yuan* per square meter. How do you explain the large price differences to me?
A: _____.
(那些价格低的是人造大理石,透明度不好,且没有光泽。)
B: Oh, I know. Can you tell me how to distinguish the two different kinds of marbles?
A: _____.
(最简单的方法就是滴上几滴稀盐酸,天然大理石会剧烈起泡,人造大理石起泡弱甚至不起泡。)
B: Can I do a small experiment on the samples of marbles here by using diluted hydrochloric acid?
A: _____.
(当然可以。俗话说,真金不怕火炼。)
(After the experiment)
B: Well, I'll accept the price and place an initial order of 10,000 square meters.
A: _____. (太好了。跟你做生意真是我的荣幸。)
B: The pleasure is ours. Can you deliver the goods by March 31st?
A: _____. (绝对没问题,我们是不会误事的。)

2. Read and interpret the following passages.

(1) Fired bricks are used extensively for houses in developed countries. Their size and type are governed by national standards and there is a move to set up international standards. The size and proportions are broadly chosen so that a bricklayer can hold a brick using only one

hand and the brick can bond with others lying parallel and at right angles to the wall face.

Most bricks are made from clay or shale and are burned in a kiln. Some, however, are made of silica sand and lime and these are known as calcium silicate bricks. Building blocks are a little larger than bricks and are generally made of concrete.

（2）石材可分为天然石材和人工石材（又名人造石），石材是建筑装饰的高档产品，天然石材分为花岗岩、大理石、砂岩、石灰岩、火山岩等，随着科技的不断发展和进步，人造石的产品也不断日新月异，质量和美观已经不逊色天然石材。随着经济的发展，石材早已经成为建筑、装饰、道路、桥梁建设的重要原料之一。

3. Pair work.

Suppose you are a material man. Talk with a material engineer of a construction company and try to persuade him into purchasing your building materials.

Supplementary Materials 补充材料

Tables of Common Building Materials
常见建筑材料一览表

CATALOGUE(类别)	EXAMPLES（举例）
Bricks and Tiles（砖瓦）	red brick（红砖） clay brick（粘土砖） glazed brick（ceramic tile）（瓷砖） fire brick（防火砖） hollow brick（空心砖） facing brick（面砖） flooring tile（地板砖） clinker brick（缸砖） mosaic（马赛克） glazed tile（琉璃瓦） ridge tile（脊瓦） asbestos tile（shingle）（石棉瓦）
Lime, Sand and Stone（灰、砂和石）	gypsum（石膏） marble（大理石） white marble（汉白玉） rubble（毛石） granite（花岗岩） crushed stone（碎石） vermiculite（蛭石） gravel（砾石） terrazzo（水磨石） cobble（卵石） course sand（粗砂） fine sand（细砂） medium sand（中砂）
Cement, Mortar and Concrete（水泥、砂浆和混凝土）	portland cement（波特兰水泥） silicate cement（硅酸盐水泥） white cement（白水泥） cement mortar（水泥砂浆） lime mortar（石灰砂浆） cement-lime mortar（水泥石灰砂浆） thermal mortar（保温砂浆） water-proof mortar（防水砂浆） acid-resistant mortar（耐酸砂浆） alkaline-resistant mortar（耐碱砂浆） bituminous mortar（沥青砂浆） plain concrete（素混凝土） reinforced concrete（钢筋混凝土） lightweight concrete（轻质混凝土） fine aggregate concrete（细石混凝土） asphalt concrete（沥青混凝土） foamed concrete（泡沫混凝土） cinder concrete（炉渣混凝土）
Asphalt and Asbestos（沥青和石棉）	asphalt felt（沥青卷材） asphalt filler（沥青填料） asphalt grout（沥青胶泥） asbestos sheet（石棉板） asbestos fiber（石棉纤维）
Timber（木材）	cypress（柏木） white poplar（白杨） birch（桦木） fir（冷杉） oak（栎木） willow（榴木） elm（榆木） cedar（杉木） teak（柚木） camphor wood（樟木） preservative-treated lumber（防腐处理的木材） plywood（胶合板） tongued and grooved board（企口板） laminated plank（层夹板） glue-laminated lumber（胶合层夹木材） fiber-board（纤维板） log（原木） round timber（圆木） square timber（方木） plank（板材） batten（木条） lath（板条） board（木板） red pine（红松） white pine（白松） spruce（云杉） deciduous pine（落叶松） bamboo（竹子）

续表

CATALOGUE(类别)	EXAMPLES(举例)
Metallic Materials（金属材料）	alloy steel（合金钢） titanium alloy（钛合金） stainless steel（不锈钢） corrugated steel bar（竹节钢筋） deformed bar（变形钢筋） plain round bar（光圆钢筋） steel plate（钢板） thin steel plate（薄钢板） low carbon steel（低碳钢） cold bending（冷弯） steel pipe (tube)（钢管） seamless steel pipe（无缝钢管） welded steel pipe（焊接钢管） iron pipe（黑铁管） galvanized steel pipe（镀锌钢管） cast iron（铸铁） steel bar（圆钢） square steel（方钢） steel strap（钢带），flat steel（扁钢） steel section (shape)（型钢） channel（槽钢） angle steel（角钢） equal-leg angle（等边角钢） unequal-leg angle（不等边角钢） I-beam（工字钢） wide flange I-beam（宽翼缘工字钢） T-bar (Z-bar)（丁字钢） light gauge cold-formed（冷弯薄壁型钢） pig iron（生铁） wrought iron（熟铁） galvanized steel sheet（镀锌铁皮） galvanized steel wire（镀锌铁丝） steel wire mesh（钢丝网） manganese steel（锰钢） high strength alloy steel（高强度合金钢） gold（金） platinum（白金） copper（铜） brass（黄铜） bronze（青铜） silver（银） aluminum（铝） lead（铅）
Building Hardware（建筑五金）	nails（钉子） screws（螺丝） flat-head screw（平头螺丝） bolt（螺栓） spiral-threaded roofing nail（螺纹屋面钉） cinch bolt（胀锚螺栓） annular-ring gypsum board nail（环纹石膏板钉） washer（垫片） common bolt（普通螺栓） high strength bolt（高强螺栓） insert bolt（预埋螺栓）
Paint（油漆）	primer（底漆） rust-inhibitive primer（防锈底漆） varnish（透明漆） anti-corrosion paint（防腐漆） mixed paint（调和漆） flat paint（无光漆） aluminum paint（银粉漆） enamel paint（磁漆） drying oil（干性油） thinner（稀释剂） tar（焦油）asphalt paint（沥青漆）Chinese wood oil（桐油） red lead（红丹） lead oil（铅油） putty（腻子）
Facing and Plastering Materials（饰面及粉刷材料）	granitic plaster（水刷石） artificial stone（斩假石） lime wash（刷浆） casein（可赛银） white wash（大白浆） hemp cuts and lime as base（麻刀灰打底） lath and plaster（板条抹灰）
Anti-corrosion Materials（防腐蚀材料）	polythene, polyethylene（聚乙烯） nylon（尼龙） PVC (polyvinyl chloride)（聚氯乙烯） polycarbonate（聚碳酸酯） polystyrene（聚苯乙烯） acrylic resin（丙烯酸树脂） vinyl ester（乙烯基酯） rubber lining（橡胶内衬） neoprene（氯丁橡胶） bitumen paint（沥青漆） epoxy resin paint（环氧树脂漆） zinc oxide primer（氧化锌底漆） anti-rust paint（防锈漆） acid-resistant paint（耐酸漆） alkali-resistant paint（耐碱漆） sodium silicate（水玻璃） resin-bonded mortar（树脂砂浆） epoxy resin（环氧树脂）

模块六 建筑材料

MODULE 7　Building Machinery
模块七　建筑机械

Learning Objectives 学习目标

In this module, learners should:
- know the Chinese and English names of various types of building machines.
- be capable of making English dialogues in aspects of introducing, operating and repairing building machines.

在本模块内，学习者应该能：
- 掌握各类建筑机械的中英文名称。
- 能进行常用建筑机械介绍、操作及修理等方面的英语对话。

Special Terms 专业词汇

starter　启动机
fork-lift　装载机
trolley　台车，手推车
electric dipper　电铲
pulley　滑车
hydraulic pump　液压泵
universal crane　万能起重机
derrick crane　悬臂起重机
travelling hoist　移动式卷扬机
windlass　卷扬机，起锚机
power capstan　动力绞盘
snatch block　辘轳紧线滑轮
automatic ram pile driver　自动冲锤打桩机
pile drawer　拔桩机
pile hoop/band　桩锤
electric rammer　电夯机
lane maker　车道画线机

dumper　翻斗车
trailer　拖车，挂车
semi-trailer　半挂车
mixer　搅拌机
loader-dozer　带式输送机
tipper truck　自卸车
electric crane　电动起重机
platform hoist　平台式起重机
builder's lift　施工用升降机
bridge crane　桥式起重机
builder's winch　施工绞车
overhanging pile driver　伸臂式打桩机
pile frame　打桩架
jack bit　钻头
hydraulic drill　液压钻机
track-lift　叉式升降机，铲车
stone breaker　碎石机

asphalt layer 沥青铺面机	road paver 铺路机
road roller 压路机	road ripper 松土机
road scraper 刮路机	tar sprayer 焦油浇注机

machine 是指一部机器,而 machinery 是机器的总称(machine system),一套机械系统(set of machines)。如:The machinery in the factory consists of several different kinds of machines. 工厂里的机械设备包括许多种不同的机器。

Situational Conversations 情景对话

James: Is this the mechanized building site, Mrs. Li?

Li Qin: Yes. Do you need some help?

James: Yea. There are so many machines on the site, just like an exhibition of construction machinery. I wonder whether every procedure on the site is completely done by machines.

Li Qin: Oh, right. I suppose you must be the first time to come here.

James: That's right. Although I heard of it before, I have never seen myself. I am very lucky today to be a real eye opener.

Li Qin: The building industry has undergone great changes from strenuous hand labor in the past to mechanized construction nowadays.

James: So you keep abreast of the time as well. Can you tell me what kinds of construction machines there are on your site?

Li Qin: With pleasure. There are cranes, conveyers, concrete machines, earth and rock-moving equipments and so on.

James: Quite a lot. What do you do on the construction site?

Li Qin: I am a dumper driver.

James: Very nice. Do you have a license?

Li Qin: Of course, I do. Every mechanics on the site must have a relevant certificate to go on duty.

James: It means that you take up the post through competition, don't you?

Li Qin: You are right. First we have to be trained at least one year, and then we are strictly examined in the rules of operating procedure. Only after passing the examination, can we finally get the license to operate the machines.

James: The regulations are required as strictly as that in my country. By the way, besides a dumper, are you capable of operating other machines?

Li Qin: Yes, I can operate a lot of machines well, such as concrete mixer, hoister, and so on.

James: You are a general-purpose manipulator. Let me see how well you drive your dumper, will you?

Li Qin: I really don't deserve it. But I'm very happy to show my operative skills of dumper.

James: Hey, you are really something. You have skillful operations and perfect techniques. But I suggest that before operation you carefully test the machine's performance and in driving you concentrate your efforts without slackening any vigilance.

Li Qin: Thanks. I will never forget it and follow what you suggested in future.

Questions

1. What does a mechanized building site mean?
2. What suggestions did James offer to Li Qin?

Notes 注释

1. the mechanized building site 机械化的建筑工地。后缀-ize(-ise)可以加在名词或形容词的后面构成动词,表示"照……样子做"、"按……方式处理"、"使成为……"、"变成……状态"、"……化"的意思。例如:dramatic(戏剧的)→dramatize(改编成剧本),modern(现代的)→modernize(现代化),civil(文明的)→civilize(使文明,变为文明)。某些以-y结尾的词,加-ize(-ise)后缀时,要去掉-y再加-ize(-ise),例如:sympathy(同情心)→sympathize(同情)。
2. yea 为 yes 的过时用法(old-fashioned),意思为"是,对"。
3. "… just like an exhibition of construction machinery." 就像建筑机械的展览会。
4. a real eye opener 大开眼界。
5. "… has undergone great changes …" 经历了巨大的变化。undergo 意思为"经历,经验;遭受,承受",如"Everyone will undergo highs and lows in his work or life." 每个人在工作和生活中都会经历起伏。
6. keep abreast of the time 与时俱进。此处 abreast 为副词,意思为"并排,并肩"。
7. earth and rock-moving equipments 土石方机械。
8. take up the post through competition 竞聘上岗。

9. a general-purpose manipulator 万能的机械手。
10. You are really something. 你真了不起。
11. I suggest that before operation you carefully test the machine's performance and in driving you concentrate your efforts without slackening any vigilance. 我建议你在操作机械之前，必须检查机械的性能；机械驾驶中，必须集中精力，不可麻痹大意。concentrate one's efforts on doing sth 集中精力做……，如"We must concentrate our efforts on improving the quality of our products."我们必须集中力量，提高产品质量。slacken/relax one's vigilance 麻痹大意；maintain sharp vigilance 保持高度警惕；redouble one's vigilance 加倍警惕。

Useful Sentences 必学句型

1. I wonder whether every procedure on the site is completely done by machines. 我想知道建筑工地上的每道工序是否全由机器来完成。
2. I suppose you must be the first time to come here. 我猜你一定是第一次来这里。
3. The building industry has undergone great changes from strenuous hand labor in the past to mechanized construction nowadays. 建筑业经历了巨大的变化，从过去繁重的手工操作到今天的机械化施工。
4. It means that you take up the post through competition, don't you? 意思是说，你通过竞争上岗，不是吗？
5. Only after passing the examination, can we finally get the license to operate the machines. 只有通过考试，我们才能拿到操作机械的执照。
6. Are you capable of operating other machines? 你能操作其他机械吗？
7. Let me see how well you drive your dumper, will you? 让我看看你是如何驾驶翻斗车的，可以吗？
8. I really don't deserve it. 不敢当。
9. I'm very happy to show my operative skills of dumper. 我很高兴展示翻斗车操作技能。
10. I suggest that you (should) do/not do... 我建议你应该做/不该做……

Exercises 练习

1. Complete the following dialogue in English.

A: What is the matter, sir?
B: _____. (混凝土搅拌机出现了故障，不能正常运转。)
A: Let me start it first, and see what mechanical failure on earth it is.

B：_____?（瞧！马达运转很正常，到底哪里有毛病?）

A：I can't explain it exactly now. I will take some time to check it.

B：_____.
（假如搅拌不出混凝土，这可就耽误大事了，因为工地上绝大多数建设者只好停工待料，所以我想知道得花多长时间才能修好。）

A：I am not sure. Maybe a few minutes, maybe half an hour.

B：_____?
（这可把人急死啦！为什么在马达转动正常状态，混凝土拌和筒不转呢?）

A：Let me think it over.

B：_____?（是不是皮带太松弛不起作用了?）

A：I think so. Why not change a new one?

B：It is a good idea.

(After a while)

A：_____.（新的皮带已换好，请重新启动一下。）

B：Oh, it is OK. Thank you for your help.

A：_____.
（哪的话，我的工作职责就是为施工服务，保障机械正常运转，施工正常运行。）

C：_____?
（劳驾，我的翻斗车刹车不灵，挂挡也困难，需要修理。你能过来看一看吗?）

A：I'm busy and I've a lot of repairing work to do. However, I find it is difficult to refuse because of my duty. Shall we go to check it up?

C：_____.
（那太好了！多谢你给我这个面子。咱们走。）

A：Don't stand on ceremony. Serving construction is my first thing to do.

2. **Read and interpret the following passage.**

Scrapers and Graders

For building level and modern roads, the specialized earth movers employed are scrapers and graders. A scraper may be self-propelled or pulled by a tractor. It has a knifelike cutter that planes off a layer of soil into an internal reservoir that can hold up to 1,400 cubic feet (40 cubic meters) hydraulic rams and the machine can transport its load to a nearby site, where it is dumped.

For precise finishing of the road foundation before concreting, a grader is used. It has an angled blade 2~4 m wide, hydraulically controlled and slung between its wheels. Most graders are self-propelled.

3. **Pair work.**

Suppose A acts as a machine driver, B acts as a repairman who wants to know the trouble of a bulldozer. Use the following expressions：

A：*Can you help me, sir?*

B：*Yes, I'd like to ...*

A: *Please check my ... and see what is the trouble with ... .*
B: *OK. Let me ...*

Supplementary Materials 补充材料

Tables of Common Building Machinery
常见建筑机械一览表

CATALOGUE(类别)	EXAMPLES（举例）
Road Machinery（路面机械）	stabilized soil mixer(稳定土拌和机) road cutter（路面切割机） road-marking vehicle（划线车） snow remover（除雪机） asphalt distributor（沥青洒布车） asphalt dumping equipment（沥青脱桶设备） asphalt pavement repairing vehicle（沥青路面修补车） asphalt mixture transfer vehicle（沥青混合料转运车） groover（刻纹机） paving machine（摊铺机） milling machine（铣刨机） slurry seal machine（稀浆封层机） pavement maintenance vehicle（路面养护车） pavement breaker（路面破碎机） road block removal truck（道路清障车） garbage-treatment car（垃圾处理车） breakstone disperser（碎石撒布机） sweeping vehicle（清扫车）
Digging Machinery（挖掘机械）	excavating loader（挖掘装载机） hydraulic wheel excavator（轮胎式液压挖掘机） trencher(挖沟机) hydraulic crawler excavator（履带式液压挖掘机）
Concrete Machinery（混凝土机械）	concrete mixing truck（混凝土搅拌运输车） shotcrete machine（混凝土喷射机） concrete pump（混凝土输送泵） concrete breaker（混凝土粉碎机） concrete paver(混凝土摊铺机) concrete mixer（混凝土搅拌机） concrete pump truck(混凝土泵车) concrete trailer pump（混凝土拖泵）
Hoisting Machinery（起重机械）	windlass（卷扬机） truck crane（汽车起重机） crawler crane（履带式起重机） elevator（升降机） lift car(升降车) pipe crane（吊管机） aerial platform vehicle（高空作业车） tower crane（塔式起重机） tyre crane（轮胎式起重机） towing machine（牵引机） forklift truck（叉车） gantry crane（门式起重机）
Earth Moving Machinery（铲土运输机械）	transport vehicle(运输车) scraper（铲运机） grader（平地机） dumper（翻斗车） tyred loader（轮胎式装载机） crawler loader（履带式装载机） skid loader（滑移式装载机） bulldozer(推土机) dump truck（自卸卡车） conveyor(输送机)
Compaction Machinery（压实机械）	vibrating tamper(振动夯实机) vibratory roller（振动压路机） static roller（静力式压路机） impact compactor（冲击夯实机） compactor（压实机） roller compactor（碾压机） tyre roller（轮胎压路机）
Drilling Machinery（钻探机械）	heading machine(掘进机) multifunctional drilling rig（多功能钻机） rotary drilling rig（旋挖钻机） percussive drilling rig（冲击式钻机） construction drill（工程钻机） rotary-percussive drill（冲击回转钻机） water well rig（水井钻机） anchor drill（锚固钻机） opencast driller（潜孔钻机）
Decoration Machinery（装修机械）	electric nacelle（电动吊篮） mud pump（泥浆泵） mortar pump（砂浆泵） winch（绞车） heater（加热器） edger（磨边机） spraying pump（喷涂泵） plastering machine（抹灰机）
Pile Driving Machinery（桩工机械）	pile hoop/band（打桩锤） pile frame（桩架） pile driver（桩机） hydraulic shear（液压剪） diaphragm-wall grab（连续墙抓斗）

续表

CATALOGUE(类别)	EXAMPLES(举例)
Pre-stressed Machinery（预应力机械）	hydraulic tong(液压钳)　reinforcing steel adjusting cutter（钢筋调直切断机）　jack(千斤顶)　anchor device（锚具）　reinforcing steel bending machine（钢筋弯曲机）　cold rolling mill（冷轧机）　tube straightening machine（钢管矫直机）　cutting machine（切割机）　hydraulic machine（液压机）　screw machine（滚丝机）　roller（滚丝轮）　steel sleeve（钢套筒）
Rock Drilling Machinery（凿岩机械）	compressor(压缩机)　ball mill（球磨机）　magnetic separator（磁选机）　hydraulic crusher（液压破碎机）　breaking hammer（破碎锤）　rock drill（凿岩机）

MODULE 8　Architectural Drawings
模块八　建筑图纸

Learning Objectives 学习目标

In this module, learners should:
- know the Chinese and English names of various types of architectural drawings and drawing instruments.
- be capable of discussing in English problems of making and reading architectural drawings.

在本模块内，学习者应该能：
- 掌握各类建筑图纸及绘图仪的中英文名称。
- 能用英语谈论建筑图纸的绘制及识别等问题。

Special Terms 专业词汇

diagram　示意图	sketch　草图
topographical map　地形图	earth-work drawing　土方工程图
developed drawing　展开图	formwork drawing　模板图
standard drawing　标准图	plan　平面图
schematic plan　平面示意图	sectional plan　平剖面图
plan of provision of holes　留孔平面图	section　剖面
longitudinal section　纵剖面	cross (transverse) section　横剖面
elevation　立面	front elevation　正立面
side elevation　侧立面	perspective drawing　透视图
general layout　总图	building drawing　建筑图
roof/foundation plan　屋面/基础平面图	typical drawing　定型图
installation drawing　安装图	equipment drawing　设备图
process flow diagram　工艺流程图	reinforcement drawing　配筋图
dimensioned drawing　标有尺寸的图纸	make/read drawings　制/识图
legend　图例	scale of a drawing　图纸比例
copy of a drawing　图纸副本	drawing instruments　绘图仪器
drawing pen　绘图笔	drawing-compasses　绘图圆规

T-square 丁字尺
drawing paper 绘图纸
French curve 曲线尺
drawing scale 绘图比例尺
tracing paper 描图纸
drawing board 绘图板

figure 通常指几何图形或书中插图；graph 一般指曲线图、标绘图，也可指图解；view 一般用于机械图或各种结构图中的各向视图；profile 一般指零（部）件的外形轮廓图，剖面形状图；pattern 用于指图型、图案、花纹等；drawing 指各种工程图纸及有关工程设计的附图、插图；map 指地图、天体图、布局图以及一些专用图形。

Situational Conversations 情景对话

Jordan: Hi. Can you do me a favor, Engineer Li?

Li Can: At your service.

Jordan: I don't know the exact position of the switch board. Will you scratch it on the wall?

Li Can: It should be scratched in accordance with your drawing. Where is the drawing?

Jordan: Here it is, Engineer Li.

Li Can: Sorry. You have got a wrong drawing.

Jordan: What is the problem?

Li Can: It is a plan, but what I need is an elevation, where the switch board is clearly marked. Would you please get it for me now?

Jordan: OK. Here you are.

Li Can: Thank you. (After a while) Look, the switch board is near the corner of the walls.

Jordan: You are very observant. I do admire you very much.

Li Can: If you were in my position, you'd have done the same, I am sure.

Jordan: That's true. But how high is the switch board to the floor?

Li Can: It is 1.5 m.

Jordan: How do you know the exact size?

Li Can: Because what you gave me for the second time is a dimensioned drawing. If you don't believe it, you can get a drawing scale to measure it yourself.

Jordan: In fact, there is no need at all to do that. So reading and studying drawing carefully is an essential prerequisite for construction well, isn't it?

Li Can: Yes, absolutely. As every drawing is meticulously designed, the sizes and figures on the drawing are also calculated exactly, we constructors should regard it as the norm and the guide of our construction works.

Jordan: That means construction is the translation of design into reality, am I right?

Li Can: Quite right. It seems that you don't read the drawing well.

Jordan: Oh, just so-so.

Li Can: Personally, I think you should make efforts to read the drawing well. Only in this way, can you do your work well. Don't you think so?

Jordan: Sure. I will follow your advice and redouble my efforts to make up for knowledge of building drawings.

Li Can: If you have any drawing problem in your future work and study, please don't hesitate to call me, and I will do my best to help you.

Jordan: You are very kind. Thank you very much.

Li Can: Not at all. I am honored to do something useful for you.

Questions

1. What is an essential prerequisite for construction well?
2. What does "Construction is the translation of design into reality" mean?

Notes 注释

1. do me a favor 帮忙，如 "Would you do me a favor to translate the poem into English?" 你能不能帮忙把这首诗翻译成英语？
2. "At your service." 愿为您效劳。
3. switch board 配电控制板。
4. in accordance with 根据、按照，类似表达还有 according to, in the light of, in line with 等。
5. very observant 观察力非常敏锐。如 "Journalists are trained to be observant." 新闻记者都要训练成有敏锐观察力的人。

6. I do admire you very much. 我非常佩服你。"do/does/did＋动词原形"表示强调，如"Do drop in if you happen to be passing!"如果你碰巧经过时进来坐坐。
7. a dimensioned drawing 标有尺寸的图纸。
8. a drawing scale 比例尺。
9. So reading and studying drawing carefully is an essential prerequisite for construction well, isn't it? 因此说，认真识图和钻研图纸是搞好施工的必要前提，不是吗？
10. As every drawing is meticulously designed, the sizes and figures on the drawing are also calculated exactly, we constructors should regard it as the norm and the guide of our construction works. 因为每一张图纸都是精心设计出来的，图纸上的尺寸和数据也是精确计算出来的，所以我们施工人员应该把图纸看作我们施工的指南和准则。regard … as 把……认作，类似表达还有 assume as, consider as 等。
11. "… construction is the translation of design into reality." 施工就是把设计变成现实。"translate A into B"把 A 翻译为 B, 把 A 转化为 B, 如"We must make efforts to translate our ideal into reality."我们必须努力把理想转化为现实。
12. redouble my efforts 加倍努力。
13. make up 弥补，如"Hard work can often make up for a lack of ability."努力工作经常可以弥补能力的不足。
14. "… please don't hesitate to call me." 只管给我电话。又如"I will not hesitate to recommend this brand."我毫不犹豫向您推荐这个品牌。

Useful Sentences 必学句型

1. Will you do me a favor to lift the heavy box? 你能帮我提一下这个重箱子吗？
2. What is the problem/What is wrong/What is the matter with the machine? 机器出了什么问题？
3. If you were in my position, you'd have done the same, I am sure. 我相信如果你处在我的位置上，也会这样做。
4. Personally, I think you should make efforts to read the drawing well. 我个人觉得你应该努力学会如何更好地识图。
5. Only in this way, can you do your work well. 只有这样，才能做好你的工作。
6. I will follow your advice and redouble my efforts to make up for knowledge of building drawings. 我会听取您的建议，加倍努力补习关于建筑图纸方面的知识。
7. If you have any questions, don't hesitate to ask. 有什么问题只管问。
8. I am honored to do something useful for you. 能为你做些有用的事情我深感荣幸。

Exercises 练习

1. Complete the following dialogue in English.

A: Excuse me! Can you answer me some questions about building drawings?

B: _____.

(当然可以。关于建筑图纸你想了解什么?)

A: First, I want to know the more scientific definition of building drawings.

B: _____.

(所谓的建筑图纸就是将一幢拟建建筑物的内外形状和大小,以及各部分的结构、构造、装饰、设备等内容,按照有关规范规定,用正投影方法,详细准确地画出的图样。)

A: So building drawings are very important to the construction works, aren't they?

B: _____.

(你说的没错。建筑图纸一直被看作是施工的指南和准则。)

A: How many parts are there in a complete set of building drawings?

B: _____.

(一套完整的施工图,根据其专业内容或作用不同,一般包括图纸目录、设计总说明、建筑施工图、结构施工图及设备施工图。)

A: How can I tell the differences between the building construction drawings and the structural working drawings?

B: _____.

(建筑施工图表示的是建筑物的内部布置情况,外部形状,以及装修、构造、施工要求等内容。)

A: What about structural working drawings?

B: _____.

(结构施工图表示的是承重结构的布置情况、构件类型、尺寸大小及构造做法等内容。)

A: To make these complicated drawings, some precise instruments are inevitable, am I right?

B: _____.

(是的,常用的绘图仪器有绘图笔、绘图圆规、丁字尺、曲线板等。)

A: I know. They are mainly used in manual drawings, aren't they?

B: _____.

(没错,现在的建筑图纸多是通过计算机 AutoCAD 软件绘制出来的。相对于手工绘图,其优点是不言而喻的。)

A: What is AutoCAD, I want to know?

B: _____.

(AutoCAD 是美国 Autodesk 公司开发的用于二维及三维设计、绘图的自动计算机辅助设计软件。)

A: Will you mind teaching me to make building drawings by AutoCAD sometime when you are free?

B: _____.

(当然不介意,如有需要,只管给我打个电话,我一定会不遗余力地帮你。)

2. Read and interpret the following passage.

Building Drawings

Building drawings involve a variety of drawings such as plan, elevation, cross section, layout, bird's eye view, standard drawing, working drawing … Drawings play an important part in construction. Therefore, they are regarded as the norm and the guide of the construction. In other words, construction is the translation of design into reality.

3. Pair work.

Imagine A wants to do his construction work well without drawings, B thinks that it is impossible. They are arguing about it.

Supplementary Materials 补充材料

Dialogue Expressions of Engineering Drawings
工程图纸对话用语

1. We completed this task according to the drawing numbered SD-76.
   我们按照图号 SD-76 的图纸完成了这项工作。

2. This is a floor plan (general layout, general arrangement, detail, section, installation, flow sheet, PID, assembly, civil construction, electrical, control and instrumentation, projection, piping, isometric).
   这是一张平面布置(总平面、总布置、细部、剖面、安装、流程、带仪表控制点的管道、装配、土建、电气、自控和仪表、投影、配管、空视)图。

3. That is a general view (front, rear, side, left, right, top, vertical, bottom, elevation, auxiliary, cut-away, birds eye).
   那是全视(前视、后视、侧视、左视、右视、顶视、俯视、底视、立视、辅助、内部剖视、鸟瞰)图。

4. How many drawings are there in the set?
   这套图纸有几张?

5. Is this a copy for reproduction?
   这是一份底图吗?

6. What is the edition of this drawing?
   这张图纸是第几版?

7. Is this drawing in effect?
   这张图纸有效吗?

8. Is this drawing a revised edition?
   这是修订版吗?
9. Will the drawing be revised yet?
   这张图纸还要修订吗?
10. Are there some modifications (revisions) on the drawing?
    这张图纸上有些修改(修正)吗?
11. The information to be placed in the title block of each drawing includes: drawing number, drawing size, scale, weight, sheet number and number of sheets, drawing title and signatures of persons preparing, checking and approving the drawing.
    每张图纸的图标栏内容包括:图号、图纸尺寸、比例、重量、张号和张数、图标以及图纸的制图、校对、批准人的签字。
12. There are various types of lines on the drawing, such as, border lines, visible lines, invisible lines, section lines, central lines, down-lead lines, dimension lines, broken lines and phantom lines.
    图纸上有各种形式的线条,诸如:边框线、实线、虚线、剖面线、中心线、引出线、尺寸线、断裂线、假想线。
13. We have not received this drawing (instruction book, operation manual), so please help us to get it.
    我们还未收到这张图纸(说明书、操作手册),请帮助我们取得。
14. Please explain the meaning of this abbreviation (mark, symbol) on the drawing.
    请解释图纸上这个缩写(标记、符号)的意义。
15. Please make a sketch of this part on the paper.
    请将这个零件的草图画在纸上。
16. Would you lend me your drawings?
    可否将你的图纸借给我?
17. Please bring us those drawings.
    请把那些图纸带给我们。
18. As the copy of the drawing is blurred, it is not very clear.
    这张图纸的复印件被弄模糊了,不太清晰。
19. Please give us a copy of this information (technical specification, instruction, manual, document, diagram, catalog).
    请给我们一份这个资料(技术规程、说明书、手册、文件、图表、目录样本)的复印本。
20. We regard these drawings very useful in construction works.
    我们认为这些图纸在施工中是很有用的。
21. A working drawing must be clear and complete.
    工作图纸必须简明完整。
22. Just look at this drawing.
    看看这张图纸吧。
23. Please have a look at the drawing.

请看这张图纸。
24. Please make a copy of this drawing.
    请把这张图纸复制一份。
25. I have done six copies of this drawing.
    这张图纸我已复制六份。

MODULE 9　Construction Tendering
模块九　建筑招投标

Learning Objectives 学习目标

In this module, learners should:
- know the Chinese and English names of tendering documents.
- be capable of consulting and discussing in English the relevant contents of tendering documents.

在本模块内，学习者应该能：
- 了解建筑标书文件的中英文名称。
- 能用英语咨询投标事宜以及谈论标书相关内容。

Special Terms 专业词汇

tender document　标书文件
lose a tender　未中标
tender opening　开标
tender decision　决标
tender invitation　招标
tender board/committee　投标委员会
tender in date　截标日期
tender validity period　标书有效期
tender deposit　投标按金
tender rate　标额
tender negotiation　投标协商
international tender　国际招标
competitive tender　竞争招标
Tender Selection Board　投标遴选委员会
tenderer/ee　投标者/招标者
tender guarantee　投标保证书
tender for construction　投标承建

tender accepted　中标
tender quotation　报标
tender discussion　议标
tender submission　投标
tender assessment　评标
tender conditions　标书条件
tender out date　出标日期
tender period　投标期
tender price index　投标价格指数
tender offers　投标开价
joint tender　联合招标
advertised tender　公开招标
tender procedures　投标程序
tender selection criteria　选标准则
successful tenderer　中标人
tender reference　招标编号
tender for purchase　投标承购

tender notice   招标告示；招标公告
tender referral   标书转介
tender specifications   标书规格
tender recommendation   标书举荐
tender schedule   标书附表
base price limit on tender   标底

tender/bid 可用作名词和动词，表示"投标"或"招标"，是国际贸易中常见的一种贸易形式。它常用在国家政府机构、国有企业或公用事业单位采购物资、器材或设备和交易中，更多地用于国际承包工程。在美国通常用 bid，而在英国则多用 tender。

Situational Conversations 情景对话

George: Mr. Wu, many companies have been invited to the tender for the pavilion constructions of the 2010 Shanghai World Expo. Wouldn't you like to submit your tender?

Wu Lin: Of course we would. But first of all, we want to know what we have to do before sending our tender.

George: As is often the case, you have to submit your relevant materials on cost, construction time and the volume of works concerning some already constructed big projects by your company.

Wu Lin: I see. We will do that as soon as possible. Besides, can you tell me some requirements of the tender committee?

George: OK. How do you assess the volume of work on the project?

Wu Lin: The work volume is assessed on the basis of the acquired data. When will you arrange the registration formalities for our company?

George: As soon as we receive your relevant materials, I suppose.

Wu Lin: When is the tendering deadline?

George: Ten days before the tender opening.

Wu Lin: And when are you going to open the tender then?

George: On Jan, 1st, 2007.

Wu Lin: I've born in mind. How do you rate our chances of success?

George: It is very hard to say. That depends on your tender and sincerity. You have rich experience and solid strength in this field, so I suppose you must have a greater probability of success in winning the tender.

Wu Lin: I hope so.

George: Good luck and success to you and your company.

Wu Lin: Thanks a lot. We are sure to seize the opportunity.

Questions

1. What does Mr. Wu's company have to do before sending the tender?
2. When is the last tendering day of the pavilion constructions of the 2010 Shanghai World Expo according to the conversation?

Notes 注释

1. the pavilion constructions of the 2010 Shanghai World Expo 2010 年上海世博会的场馆建设。
2. "As is often the case,..."意思为"通常情况",如"As is often the case, the careless girl forgot to bring her dictionary."正如往常一样,这个粗心的女孩又忘了带上字典。
3. the tender committee 投标委员会。
4. on the basis of 意思为"以……为基础;根据;按照;依据",如"Don't evaluate a person on the basis of appearance."不要以相貌取人。
5. arrange the registration formalities 办理注册手续。类似的说法还有"go through formalities of",如"Please receive the notice herewith and go through formalities of dismissal within three days."请您接到通知后三天内办理离职手续。
6. the tendering deadline 投标的截止日期。
7. I've born in mind. 我记住了。"bear in mind sth./that clause" 记住,如"You must bear in mind all these wise sayings."这些至理名言你可要谨记在心。"Bear in mind that the performance begins at 10:30."记住演出十点半开始。
8. solid strength 雄厚的实力。
9. seize/grasp the opportunity 抓住机遇。

Useful Sentences 必学句型

1. <u>Wouldn't you like to submit</u> your tender? 难道你们不想参与投标吗?
2. <u>But first of all, we want to know what</u> we have to do before sending our tender. 但是,首先我们想了解一下在投标前应该做哪些准备工作。
3. <u>We will finish the work as soon as possible.</u> 我们会尽快把工作做完。
4. <u>How do you assess the volume of work</u> on the project? 你们如何评估工程项目的工程量呢?
5. <u>The work volume is assessed on the basis of</u> the acquired data. 工程量是根据已积累的相关数据资料来确定的。
6. <u>When will you arrange</u> the registration formalities <u>for</u> our company? 你什么时候为我们公司办理投标登记手续?
7. <u>We must bear in mind that</u> wasting time is equal to wasting our life. 我们必须记住浪费时间等于浪费生命。
8. <u>How do you rate</u> our chances of success? 你看我们中标的可能性有多大?
9. <u>I suppose you must have a greater probability of success in</u> winning the tender. 我认为你们中标的几率很高。
10. <u>Good luck and success to</u> you and your company. 祝你及贵公司好运,能够成功中标。

Exercises 练习

1. **Complete the following dialogue in English.**

    A: Good afternoon! Nice to meet you again!
    B: _____.
    (下午好!很高兴再次见到您!首先,祝贺贵公司已通过我们的资格预审进入大龙电站工程的投标阶段。)
    A: Thank you! Is it possible for us to know how many companies are still in the circle for competition and who they are?
    B: _____. (当然不能,那是我们的商业秘密。)
    A: I am sorry. I did so just from curiosity, no other purpose. Please forget it.
    B: _____.
    (现在让我们回到标书问题上。您看有很多卷。卷1是依据FIDIC拟订的合同条件,对承包商和业主双方都是公平的,我们希望贵公司能赞同这些条件。)
    A: We will study it carefully and have our comments if it is allowed.
    B: _____.

（好的，让我们继续谈论标书。卷 2 是工程量单，有 18 节 989 个单价条目。）

A：Is the contract price a lump sum or a rate-based one?

B：_____.

（此为单价合同，即合同中的总工程量取决于承包商实际完成的工程量，因为电站结构非常复杂，工程量也很大，在施工期间一定会有些变动。）

A：Compared with the lump sum price contract, the rate-based one is good for us, as it can reduce our risk.

B：_____.

（卷 3 是工程范围。贵公司应该根据我们在此卷中表示的总体计划表提供每座建筑物的详细施工进度计划表。）

A：Can we make some adjustments to the key dates marked in the General Guiding Schedule for some individual buildings without affecting the completion of the whole works?

B：_____.

（不行。工程最重要部分的关键日期是固定的，毫无修改余地。关键日期延期导致的违约金有不同级别的罚款。）

A：OK. Let us go on to the tender documents.

B：_____.

（卷 4 和卷 5 是技术规格书。由于本电站的设计是由英国工程公司完成的，因此在所有的工程中采用的主要是英国规范。本卷列有本工程所采用的英国规范的清单。）

A：We will collect all necessary information about the standard and get familiar with the specifications of the project.

B：_____.

（卷 6 是质保手册。本项目定义了 3 种级别的质量保证等级。）

A：Would you give us some explanations about the quality assurance?

B：_____.

（第一级 QA1 用于诸如锅炉炉架等与发电直接有关的结构；第二级 QA2 用于如主厂房等电站中重要的结构；第三级 QANC 同于普通土建工程结构。）

A：We will work out our quality assurance program for this project in accordance with these grades.

B：_____.

（卷 7 为图纸。所有图纸均盖有"投标专用"图章。一旦中标，您将得到盖有"施工专用"图章的图纸。）

A：That's just what we want to obtain.

B：_____.

（这就要看你们把招标书的卷 8 完成得怎样。如果没有竞争力，你们将不能得到"施工专用"图纸。）

A：What is Volume 8 mainly about?

B：_____.

（卷 8 为投标书，包括协议书、施工方案、质量和安全措施及工程量单等四部分内容。）

A：We will do our best to fulfill and submit the above material according to the requirement, as ours is an experienced company for power station construction. By the way, could we ask for the tendering whether you will favorite the lowest price or not?

B：_____.

（我们将根据对标书的全面分析和评定来做决定。我们希望贵公司尽力填好标书的所有部分，并在今天以后的 30 个日历天的中午 12 点之前交给我们。）

A：Ok, we will.

2. Read and interpret the following passage.

Reply to the Tender Submission

Dear Sir：

Having read the terms and conditions in the official form supplied by your Preparatory Department, we enclose our tender for the construction of Tailai Guest House in Saibai Road and trust that it will be accepted.

Yours sincerely

Encl：as stated.

3. Pair work.

You are a vice-manager in charge of tender in the group corporation, and you and your assistors are preparing the tender of International Hotel. Try to say that you must prepare before submitting the tender.

Supplementary Materials 补充材料

Bid Form
投标书格式

致：（招标机构）
To：(name of Tendering Agent)

根据贵方为（项目名称）项目招标采购货物及服务的投标邀请（招标编号），签字代表（姓名、职务）经正式授权并代表投标人（投标人名称、地址）提交下述文件正本一份及副本 _____ 份。

In compliance with your IFB No. _____ for (Goods to be supplied) for the _____ Project, the undersigned representative (_full name and title_) duly authorized to act in the name and for the account of the Bidder (name and address of the Bidder) hereby submit the following in one original and copies：

1. 开标一览表
Summary Sheet for Bid Opening;

2. 投标分项报价表
Bid Schedule of Prices;

3. 货物说明一览表
Brief Descriptions of the Goods;

4. 技术规格响应/偏离表
Responsiveness/Deviation Form for Technical Specifications;

5. 商务条款响应/偏离表
Responsiveness/Deviation Form for Commercial Terms;

6. 按招标文件投标人须知和技术规格要求提供的有关文件
All the other documents required in response to *Instructions To Bidders and Technical Specifications*;

7. 资格证明文件
Qualification Documents;

8. 由(银行名称)出具的投标保证金保函,金额为(金额数和币种)。
Bid Security in the amount of _____ issued by (name of issuing bank).

在此,签字代表宣布同意如下:
By this letter, the undersigned representative hereby declares and agrees:

1. 所附投标价格表中规定的应提供和交付的货物投标总价为(注明币种,并用文字和数字表示的投标总价)。
   That the Total Bid Price for the supply and delivery of the Goods specified in the attached Bid Schedule of Prices is (specify currency or currencies), that is (in words).

2. 投标方将按招标文件的规定履行合同责任和义务。
   That the Bidder will take full responsibility for performance of the Contract in accordance with all provisions of the Bidding Documents.

3. 投标人已详细审查全部招标文件,包括(补遗文件)(如果有的话)。我们完全理解并同意放弃对这方面有不明及误解的权利。
   That the Bidder has examined in detail all the documents including amendments (if any) and all information furnished for reference as well as relevant attachments and that he is perfectly aware that he must renounce all right of invoking ambiguities or misunderstandings in this respect.

4. 本投标有效期为自开标日起(有效期日数)日历日。
   That his bid is valid for a period of _____ calendar days from the date of bid opening.

5. 投标人同意投标人须知中第15.7条款关于没收投标保证金的规定。
   The bidders agree the provision about bid security forfeiture of Clause 15.7 in ITB.

6. 根据投标人须知第2条规定,我方承诺,与买方聘请的为此项目提供咨询服务的公司及任何附属机构均无关联,我方不是买方的附属机构。
   That, pursuant to ITB Clause 2, he declares that, he is not associated with a firm or any its affiliates which have been engaged by the Tendering Agent/the Purchaser to provide consulting services for this Project, and we are not a dependent agency of the Purchaser.

7. 投标人同意提供贵方可能要求的与其投标有关的一切数据或资料。投标人完全理解贵方不一定接受最低价的投标或收到的任何投标。

That he agrees to furnish any other data or information pertinent to its Bid that might be requested by (the Tendering Agent) and that he understands that you are not bound to accept the lowest or any bid you may receive.

8. 与本投标有关的一切正式信函请寄：

That all official correspondence pertinent to this bid shall be addressed to:

地　　址：Address ＿＿＿＿＿＿＿＿＿＿　　　传　真：Fax ＿＿＿＿＿＿

电　　话：Tel ＿＿＿＿＿＿＿＿＿＿＿　　　电子函件：E-mail ＿＿＿＿＿

投标人代表签字：
Name of Representative：＿＿＿＿＿＿

投标人名称：
Name of the Bidder：＿＿＿＿＿＿

公章：
Official Seal ＿＿＿＿＿＿＿＿＿＿

日期：
Date ＿＿＿＿＿＿＿＿＿＿＿＿

MODULE 10　Construction Contract
模块十　建筑合同

Learning Objectives 学习目标

In this module, learners should:
- know the Chinese and English names of the contract clauses.
- be capable of negotiating and signing in English the engineering contracts.

在本模块内，学习者应该能：
- 了解合同条款的中英文术语。
- 能用英语洽谈与签订各类工程合同。

Special Terms 专业词汇

construction contract　建筑合同
contract management　合同管理
contract clauses　合同条款
contract period　合同期限
contract party　合同当事人
long-term contract　长期合同
terminal/fixed term contract　定期合同
negotiate a contract　洽谈合同
tear up a contract　撕毁合同
terminate a contract　终止合同
make a contract　订立合同
sign a contract　签署合同
infringe/break a contract　违反合同
prolong a contract　延长合同
originals of the contract　合同正本
renewal of contract　合同的续订
contract of carriage　运输合同
contract for goods　订货合同

decoration contract　装饰合同
contract provisions/stipulations　合同规定
contract number　合同编号
expiration of contract　合同期满
contractual obligations　合同义务
short-term contract　短期合同
void contract　无效合同
approve a contract　审批合同
complete a contract　完成合同
hold a contract　信守合同
revise a contract　修改合同
cancel a contract　取消合同
execute/perform a contract　履行合同
countersign a contract　会签合同
copies of the contract　合同副本
contract of employment　雇佣合同
contract of arbitration　仲裁合同
contract for purchase　采购合同

contract for service 劳务合同
contract of sale 销售合同
contract for future delivery 期货合同
contract of insurance 保险合同

"协议(agreement)"和"合同(contract)"经常用作同义词,但"协议"这一术语含义更广,协议可能缺乏合同的必备条款(essential clauses)。而称为合同的文体肯定少不了必备条款,有的合同将其单列,称为一般条款(general provisions)。具备合同成立要求的具有强制执行力的协议才是合同。

Situational Conversations 情景对话

Mr. Green: Today let us discuss the contract conditions, shall we?

Mr. Wang: It is good to have a chance to talk about this important topic. We thought it has been fixed already.

Mr. Green: Not yet, it is still open for discussion. First I would like to make it clear that in principle the contract conditions are complied with the "FIDIC" document.

Mr. Wang: We quite appreciate that because the "FIDIC" is relatively fair for both client and contractor.

Mr. Green: I am sure that you must have read these conditions carefully and you can present your comments now.

Mr. Wang: Frankly speaking, we do have some different opinions on the conditions if you don't mind. Firstly, in Clause 10, 15% of the performance bond is higher than the usual practice, so I wonder whether it can be modified to 10% or not.

Mr. Green: We will consider what you proposed for this clause.

Mr. Wang: For Clause 41, we think that it is a little bit too tight for the contractors to commence the works within 10 days after the signing of the contract.

Mr. Green: We don't think so. It is quite enough for your people to move in and set up the construction equipment on the site to start works within 10 days. For such a tight construction program, we cannot allow any delay for commencement.

Mr. Wang: In such a case we will withdraw our opinion for this clause. In clause

	47, the amount of the liquidated damages for delay is much higher than normal, so we cannot agree with it.
Mr. Green:	Can you tell me what the normal amount is?
Mr. Wang:	For example, we have completed the same kind of project last year. The payment for the liquidated damages is only half of this one.
Mr. Green:	How about the size of the project? I guess it may be the half of this one. Because any delay of such a large project is a very heavy loss for the owner, it is definitely necessary to have such a high amount of liquidated damages. Are there any comments for other clauses?
Mr. Wang:	It is mentioned in Clause 61 that the engineer will supply all drawings in accordance with the works progress defined in the schedule. The question is what we can do if the delay of the drawing supply really happens.
Mr. Green:	We will do our best to avoid it.
Mr. Wang:	Therefore, our proposal is to add a sub-clause like that in case the contractor suffers delay of drawings supply he is entitled to have an extension of time to the contract period and obtain an amount of compensation for the cost on catching up the progress.
Mr. Green:	We agree with your proposal in principle. But the time extension and cost increase must be determined by the engineer after due consultation with the employer and the contractor. This point must be added into the sub-clause.
Mr. Wang:	OK, we agree to your modification to this new sub-clause.
Mr. Green:	Are there any more comments on the contract conditions?
Mr. Wang:	I have no different opinions at the present.
Mr. Green:	OK, now let us finish the discussion of the contract conditions. If you have something to say, you can put them in your letters, and we will arrange another discussion when necessary.
Mr. Wang:	That's fine.

Questions ● ● ● ●

1. How does Mr. Wang think of the performance bond in Clause 10?
2. Does Mr. Green agree with Mr. Wang's modification of the liquidated damages for delay? Why or why not?
3. What are the final proposals to Clause 61?

Notes 注释

1. open for discussion 敞开讨论，be open to public 向公众开放，be open with me about the accident 对这次事故向我坦言。
2. be complied with 符合，如"Everyone should comply with the law."每个人都应该遵守法律。类似的表达还有"in compliance with"，"in conformity with"等。
3. FIDIC 是国际咨询工程师联合会（Fédération Internationale Des Ingénieurs Conseils）的法文缩写。FIDIC 的本义是指国际咨询工程师联合会这一独立的国际组织。习惯上有时也指 FIDIC 条款或 FIDIC 方法。
4. "… you can present your comments now."现在你可以提出你们的意见。
5. the performance bond 履约担保金。
6. withdraw our opinion for this clause 撤销我们对此项条款的看法。withdraw 撤走，拿走，退出，如"He has decided to withdraw from the competition."他已决定退出竞赛。
7. the amount of the liquidated damages for delay 违约罚金的数额。
8. "… supply all drawings in accordance with the works progress defined in the schedule."根据计划表中规定的工程进度提供所有的图纸。
9. add a sub-clause 增加如下副条款。
10. consultation with the employer and the contractor 与业主和承包商协商。in consultation with 与某人协商，如"The scheme was developed in close consultation with the local community."该计划是在同当地社区密切磋商中逐渐形成的。

Useful Sentences 必学句型

1. It is good to have a chance to talk about this important topic. 有机会讨论合同条件太好了。
2. First I would like to make it clear that in principle the contract conditions are complied with the "FIDIC" document. 首先，我想说明一下该合同条件是符合 FIDIC 基本原则的。
3. Frankly speaking, we do have some different opinions on the conditions if you don't mind. 坦率地讲，如果你不介意的话，我们对这个合同条件确实有不同的看法。
4. I wonder whether it can be modified to 10% or not. 我想知道能否将履约担保金调整为 10%。
5. For such a tight construction program, we cannot allow any delay for commencement. 对工期如此紧张的施工项目，我们不允许延长进场时间。
6. In such a case we withdraw our opinion for this clause. 既然这样，我们撤回针对这一条款的建议。

7. Because any delay of such a large project is a very heavy loss for the owner, <u>it is definitely necessary to</u> have such a high amount of liquidated damages. 因为这项巨大工程的任何延期对业主来说都是非常大的损失,所以采用较高的违约金是绝对有必要的。
8. In case the contractor suffers delay of drawings supply <u>he is entitled to have</u> an extension of time to the contract period and obtain an amount of compensation for the cost on catching up the progress. 若承包商因图纸提供延期受到损失,他有权使合同工期顺延,补偿为赶工增加的费用。
9. We agree with your proposal <u>in principle</u>. 我们原则上同意你所提的建议。

Exercises 练习

1. Complete the following dialogue in English.

A: This contract is valid for a period of two years from Jan. 1ˢᵗ, 2004 to Dec. 31ˢᵗ, 2005, right?

B: _____.

(对。这份合同有两份原件,每份均用英汉两种文字打印,两种文本均有同等的法律效力,双方各持一份。)

A: OK. I think the payment terms in the contract are also very important, aren't they?

B: _____.

(是的。这份合同基本上包括了在洽谈期间达成的所有款项。这是一份合同副本,请你在签署之前再审阅一次好吗?)

A: I don't think it is necessary and I don't believe there are conflicts between this contract conditions and normal international contract documents. We have settled all the points under dispute.

B: _____.

(那好,如果在工作运作中出现新问题的话,我们可以随时解决。)

A: _____.

(好的。但是我觉得合同中最好加上这样一句:如果一方未履行本合同条款,另一方则有权终止合同。)

B: I think you are right.

A: _____.

(一些原则性问题经双方同意后可以写入合同的补充文件中。)

C: Fine. Everything is ready. Contract parties of A and B, please come and sign here.

A: I wish to cooperate closely with you.

B: _____.

(我们一定信守合同,保证质量,密切合作,增进友谊。)

2. Read and interpret the following passage.

Contract of Building the Friendship Hotel

A contract is hereby concluded between Huaxia Travel Service (hereafter to be called the first party) and Tianshan Construction Corporation (hereafter to be called the second party) for building the Friendship Hotel. The two contracting parties agree to the following terms:

1. The first party entrusts the second party with building the Friendship Hotel, the designing drawing of which is to be submitted by the first party.

2. Both contracting parties agree that the building cost is fixed at $ 6,000,000 only (six million U. S. dollars), thirty percent of which is to be paid by the first party to the second party within ten days after signing the present contract, all the rest to follow up two weeks after the completion of the hotel.

3. All the building materials to be used for the hotel are to be supplied on time by the first party. But they meet the agreed standards and specifications.

4. The building works of the hotel must be completed in 12 months after signing the contract. The hand-over will take place on Oct. 1st, 1995.

5. The said hotel is guaranteed for fifty years against collapse or leakage, for which, if found in any form, maintenance and repairs must be done by the second party.

6. Signed on Oct. 1st, 1994, at London, the present contract is made in duplicate in Chinese and English languages. Both texts have the equal legal effects.

Yang Ming	David Smith
(signed)	(signed)
For Huaxia Travel Service	For Tianshan Construction Co.

Supplements Omitted

3. Pair work.

Imagine A acts as an engineering contractor, B acts as a promote client. After both sides fully discuss and consult the contract terms, they decide to sign it. Try to talk something while they are signing the contract.

Supplementary Materials 补充材料

Building Construction Contract
建筑施工合同

发包方(甲方)×××××
Party A: ××××

承包方(乙方)××××

Party B：××××

本合同由如上列明的甲、乙双方按照《中华人民共和国合同法》、《建筑安装工程承包合同条例》以及国家相关法律法规的规定，结合本合同具体情况，于××年×月×日在××签订。

This contract is signed by the two Parties in xxxx on xxxx according to the *Contract Law of the People's Republic of China*, the *Regulation on Building and Installation Contracting Contract*, and other relevant national laws and regulations, as well as the specific nature of this project.

第一条　总则

Article 1　General Principles

1.1　合同文件

Contract Documents

本合同包含合同、展示、施工图纸、作法说明、招投标文件以及合同所指的其他文件，它们均被视为合同的一部分。合同文件应该能够相互解释，互为说明。组成本合同的文件及优先解释的顺序如下：本合同、中标通知书、投标书及其附件、标准、规范及有关技术文件、图纸、工程量清单及工程报价单或预算书。合同履行中，发包人和承包人有关工程的洽商、变更等书面协议或文件视为本合同的组成部分。

This contract includes the contract itself, exhibits, construction drawings, explanations of work procedures, tender documents, as well as other documents specified by the contract. The contract documents should be mutually explainable and mutually descriptive. The documents that constituted the contract and the priority hierarchy of explanations of the documents are as follows: this contract; the official letter of winning the tender; letter of bidding and its annex, standards, guidelines, and relevant technical documents, drawings, Bill of Quantity (BOQ), quotation of prices, and project budget. During the implementation of the contract, any written agreements or documents between two parties such as change-orders are also regarded will be deemed as part of this contract.

1.1.1　项目概况

Project Introduction

1.1.2　工程名称：××××

Name of Project：××××

1.1.3　工程地点：××××

Location of Project：××××

1.1.3.1　工程范围：除了本合同其他条款另有说明外，乙方应提供为履行合同所需的所有服务、用品以及其他保障工程进行所需的必要花费以完成下列工作：

Scope of the project: unless otherwise explained by other articles in this contract, Party B shall provide all services, utensils, and other necessary cost for the implementation of this contract; the scope of project includes, but not limited to:

※室内装饰工程，详见附件一和附件二

Inner decoration, see Appendixes 1 & 2

※室外装饰工程(门窗、屋面、台阶等),详见附件一和附件二

Façade (including doors, windows, roof and stairs) see Appendixes 1 & 2

※电器工程,详见附件一和附件二

Electronic Engineering, see Appendixes 1 & 2

※空调工程,详见附件一和附件二

Air Conditioning System, see Appendixes 1 & 2

※给排水及采暖工程,详见附件一和附件二

Water Supply, Sewage and Heating System, see Appendixes 1 & 2

※消防工程

Fire Control System, see Appendixes 1 & 2

※其他图纸上所列项目(任何对原定设计的变更应提供新的图纸并由甲方的签字确认)以上所有的工程项目以下统称为"工程"。

Other items listed in the construction drawings (any changed drawings shall be provided and confirmed by Party A). All these aforementioned items are generally referred as "project" hereafter.

1.1.3.2　承包方式:乙方以包工包料、包工程质量、包安全、包文明施工的方式承包工程

Nature of Contracting: Party B shall be responsible for both labor and materials for this project, and will be responsible for the quality of this project, safety, as well as code of conduct during the construction project.

1.1.4　甲方工地代表由甲方指派。

On-site representative of Party A shall be appointed by Party A.

1.1.5　开工日期××××

Date of the project beginning:××××

1.1.6　竣工日期××××

Date of the project completion:××××

1.1.7　工程质量:质量合格,达到本合同要求和国家质量验收标准,并确保竣工验收一次合格。验收内容包括但不仅限于:①隐蔽工程;②分项工程;③实验报告;④材料检验报告。如果由于验收未能一次通过而导致后续工程开工的延迟,乙方将按照每日工程总款的2‰金额赔偿给甲方作为罚金,但最多不超过工程总价款的5%。

Quality of Project: The quality should be "Excellent", and shall meet the requirements by this contract and the National Quality Standards, and should be guaranteed to be accepted at the first attempt upon project completion, and shall also LEED certified. The scope of as-built acceptance includes, but not limited to: ①concealed work, ②itemized project, ③reports of experiments, and ④reports of material testing. In the event of project fails to be accepted at the first inspection and thus incurs delays beginning of the subsequent projects. Party B shall compensate Party A at the daily rate of 2‰ of the total contract amount as penalty, but the total amount shall not exceed 5% of the total contract amount.

1.1.8　工程资质:在实施此合同所涉及的工程时,乙方应确保其具有相关资质。如乙方因为不具备相关资质导致甲方的损失或工程进度的滞后,乙方承担全部责任。

Qualifications: Party B represents and warrants it is competent and legitimate to carry out the services that set forth under this Agreement when implementing this contract. Party B shall be responsible for any delay of the construction induced by their insufficient qualifications.

1.2 合同价款：

Contract Amount:

本合同价款为人民币××××，为固定总价合同价款。

The total contract amount is ××××, which is fixed contract amount.

本合同包括设备材料费、人工费、机械费、管理费、利润、税金、代办费用、保险费、运输费、劳务费用、总承包服务费以及为完成工程所必需的其他一切费用，和工程各系统检验检测、安装调试等费用。该款项为甲方应付给乙方的全部费用，并已经包含物价变动因素。

This agreement includes the cost of equipment and materials, labor cost, machinery cost, management cost, profit, tax, government charges on behalf of Party A, insurance, transportation, labor, subcontract service fee, and all other cost for the completion of the project, as well as every system testing, installation, and commissioning costs. This total contract amount is exact amount that Party A shall pay to Party B and it includes the fact of price fluctuation.

1.3 工程结算

Final Audit of Project

1.3.1 本工程计价依据 GB 50500-2008《建设工程工程量清单计价规范》采用固定总价，除施工期间甲方要求变更现有图纸及发生的增减项洽商，甲方将作价格调整。

This project is using fixed total amount according to *GB50500-2008 the Pricing Guidelines by Code of Quantity in Construction Projects*, except that Party A may make price adjustment in the event of the existing construction drawings are changed or add or remove any construction work according to the request of Party A.

1.3.2 所有的人工费用都不得以任何理由进行调整，结算时只接受投标文件中约定的价格。

All labor cost shall NOT be adjusted in any event. Only the prices stimulated in the bidding documents are accepted at the final audit after completion.

1.3.3 因工程调整而产生的工程洽商，如洽商费用超过人民币五万元整，则洽商文件必须在工程中期验收当日被提交给甲方，所产生的洽商费用在交付中期款时一并核算结清。如洽商费用低于五万元人民币整，则洽商文件必须在工程验收当日内提交给甲方，所产生的费用在交付工程验收款时一并核算结清。

If the cost of change orders are over RMB 50,000 *yuan*, then all change orders issued because of the construction adjustments shall be submitted to Party A on the same day of the construction mid-term check and acceptance, and the approved amount will be paid to Party B with the construction mid-term payment; if the costs of the change orders are less than 50,000 *yuan*, then all change orders issued because of the construction adjustments shall be submitted to Party A on the same day of the construction completion check and acceptance, and the approved amount will be paid to Party B with the construction completion payment.

第二条 政府批复
Article 2　Government Approvals

2.1　乙方负责协助甲方办理此项施工需要办理的所有政府报批,包括但不仅限于消防、环保的报批与其他与本工程相关的报批,甲方负责政府行政审批的费用。

Party B shall be responsible to process government approvals related to the project, including but not limited to: fire control, environment protection and other approvals related to this Project. Party A is responsible for the costs of these approvals.

2.2　乙方负责其工程报备

Party B shall be responsible for construction applications, approvals and related costs.

2.3　乙方应承担2.2所述报备不全而导致的政府罚金,并且不能顺延工期。

Party B shall be responsible for any government fines due to incomplete approval processes, and should NOT cause delay in the construction period.

第三条 甲方的权利和义务
Article 3　Rights and Obligations of Party A

3.1　向乙方提供经确认的施工图纸或做法说明五份,并向乙方进行现场交底,向乙方提供施工所需要的水电设备,并说明使用注意事项。

Party A shall provide FIVE copies of confirmed construction drawings and explanations of work procedures, and shall conduct technical clarification. Party A shall provide Party B with necessary water and power equipment and the instructions on using the equipment.

3.2　指派××××为甲方驻工地代表,负责合同的履行。对工程质量、进度进行监督检查,办理验收、变更事宜。甲方的工地代表如果认为乙方的某雇员行为不当或散漫不羁,或甲方认为该雇员不能胜任,则乙方应立即进行撤换,并且未经甲方实现书面许可,乙方不得在施工中再行雇佣该等人员。被撤换的任何人员应尽可能立即由甲方代表所批准的胜任的人员代替。

Party A appoints xxxx as the on-site representative to supervise the fulfillment of contract obligations, to oversee the quality control and check the project progress, and to handle issues such as acceptance and variations. In the event of the on-site representative of Party A believes that any employee of Party B has improper conduct or misbehaviors, or if Party A consider such employee is not competent for the relevant work, Party B shall dismiss and replace this employee immediately; and unless having received consent by Party A in writing in advance, Party B shall no longer hire the specified employee in the following phase of this project. Party B should make every effort to replace the dismissed employee with competent personnel authorized by on-site representative of Party A.

3.3　甲方按照付款约定向乙方支付工程款。

Party A should make payments to Party B according to the payment terms.

3.4　如甲方认为乙方确已无能力继续履行合同的,则甲方有权解除合同,乙方必须在接到甲方书面通知后两周内撤离场地以便甲方继续施工。对乙方完成工程量的结算不作为撤离场地的条件，结算应在竣工一个月之内完成，付款方式按照本合同条款。

In the event of Party A consider Party B is indeed unable to further fulfill its contract obligations, then Party A has the right to terminate the contract, and Party B should vacate the project site within two weeks after receiving Party A's notice, so that Party A can resume construction as soon as possible. Confirmation of finished quantity shall NOT be regarded as a prerequisite to Party B's vacation of the project site, and the confirmation should be processed within one month after the project completion. Payment shall be made according to the payment terms in this contract.

3.5 甲方有权要求乙方按照甲方的组织设计和施工工期进行施工，乙方如对甲方的要求和指令不予执行的，则按照乙方违约处理，乙方应承担违约责任。

Party A has the right to instruct Party B to do the construction according to Party A's organization and planned construction period; in the event of Party B ignores and refuses to observe Party A's instructions, Party B will be deemed as breach of the contract, and Party B shall be held responsible for the liabilities of breaching the contract.

3.6 甲方有权要求乙方服从甲方的统一安排和管理，乙方的施工人员必须遵守各项规章制度。对于乙方施工人员违规操作所产生的后果，乙方承担全部责任。甲方有权从工程总价款中扣除相应的款项。

Party A has the right to instruct Party B to observe the general arrangement and management by Party A, and the construction staffs of Party B must observe all rules and regulations. Party B shall be fully responsible for the consequences of such violations by the staff of Party B. Party A has the right to directly deduct the corresponding amount from the total contract amount.

3.7 甲方所有的通知可以以书面或口头形式发出，乙方接获甲方的通知后应根据通知规定的内容执行。

All notices from Party A can be made both in writing and orally, but the oral instructions are only applicable to the representative of Party A. Party B shall, upon receiving notices from Party A, execute the corresponding matters according to the content of the notices.

3.8 未经甲方同意，乙方不得将工程转让或分包，对于乙方将工程擅自转让或分包的，甲方有权解除合同，乙方必须接受并承担由此造成的一切后果。

Party B shall NOT transfer or subcontract the project to any third party without the consent of Party A; in the event of Party B transfers or subcontracts the project to any third party without the consent of Party A, Party A has the right to terminate the contract, and Party B must accept and be responsible for any consequence of such violation.

3.9 甲方有权制定专业分包商，并按照乙方在投标文件中承诺的配合管理费率向乙方支付配合管理费。

Party A has the right to appoint special sub-contractors, and shall pay the management fee to Party B according to the rate of subcontract management and coordination fee stipulated in the bidding documents.

3.10 按照招标文件中的相关条目，甲方有权自行采购材料供给乙方，并按照乙方在投标文件的相关条目中涉及的人工费、机械费、辅助材料费等向乙方支付费用。甲方没有义务向乙方支付其他费用。

Party A has the right to purchase and provide Party B with materials on its own, and shall pay labor cost, machinery cost, and accessory cost to Party B according to the relevant terms in the bidding documents. Party A has no obligations to pay any other costs to Party B.

第四条 乙方的权利义务

Article 4　Rights and Obligations of Party B

4.1 参加甲方组织的施工图纸或做法说明的现场交底，拟定施工方案和进度计划，交由甲方审定。施工过程中，乙方按照甲方的有关指示及修改变更要求进行相应调整。

Party B shall participate in the technical clarification on construction drawings and explanations of work procedures organized by Party A, and should develop the construction plan and the progress schedule for Party A to review. During construction, Party B should make such adjustment to the construction plan and the progress schedule per Party A's instruction and change-orders.

4.2 指派××××为乙方驻工地代表，负责合同的履行，按照要求组织施工，保质保量、按期完成施工任务。解决由乙方负责的各项事宜。乙方驻工地代表在本公司的工作时间不得少于90％工作日。

Party B appoints xxxx as the on-site representative of Party B to take charge of fulfilling the contract obligations. The on-site representative of Party B shall organize the construction according to contract requirements so that the project can be completed according to the quality and quantity requirements and on a timely manner. The on-site representative of Party B shall work on the project site for no fewer than 90％ of the total working days.

4.3 严格执行施工规范、安全操作规程、防火安全规定、环境保护规定。严格按照图纸或做法说明进行施工，做好各项质量检查记录，参加竣工验收，编制竣工资料及工程结算。

Party B shall strictly observe construction guidelines, safety requirements, fire safety regulations, environment protection regulations and LEED requirements. Party B shall do the construction by strictly adhering to the construction drawings and explanations of work procedures, and shall effectively record each QA/QC inspection. Party B shall attend the completion acceptance, and develop at-built submittals and final project audit.

4.4 根据甲方和设计方一致通过的设计图纸进行施工，遵从甲方工地代表和设计方的指示，如乙方发现在工程标准和设计图之间存在不一致时，应以书面形式通知甲方和设计方。

Party B shall carry out the construction according to the design drawings agreed upon by both Party A and the designer, shall observe the instructions of designer and the representative of Party A; in the event of Party B finds inconsistence between project standards and design drawings, Party B should inform the designer and Party A in writing.

4.5 遵守国家或地方政府及有关部门对施工现场管理的规定及甲方的规章制度，妥善保护好施工现场周围的建筑物、设备管线等不受损坏。做好施工现场保卫、消防和垃圾消纳等工作，处理好由于施工带来的扰民问题及与周围单位（住户）的关系；如果由于乙方导致任何设施、设备或管道在工地内外受损,将由乙方赔偿损失。乙方负责与甲方的施工协调事项,并独自完全承担所有相关责任。

Party B shall observe policies of on-site management by the state and local government authorities as well as Party A's rules and regulations; Party B shall compensate for the losses to any facilities, equipment or pipelines both inside and outside of the construction yard caused by party B. Party B shall be responsible for the coordination of construction issues with party A, and shall independently and fully assumes corresponding responsibilities.

4.6　对任何原建筑物结构的拆改或设备管道的挪移,乙方应向甲方申报;在甲方批复前,不得擅自动工。

Party B should report to party A of any demolition of or variation to any original building structure or re-position of equipment pipes; Party B will refrain from any such work prior to receiving Party A's approval.

4.7　乙方应保护所有设备以及工程成品,并承担竣工移交前所引起损坏的损失赔偿。

Party B should protect all equipment and finished parts, and shall assume compensation responsibilities of any losses prior to completion hand-over.

4.8　乙方负责用扩展保险责任批单为与建筑物相关的工程以及工程所需的材料购买工程一切险,乙方及乙方分包商(以下简称"分包商")应对工程进行中自己或其他方的财产出资购买相应的保险,这些财产包括:工棚、铁架塔、脚手架、工具及其他的一些材料。

Party B shall purchase Construction All Risks Insurance for the project and required materials related to the building structure by using extended coverage endorsement; during construction, Party B and its subcontractors (hereafter abbreviated as "subcontractors") should purchase corresponding insurance for their own or other parties' properties, such as temporary construction barracks, iron frames and towers, scaffolding, utensils and other materials.

4.9　从工程开始至工程竣工验收报告上所列明的日期止,乙方应全权负责整项工程。不管任何原因导致的工程的损坏,乙方负责修理还原,以使整个工程竣工时能完全依照合同要求以及甲方工地代表的指示,状况良好。

From the beginning of construction to the completion date stipulated by the as-built acceptance report, Party B will be fully responsible for the entire project. Party B shall fix and reinstate any damages to the project items regardless of the cause, so that the project shall be in good condition upon completion, according to the contract requirements and the instructions of Party A's representative.

4.10　除非合同另有规定,乙方应就下列事项独自完全承担如下赔偿责任,并确保甲方完全免责:与因工程施工及维修而对人身造成的任何伤害或损害或对财产造成任何损害有关的所有损失及权利要求。但在下列情形下的赔偿或补偿除外:

Unless otherwise specified, Party B should independently and fully assume the following compensation liabilities, and exempt Party A from all liabilities: all injury and rights claims related to any personal injuries or property damage or loss as a result of the construction project, except for the following compensation or reimbursement:

4.10.1 工程或其任何部分永久性使用或占用工地。

Permanent use or occupation of land by the project or any part of the project.

4.10.2 甲方享有在任何土地上、下、里或穿越其施工的权利。

Party A has the right to traverse the construction site from above, beneath, or inside the site.

4.10.3 根据合同规定对财产的损伤或伤害是工程施工或维修之不可避免的后果。

The property damage or loss is an inevitable loss caused by the construction or repair according to the contract requirements.

4.11 乙方保证施工现场清洁,符合环境卫生管理的有关规定,交工前清理现场达到甲方要求,如达不到甲方的要求,乙方承担因自身违反规定造成的损失和罚款。

Party B shall keep the construction site clean and meet the regulations of environment sanitation, and make sure the condition of the site meets the requirements of Party A. If the condition of the construction site does NOT meet the requirements of Party A, Party B shall be responsible for any loss or fine as a result of its own violation of such regulations.

4.12 乙方必须要按照施工图所显示的设计要求施工,并符合施工规范规定。所有因对施工图的误解或疏忽引起的施工错误,须返工者,其一切费用均由乙方自负,且不得因此延长完工期限。

Party B MUST adhere to the design requirements in the construction drawings, and must meet the requirements of construction guidelines. Party B shall be fully responsible for any cost of rework on construction mistakes as a result of misunderstanding of the construction drawings or negligence, and shall NOT delay the completion of the project.

4.13 乙方应与每位施工人员订立务工合同,办理合法务工证件并承担费用。

Party B should sign labor contract with all its construction staffs, and issue proper work certificate. Be responsible for the corresponding cost.

4.14 乙方应每月按时向每位施工人员发放工资,如果乙方未按规定发放工资而给甲方带来的任何损失,则乙方承担完全赔偿责任。

Party B should make salary/wages payment to all construction staffs in time on a monthly basis, and will be fully responsible for any liabilities caused by any loss or damage to Party A as a result of Party B's failure to pay salaries and wages according to the requirements.

4.15 在履行本合同过程中如对任何第三人造成任何侵害和损失,或违反任何相关国家法律法规,乙方对其行为和行为后果承担全部责任。

Party B shall take full responsibility for its actions or consequences caused by its actions which cause infractions to any third party and cause any violations to related state laws and regulations when implementing this contract.

4.16 乙方应对本工程所有的分包商负有管理和提供总包服务的义务,包括但不限于材料报审、工程预验收和报审、分包付款申请的审批、工程资料编制等。

Party B shall take the responsibilities of sub-contractor management and providing services designated to general contractor, which includes but not limited to: submitting and acquiring construction materials' approval, construction pre-examination and submitting for approval, review and approve payment applications from sub-contractors and construction document filing, etc.

第五条 付款条约
Article 5　Payment Terms

5.1　双方商定本合同价款编制采用工程量清单计划规范，固定合同总价，除施工期间甲方要求变更现有图纸，甲方将作价格调整。

The parties agree to use fixed total amount according to *GB50500-2008 the Pricing Guidelines by Code of Quantity in Construction Projects*, except that Party A may make price adjustment in the event that the existing construction drawings are changed according to the request of Party A.

5.2　本工程付款方式：工程开工后5个工作日内甲方支付总工程款的30%，室外门窗及幕墙工程验收合格后5个工作日内甲方支付总工程款的20%，室内中间验收完成后5个工作日内甲方支付总工程款的20%，工程完工验收合格并乙方向甲方提交完整的竣工资料后5个工作日内支付工程总价款的27%，工程完工验收合格保修期一年后5个工作日内支付工程总价款的70 000元。

Payment terms：Party A shall pay 30% of the total contract amount to Party B within 5 working days after signing of the contract; 20% of the total contract amount shall be paid within 5 working days after the facade is finished; 20% of the total contract amount shall be paid within 5 working days after the construction mid-term check and acceptance is completed; 27% of the total contract amount 70,000 *yuan* shall be paid within 5 working days after the construction completion check and acceptance.

第六条 开始与延期
Article 6　Beginning and Delaying of Project

6.1　整个工程应在开工后××××天内完成。

The whole project should be completed within xxxx calendar days after the beginning of the project.

6.2　非本合同规定的可以延期的情形外，如果甲方代表认为工程或其部分工程的进度太过缓慢以至无法保证工程在规定时间或延长的完工期间内完工，乙方应随即采取必要的措施，甲方代表可批准加快进度以在规定时间或约定的延长期内完成工程或其任何部分。乙方无权因采取该措施而获得额外支付。

Unless otherwise specified by the contract as acceptable conditions of delay, in the event of the on-site representative of Party A believes that the progress of the project or any part of the project substantially lags behind schedule, which may cause Party B unable to complete the project within the required construction period or any extended construction period agreed upon, Party B shall promptly take necessary measures under the authorization of the on-site representative of Party A to expedite the progress so that the project or any part of the project could be completed within the required construction period or any extended construction period agreed upon. Party B is NOT subject to any additional compensation for the measures taken.

6.3 如果由于非乙方原因导致的工程停工，比如工地停电、停水，该情形持续每满 8 小时，竣工日期往后顺延一天，乙方应有书面记录并经甲方代表签字。

Suspension of the construction work as a result of non-Party B's factors, such as power failure and water supply cut-off, the completion date shall be postponed by one day for every 8 hours of such conditions. Party B should inform Party A immediately in such events and make record of the condition in writing for the representative of Party A to sign off.

第七条 保修
Article 7 Warranty

7.1 乙方保证以一流精湛的工艺完成工程，并保证除其他机械或设备外，整个工程无瑕疵，但隐性瑕疵不受此限。乙方应按相关规定对该工程在设计使用年限内提供保修。

Party B shall complete the project with excellent workmanship and guarantees that, except for other machines or equipment, the project as a whole will be free of defect within eighteen months after the completion acceptance or prior to the last payment (whichever is later); warranty on hidden defects is not limited to this date. The warranty period shall be in accordance with the relative regulations and designed working life.

7.2 在工程建设过程中，或上述保修期内，乙方应及时修复材料或人工的瑕疵，由此引发的损失或损坏将由乙方完全赔付。

During the whole construction period or the afore mentioned warranty period, Party B shall repair any defects of material and workmanship on a timely manner; and Party B shall be fully responsible for any losses or damage caused by such defects.

7.3 在保修期内，乙方指派专人负责维护。隐性的瑕疵应在发现问题后 24 小时内修复。影响甲方正常运营的应在 4 小时内到现场修复。如果乙方未能及时修复，甲方有权自行决定雇佣第三方进行修复，由此发生的费用将由乙方来承担。

During the warranty period, Party B shall appoint special personnel for the maintenance. Hidden defects should be fixed within 24 hours after being detected, and those that have an influence on Party A's normal operation should be fixed within 4 hours on the spot. In the event of Party B fails to fix the defects on a timely manner, Party A has the right to hire a third party to do the repair, and any cost incurred shall be burdened by Party B.

第八条 关于工程质量及验收的约定
Article 8 Agreement on Quality and Acceptance

8.1 双方同意本工程将以施工图纸、作法说明、设计变更和《建筑装饰和装修工程质量验收规范》(GB 50210-2001)、《建筑工程质量验收统一标准》(GB 50300-2001)、《建筑电气工程施工质量验收规范》(GB 50303-2002)、《通风与空调工程施工质量验收规范》(GB 50243-2002)、《建筑给排水及采暖工程施工质量验收规范》(GB 50242-2002)等国家制定的施工及验收规范为质量验收标准。

The parties agrees that the construction drawings, explanations of work procedures, design change-orders and such national guidelines on construction and acceptance as *the Quality Acceptance Criteria of Construction, Decoration, and Remoduleing Projects* (GB

50210-2001), *the General Quality Acceptance Standards of Construction Projects* (GB 50300-2001), *the Quality Acceptance Guidelines of Mechanics and Engineering Projects of Construction* (GB 50303-2002), *the Quality Acceptance Guidelines of HVAC Projects* (GB 50243-2002), *the Quality Acceptance. Guidelines of Water Supply, Sewage, and Heating Systems in Construction* (GB 50242-2002) are regarded as the acceptance standards for the project.

8.2 本工程质量应达到国家质量验收标准,并确保一次验收合格。
This project should meet the national quality acceptance standards and should be accepted at the first inspection after completion.

8.3 甲乙双方应合力办理隐蔽工作和中间工程的检查与验收手续。乙方应提前24小时书面通知甲方参加各类验收,甲方如果未能及时参加隐蔽工程和中间工程验收,乙方可自行验收,甲方应予承认。若甲方要求复验时,乙方应按照要求办理复验。若复验合格,甲方应承担复验费用,由此造成停工的,工期顺延;若复验不合格,其复验费用由乙方承担,且工期不予顺延。
Two Parties shall jointly undertake the mid-term inspection and acceptance process for concealed work. Party B shall inform Party A in writing of all kinds of inspection and acceptance 24 hours in advance. In the event of Party A fails to participate in the mid-term acceptance of concealed work, Party B can do the acceptance independently; Party A should accept such acceptance. When Party A requests a re-inspection, Party B shall carry out the re-inspection accordingly. If the result of re-inspection has passed acceptance standards, Party A shall be responsible for the re-inspection cost, and the project period shall be extended by the duration of project suspension caused by such re-inspections; If the result of re-inspection has NOT passed acceptance standards, Party B shall be responsible for the re-inspection cost, and the project period shall NOT be extended.

8.4 乙方应确保甲方对于因乙方所提供的劣质材料而引发的任何事件后果完全免责,其返工费用由乙方承担,工期不予顺延。
Party B should guarantee that Party A is fully exempted from liabilities for any events as a result of materials with poor quality; the cost of re-work shall be burdened by Party B, and the project period shall NOT be extended.

8.5 工程竣工后,乙方应通知甲方验收,甲方自接到验收通知3个工作日内组织验收,并办理验收、移交手续。如甲方在规定时间内未能组织验收,需及时通知乙方,另行确定验收日期。
Upon completion of project, Party B should inform Party A to process completion acceptance; Party A shall arrange inspection and acceptance within 3 working days after receiving the notification, and shall handle the inspection and hand-over processes. In the event of Party A could NOT arrange the inspection and acceptance within the required period, Party A should inform Party B and reschedule the date for acceptance on a timely manner.

8.6 乙方在向甲方提交竣工验收申请的同时,应提交相关的竣工资料和竣工图。
Party B shall submit relevant as-built submittals and as-built drawing when submitting the

request for completion acceptance to Party A.

8.7 竣工验收后,乙方必须在7天内完成场地清退工作,并向甲方做好各项交接工作包括文件、设备和工具等。

After the completion acceptance, Party B must finish the vacation of the project site within 7 days and complete all hand-over processes including documents, equipment, and utensils.

8.8 甲方代表可对每一个工作日的工程质量进行检查检验。甲方代表对工程质量提出整改或返工通知后,乙方必须在规定时间内按要求完成。

The on-site representative of Party A may carry out the inspection of the project quality on any single workday. Having received the notification of correction or re-work due to inadequate quality from the representative of Party A, Party B shall complete the work within the required time frame.

第九条 关于材料设备的约定
Article 9 Agreement on the Supply of Materials and Equipment

9.1 本工程甲方负责采购供应的材料、设备(见附表),应为全新的合格产品,并应按时供应到现场。凡约定由乙方提货的,甲方应将提货手续移交给乙方,由乙方承担运输费用。如果由于甲方提供的材料设备质量低劣或规格差异,对工程造成损失,责任由甲方承担。甲方供应的材料,经乙方验收后,由乙方负责保管。由于乙方保管不当或被盗所造成的损失,由乙方负责赔偿。

All materials and equipment (see the attached table) that Party A orders should be brand new and qualified products, and should be delivered to the construction site as scheduled. Party A shall hand over pick-up paperwork to Party B for anything that needs Party B to pick up, and Party B shall be responsible for the cost of transportation. In the event of materials and equipment provided by Party A are poor in quality or have difference in technical specifications, and have incurred losses to the project, Party A shall be responsible for the losses. Having accepted the materials provided by Party A, Party B shall be responsible for the storage and protection of the materials. Party B shall be responsible for the compensation of any loss as a result of improper protection by Party B or theft.

9.2 本工程一般材料、设备原则上由乙方负责采购供应、场内运输及现场保管、就位等。对所选用的材料和设备的品牌及产地,乙方应事先征得甲方认可方可采购。电器材料配件、设备应优先采用名牌产品或中外合资产品。甲方有权在合同价格范围内指定部分材料采购,但不能免除乙方对工程质量、安全、成品保护、保修等相关责任。所有材料必须是全新的。

In principle Party B should be responsible for the acquisition, on-site transfer, protection, and positioning of general materials and equipment of this project. Brands and manufacturer of the materials and equipment should be confirmed by Party A prior to purchase. Famous brands or products from Joint Venture vendors are preferred for electric appliances and accessories. Party A has the right to appoint pat of the materials within the contract price range, but Party B's liabilities of project quality, safety, protection of finished goods, and warranty should NOT be exempted. All materials must be brand new.

9.3　如乙方无法满足9.2条款要求时，甲方可按9.1条款办理。
In the event of Party B fails to meet the requirement of Clause 9.2, Party A may process the issue according to Clause 9.1.

9.4　凡由乙方采购的材料、设备，如不符合相关质量要求或规格有差异，应立即停止使用。若已使用，对工程造成的损失由乙方负责。
Any materials and equipment purchased by Party B that can't meet relevant quality standards or have difference in specifications must be stopped to use. If such materials or equipment have already been used, Party B shall be responsible for the loss.

9.5　甲方在招标文件内指定材料品牌的，乙方必须按照甲方指定的品牌进行采购并施工，乙方没有权利私自使用其他品牌进行替代。
Party B shall purchase the materials and equipment that Party A has appointed according to the tender documents and do the construction and installation accordingly. Party B has NO right to replace these materials and equipment with other brands without the consent of Party A.

第十条　变更
Article 10　Variations

10.1　在工程进行中，甲方代表随时有权利对图纸和说明提出更改、增加、替换或缩减的要求，但该变更须经甲方代表以书面形式确认方能有效。
During the process of the project, the representative of Party A has the right to request for variation, addition, substitution, and reduction on the drawings and explanations at any time, but such variations shall only be regarded as effective with the confirmation of the representative of Party A in writing.

第十一条　有关安全生产和防火的约定
Article 11　Agreement on Safety and Fire Control in Construction

11.1　甲方提供的施工图纸或作法说明，应符合《中华人民共和国消防条例》和有关防火设计规范。
Construction drawings and Explanations of Work Procedures provided by Party A should meet all standards of fire control design set forth by *the Fire Code of the People's Republic of China*.

11.2　乙方在施工期间应严格遵守《建筑安装工程安全技术规程》、《建筑安装工人安全操作规程》、《中华人民共和国消防条例》和其他相关的法规、规范。
Party B must strictly adhere to *the Safety and Technical Standards of Construction and Infrastructure Installation*, *Safety Standards for Construction Workers*, *the Fire Code of the People's Republic of China*, and other relevant regulations and standards.

11.3　由于乙方在施工生产过程中违反有关安全操作规程、消防条例，导致发生安全或火灾事故，乙方应承担由此引发的一切经济损失。发生事故后，乙方应立即上报政府有关部门并通知甲方代表，同时按政府有关部门要求处理。乙方对事故负全责，并确保甲方完全免责，甲方不承担任何财务或非财务的责任。

In the event of accidents regarding safety or fire control occur due to Party B's violation of safety standards and fire code during construction, Party B shall be fully responsible for all financial losses. Upon accident happened Party B should promptly report the event to relevant government authorities and inform the representative of Party A, and should handle the issue according to government instructions. Party B shall be fully responsible for such accidents, and should guarantee that Party A is fully exempted from liabilities, and Party A shall NOT be responsible for any financial or non-financial liabilities.

11.4 乙方在开工前应提出安全措施,甲方代表有权阻止或辞退违反安全措施的乙方雇员或乙方分包商的雇员。乙方无条件同意替换雇员。

Party B should submit safety measures prior to the beginning of the project; the representative of Party A has the right to stop or dismiss employees of Party B or its subcontractors who have violated the safety measures. Party B should agree to replace such employees unconditionally.

11.5 乙方在需要动用明火作业时,应按规定向甲方审批,经批准后才可施工。

In the event of Party B needs to use open fire for operation, Party B should request consent from Party A, and can ONLY proceed with the approval of Party A.

11.6 乙方需与每个施工人员签订安全协议,并做好上岗前的安全教育工作。

Party B should sign safety agreement with each individual construction worker, and provide proper education on safety prior to first day of work.

11.7 室外施工场地和垃圾淤泥堆放场地必须限制在允许范围内,外围做实用美观的围挡防护。

Outdoor construction space and storage space for wastes should be restricted within the permitted region, and should be enclosed with decent fences for protection.

11.8 施工现场不准做饭和住宿,只允许适当人员看守现场。

No cooking and lodging is allowed on the construction site. Only authorized security personnel are permitted to stay at the site over night.

11.9 施工人员按规定通道使用指定卫生间,不准在卫生间内洗澡等。

Construction personnel should use toilets according to the approved passageway, and are NOT allowed to take showers in the restrooms.

第十二条 转让与分包

Article 12　Contract Transfer and Subcontracting

12.1 没有甲方事先的书面同意,乙方不得转让本合同的全部或其部分或其任何利益。

Party B shall NOT transfer the contract and any part of the contract and its corresponding to any third party without Party A's consent in writing.

12.2 除非合同另有规定,乙方未经甲方代表之事先的书面的同意,不得分包工程的任何部分,甲方代表的这种同意,并不得视为免除乙方在本合同项下的任何责任和义务。乙方应当为其分包商及其代理人、雇员、工人的所有行为、违约和疏忽而承担责任,这种责任应等同于其自身或其代理人、雇员、工人之行为、违约和疏忽所致责任。一般计件工作将不被视为本条款所诉的分包。甲方代表拥有完全权利,在工程开工期间向乙方随时提供为保证工程之适当、充分进行及保养所必需的进一步的详图及指导。乙方应执行并受此约束。

Unless otherwise specified, Party B shall NOT subcontract any part of the project without Party A's consent in writing. The consent of subcontract by the representative of Party A shall NOT be regarded as an exempt of Party B's any responsibilities or liabilities under this contract. Party B shall be held responsible for all behaviors, violations, and negligence of its subcontractors or their agents, employees, or workers, and such responsibility should be equivalent to that incurred by the behaviors, violations, and negligence of Party B itself or its agents, employees, and workers. Usually the piecework is not regarded as subcontracting described in this clause. The representative of Party A has full authority to provide Party B with any additional detailed drawings and instructions necessary to guarantee that the project can proceed and be maintained properly and sufficiently Party B should act accordingly and is subject to the requirement of this authority.

第十三条 违约责任
Article 13 Liabilities for Breach

13.1 甲方的违约责任

Party A's liabilities for breach

如甲方未能按合同约定方式支付合同价款，则甲方应向乙方支付滞纳金；滞纳金自工程款到期日的第二日起计算。每日滞纳金为到期款的0.2%。如由于甲方原因造成付款延期超过25日，则乙方有权解除本合同，由此造成的损失由甲方承担。

In the event of Party A fails to make payment according to the payment terms, Party A should pay a late fee to Party B; the late fee shall be calculated starting from the second day of the due date for the corresponding payment. Daily rate of the late fee is 0.2% of the corresponding payment. If the delay of the payment is caused by Party A and is delayed for more than 25 days, then Party B can terminate this contract and Party A shall take full responsibility for any loss caused by this.

13.2 乙方的违约责任

Party B's liabilities for breach

13.2.1 如乙方未能按照合同约定时间按期完工的，每逾期一天，乙方向甲方支付工程总价款的0.2%作为违约金。如由于乙方原因造成工程延期超过25日的，则甲方有权解除本合同，由此造成的损失由乙方承担。

In the event of Party B fails to complete the project according to the construction period in the contract, Party B shall pay 0.2% of the total contract amount for each day overdue as penalty for the breach. If the delay of the construction completion is caused by Party B and is delayed for more than 25 days, then Party A can terminate this contract and Party B shall take full responsibility for any loss caused by this.

13.2.2 根据甲方要求，乙方应为其所购买的工程材料向甲方提交材料的合格证以及质量检测报告。如果乙方提供的材料与合格证和质量检测报告不一致，例如价高质劣，以次充好，或假冒伪劣，乙方将被处以罚金，罚金将是工程总价款的30%。

Party B should submit to Party A the QA certificate and Report of Quality Assurance Test for the materials it has purchased; in the event of the materials provided by Party B differs from the QA certificate and the Report of Quality Assurance Test, for instance, products with poor quality and high price, inferior materials faked as superior ones, or counterfeited products, Party B shall be fined at the rate of 30% of the total contract amount.

13.2.3 如乙方未能按照本合同要求购买使用设备材料,安装建设,由此对甲方造成的损失,将由乙方采取补救措施,同时赔偿给甲方带来的经济损失。

In the event of Party B fails to purchase, use, install, and build with materials and equipment as described by this contract, Party B shall take remedial measures in response to the loss to Party A, and shall compensate Party A for the financial losses incurred.

第十四条 争议处理
Article 14 Dispute Settlement

14.1 当合同文件内容含糊不清或不相一致时,在不影响工程正常进行的情况下,由发包人承包人协商解决。

In the event that the text of the contract is vague or inconsistent, the Parties shall attempt settlement through friendly negotiation on the premise that the normal progress of the construction project is not affected.

14.2 由本合同引发的争议,应由双方友好协商解决,协商不成的,任何一方均可将争议提交位于北京的中国国际经济贸易仲裁委员会仲裁。仲裁裁决应是终局的并对双方都具有约束力。仲裁费用的承担由仲裁庭决定。

Any dispute arising from or in connection with this Contract shall be settled through friendly negotiation between the Parties, and in the event of the dispute can NOT be settled through negotiation, either party may submit the dispute to the China International Economic and Trade Arbitration Commission located in Beijing for arbitration which shall be conducted in accordance with the Commission's arbitration rules in effect at the time of applying for arbitration. The arbitral award is final and binding upon both parties. The cost of arbitration shall be burdened according to the Commission's decision.

第十五条 不可抗力
Article 15 Force Majeure

15.1 由于不可抗力诸如火灾、水灾、政府强令措施以及其他不可抗力的原因,合同不能履行的,则合同的责任义务将予以延缓。当不可抗力消失,合同将继续履行,合同的责任义务将按不可抗力所造成迟延履行的期间予以同期顺延。

If the contract cannot be fulfilled due to force Majeure, such as fire, flood, government forces and other force majeure factors, the fulfillment of obligations may be delayed. When the force majeure has disappeared, the contract shall be continued to be fulfilled, and the contract obligations shall be extended by the same period of delay caused by the force majeure.

15.2 告知不可抗力方应书面知会另一方事件的发生,同时提供适当的证明条件以及持续时间。另外,告知方应尽力减轻给对方造成的损失。

In case of force majeure, the affected party shall notify the other party of the occurrence and the evidence of existence of and the duration of the force majeure. In addition, the disclosing party shall endeavor to reduce losses possibly inflicted to the other party.

15.3 一旦不可抗力事件发生，双方应即时商谈并寻求公正的解决方法，努力减少损失。如该不可抗力情形持续超过二十天，则甲方有权决定解除合同。

In case of force majeure, the two Parties shall discuss in a timely manner in order to seek fair and square solutions and reduce possible losses as much as possible. In the event that the said "Force Majeure" cause lasts over 20 days, Party A has the right to terminate the contract.

第十六条　使用已完成工程部分
Article 16　Use of Finished Parts of the Project

16.1 甲方有权利使用任何已经完成部分的工程。
Party A has the right to use any finished parts of the project.

第十七条　通知
Article 17　Notices

有关本合同的所有通知应视为已于下列时间送达：
All notices with regard to the contract shall be regarded as delivered at the following times：

（a）如以专人递送，到达指定地址时；
Delivery by specified personnel, upon arrival at the specified location；

（b）如以传真方式，发件人的传真机打出成功传送的确认条时；
Delivery by facsimile transfer, upon successful printing of the confirmation notice by the sender's facsimile machine；

（c）如以快递方式，在发件后的第三日；
Delivery by courier service, the third day after sending out the notice；

上述通知应送至如下列所接收通知的地址或合同任一方于其后指定的地址。
All above notices should be delivered to the recipient's address listed as follows, or to an address that either Party may appoint later.

乙方代表：××××
Representative of Party B：××××
地址：××××
Address：××××
甲方代表：××××
Representative of Party A：××××
地址：××××
Address：××××

第十七条　未尽事宜
Article 18　Miscellaneous

18.1 合同未尽事宜由双方协商签订书面补充协议。补充协议与本合同具有同等效力。
Matters not mentioned herein shall be settled by supplemental agreements by the two Par-

ties. The supplemental agreements shall be equally effective as this contract.

第十九条　合同生效
Article 19　Effectively Clause

本合同以中英文书写。一式四份，双方各持两份，签字盖章后生效。如中英文相冲突的，以中文为准。

This contract is written in both Chinese and English in quadruplicate, with both texts being equally authentic and each Party shall hold two copies. The contract becomes effective from the date of signing and stamping by both Parties. In the event of any conflict between the English and Chinese, the latter shall prevail.

甲方：××××　　　　　　　　乙方：××××
Party A　　　　　　　　　　　Party B

委托代表人：
Representative：

签订日期：　　　　　　　　　　签订日期：
Date　　　　　　　　　　　　　Date

MODULE 11 Construction Laws and Regulations
模块十一 建筑法律法规

Learning Objectives 学习目标

In this module, learners should:
- know the Chinese and English terms of construction laws and regulations.
- be capable of discussing the contents of construction laws and regulations in English.

在本模块内,学习者应该能:
- 了解建筑法规的中英文术语。
- 能用英语谈论建筑法律法规的有关内容。

Special Terms 专业词汇

definition 定义
examination of premises 场地的检查
building permit 建筑许可
specifications and drawings 规格和图纸
contract assignment 合同转让
intellectual property 知识产权
liability and indemnification 责任和赔偿
property insurance 财产保险
confidentiality 保密
legal liability 法律责任
delays and extension of time 延误和延期
completion of the work 竣工
termination 终止
guarantee 担保
jobsite safety 工地安全
right to audit 审计权
severability 可分割性
entire agreement 全部协议
supplementary provisions 附则

general provisions 总则
ordinance and regulation 法令和法规
permits and inspection fees 许可证和审查费
reference specifications 参照规格
contract subletting 合同分包
fire protective measures 防火措施
indemnity bonds 赔偿担保
casualty insurance 伤亡保险
surveys and project layout 勘察和项目布局
time of completion 竣工时间
suspension of operation 中止作业
as-built records 竣工记录
acceptance of equipment 设备验收
force majeure 不可抗力
title and risk of loss 所有权和损失风险
no implied waiver 无暗示放弃
dispute resolution 争议的解决
terms and pages 条款和页数
regulations on administration 管理规定

根据《立法》的规定，法律体系框架主要分为三层：第一层为法律（law），由全国人大制定和通过；第二层为行政法规（administrative regulations），分为国务院行政法规和地方性法规；第三层为规章（rules），分为国务院部门规章和地方政府规章。注意：(1)规定（stipulations）是规范性文件，不属于法律范畴，效力低于法律。(2)条例(ordinances)是法律的名称，不是法律的种类。

Situational Conversations 情景对话

Mr. Smith: I know little about *Construction Law of the People's Republic of China*, will you introduce it to me generally?

Mr. Zhang: My pleasure! What would you like to know, Mr. Smith?

Mr. Smith: How many parts are there in total?

Mr. Zhang: There are 8 chapters, which are general provisions, building permit, contract issuance and contracting of construction project, supervision of construction project, management of construction safety and operation, quality control of construction project, legal liability and supplementary provisions respectively.

Mr. Smith: Oh, I know. What is the main purpose of the *Construction Law*?

Mr. Zhang: This law is enacted with a view to enhancing supervision and administration over building operations, maintaining order in the construction market, ensuring the quality and safety of construction projects and promoting the sound development of the building industry. Therefore, it shall be adhered to in engaging in building operations and in the exercise of supervision and administration over building operations within the territory of the People's Republic of China.

Mr. Smith: Can you explain in detail what building operations here refer to?

Mr. Zhang: The building operations referred to in this law mean the construction of all types of housing and the construction of their ancillary facilities as well as their matching installation operations of wiring, piping and equipment.

Mr. Smith: So, the building operations shall ensure the quality and safety of construction projects and ensure that they are in conformity with the state safety standards for construction projects, am I right?

Mr. Zhang: Quite right. No unit or individual shall hinder or obstruct the building operations conducted in accordance with law. That is to say, in engaging in building operations, laws and regulations shall be adhered to, and public interest of society and the legitimate rights and interests of others shall not be infringed upon.

Mr. Smith: Which department should be responsible for the building operations nationwide?

Mr. Zhang: It is the competent department of construction administration under the State Council that exercises uniform supervision and administration over building operations nationwide.

Mr. Smith: What is the general policy for constructions embodied in this law?

Mr. Zhang: Generally the state supports the development of the building industry, supports scientific and technological research in construction to improve the levels in the design of housing construction, encourages energy economy and environmental protection, encourages adoption of advanced technologies, advanced equipment, advanced techniques and new building materials and modern mode of management.

Questions

1. What is the main purpose of the Construction Law?
2. What do building operations refer to in the Construction Law?

Notes 注释

1. Construction Law of the People's Republic of China 中华人民共和国建筑法。
2. in total 总共，类似的还有"in all"。如"These products, in total, account for about 80% of all our sales." 这些产品总共约占我们全部销售额的80%。
3. There are 8 chapters, which are general provisions, building permit, contract issuance and contracting of construction project, supervision of construction project, management of construction safety and operation, quality control of construction project, legal liability and supplementary provisions respectively. 总共有8章，分别是总则、建筑许可、建筑工程发包与承包、建筑工程监理、建筑安全生产管理、建筑工

程质量管理、法律责任和附则。

4. be adhered to 坚持，如 "In construction of coal mines the principle of protecting the cultivated land and utilizing the land rationally shall be adhered to." 煤矿建设应当贯彻保护耕地、合理利用土地的原则。
5. "... engaging in building operations ..." 从事建筑活动。"engage in" 从事，参加。如 "I have no time to engage in the debate." 我没时间参加辩论。
6. "... referred to in this law"，过去分词短语（past participle phrase）作 "building operations" 的定语，意思为 "本法律所指的建筑活动"。
7. in conformity with 和……相适应，和……一致[符合]。如 "I acted in conformity with my principles." 我按照我的原则办事。
8. No unit or individual shall hinder or obstruct the building operations conducted in accordance with law. 任何单位和个人都不得妨碍和阻挠依法进行的建筑活动。"conducted in accordance with law" 过去分词短语（past participle phrase）作定语，修饰 "building operations"。
9. be infringed upon 侵犯。如 "The company's lawful rights and interests are protected by law and shall not be infringed upon." 公司的合法权益受法律保护，不受侵犯。

Useful Sentences 必学句型

1. I know little about *Construction Law of the People's Republic of China*. 我对中华人民共和国建筑法了解甚少。
2. How many parts are there in total? 总共有几部分？
3. This law is enacted with a view to enhancing supervision and administration over building operations, maintaining order in the construction market, ensuring the quality and safety of construction projects and promoting the sound development of the building industry. 为了加强对建筑活动的监督管理，维护建筑市场秩序，保证建筑工程的质量和安全，促进建筑业健康发展，制定本法。
4. Can you explain in detail what building operations here refer to? 你能详细地解释一下这里的建筑活动指的是什么吗？
5. The building operations referred to in this law mean the construction of all types of housing and the construction of their ancillary facilities as well as their matching installation operations of wiring, piping and equipment. 本法所称建筑活动，是指各类房屋建筑及其附属设施的建造和与其配套的线路、管道、设备的安装活动。
6. It is the competent department of construction administration under the State Council that exercises uniform supervision and administration over building operations nationwide. 国务院建设行政主管部门对全国的建筑活动实施统一监督管理。

7. What is the general policy for constructions embodied in this law? 这部法律所体现的国家对建筑行业的总体政策是什么？

Exercises 练习

1. Complete the following dialogue in English.

A: Can you tell me how to get the building permit for construction project?
B: _____.
（建设单位在建筑工程开工前应当按照国家有关规定向工程所在地县级以上人民政府建设行政主管部门申请领取施工许可证。）
A: Is the regulation suitable for all the cases?
B: _____.
（那倒不是。国务院建设行政主管部门确定的限额以下的小型工程除外。同时，按照国务院规定的权限和程序批准开工报告的建筑工程，不再领取施工许可证。）
A: What terms shall be met to apply for a building permit?
B: _____.
（第一，已经办理该建筑工程用地批准手续；第二，已经确定建筑施工企业；第三，有满足施工需要的施工图纸及技术资料；第四，有保证工程质量和安全的具体措施；第五，建设资金已经落实等。）
A: What about the construction project in an urban planning zone?
B: _____.
（在城市规划区的建筑工程要取得规划许可证。）
A: And is there any special regulation in the case of necessity of demolition and shifting?
B: _____.
（是的，需要拆迁的，其拆迁进度要符合施工要求。）
A: When shall the competent department of construction administration issue a building permit for the application which conforms to the terms?
B: _____.
（建设行政主管部门应当自收到申请之日起十五日内，对符合条件的申请颁发施工许可证。）
A: When shall the construction unit start the construction?
B: _____.
（建设单位应当自领取施工许可证之日起三个月内开工。）
A: What should the construction unit do for inability to start the construction in time due to unforeseen reasons?
B: _____.
（应当向发证机关申请延期。延期以两次为限，每次不超过三个月。既不开工又不申请延期或者超过延期时限的,施工许可证自行废止。)

A: And what if the suspension of construction of a construction project under construction happened due to unforeseen reasons?

B: _____ .

(建设单位应当自中止施工之日起一个月内,向发证机关报告,并按照规定做好建筑工程的维护管理工作。)

A: Should the construction unit submit a report to the permit-issuing organ when the construction project resumes construction?

B: _____ .

(是的,那是当然的。中止施工满一年的工程恢复施工前,建设单位应当报发证机关核验施工许可证。)

A: Thank you for telling me so much about regulations of the building permit within the construction law.

2. Read and interpret the following passage.

Preparatory construction procedures shall comprise reporting the progress of construction projects, commissioning construction supervisors, inviting and submitting tenders and execution of concluded construction contracts. Construction procedures shall comprise procurement of construction permits and undertaking of actual construction. Construction completion procedures shall comprise examination and acceptance of construction projects upon completion of construction and the conducting of outstanding repair and maintenance works during a specified time period.

Upon completion of the stage of reporting the progress of the construction project, works in the initial phase of construction shall be complete and the stage of preparatory construction shall commence. Upon obtaining a construction permit, the phase of preparatory construction shall be complete and the stage of completion of construction shall commence. The construction procedures of a construction project must be complete upon expiry of the specified time period for outstanding repairs and maintenance.

3. Pair work.

Imagine A acts as an American, who wants to invest a construction enterprise in China, B acts as a Chinese law expert. Try to make up a dialogue concerning regulations on administration of foreign-invested construction enterprises.

Supplementary Materials 补充材料

Regulations on Administration of Foreign-Invested Construction Enterprises
外商投资建筑业企业管理规定
第一章 总 则
Chapter 1 General provisions

第一条 为进一步扩大对外开放,规范对外商投资建筑业企业的管理,根据《中华人民共和国建筑法》、《中华人民共和国招标投标法》、《中华人民共和国中外合资经营企业法》、《中华人民共和国中外合作经营企业法》、《中华人民共和国外资企业法》、《建设工程质量管理条例》等法律、行政法规，制定本规定。

Article 1　These regulations hereof are formulated to further the opening up to the outside and standardize the administration of foreign-invested construction enterprises in accordance with such laws and regulations as *the Construction Law of the People's Republic of China*, *the Tendering and Bidding Law of the People's Republic of China*, *the Law of the People's Republic of China on Sino-foreign Equity Joint Ventures*, *the Law of the People's Republic of China on Sino-foreign Cooperative Joint Ventures*, *the Law of the People's Republic of China on Wholly Foreign-Owned Enterprises and the Regulations on Administration of Construction and Engineering Quality*.

第二条　在中华人民共和国境内设立外商投资建筑业企业，申请建筑业企业资质，实施对外商投资建筑业企业监督管理，适用本规定。本规定所称外商投资建筑业企业，是指根据中国法律、法规的规定，在中华人民共和国境内投资设立的外资建筑业企业、中外合资经营建筑业企业以及中外合作经营建筑业企业。

Article 2　These regulations shall apply to the establishment of foreign-invested construction enterprises within the territory of the People's Republic of China, the application for construction enterprise qualifications and the administration and supervision of foreign-invested construction enterprises. The term "foreign-invested construction enterprise" mentioned in these regulations refers to a wholly foreign-owned construction enterprise, or a Sino-foreign equity construction joint venture or a Sino-foreign cooperative construction enterprise established within the territory of the People's Republic of China in accordance with Chinese laws and regulations.

第三条　外国投资者在中华人民共和国境内设立外商投资建筑业企业，并从事建筑活动，应当依法取得对外贸易经济行政主管部门颁发的外商投资企业批准证书，在国家工商行政管理总局或者其授权的地方工商行政管理局注册登记，并取得建设行政主管部门颁发的建筑业企业资质证书。

Article 3　A foreign investor, which intends to establish a foreign-invested construction enterprise within the territory of the People's Republic of China and conduct construction business, shall, in accordance with laws, obtain the approval certificate from the relevant foreign trade and economic cooperation administration department and register with the State Administration of Industry and Commerce or its authorized administration of industry and commerce at local levels, and the qualification certificate from the relevant construction administration department.

第四条　外商投资建筑业企业在中华人民共和国境内从事建筑活动，应当遵守中国的法律、法规、规章。外商投资建筑业企业在中华人民共和国境内的合法经营活动及合法权益受中国法律、法规、规章的保护。

Article 4　Foreign-invested construction enterprises which engage in construction business within the territory of the People's Republic of China shall abide by the laws, regulations and rules of the People's Republic of China. The lawful operation of foreign-invested construction enterprises and their legal rights and interests within the territory of the People's Republic of China shall be protected by Chinese laws, regulations and rules.

第五条　国务院对外贸易经济行政主管部门负责外商投资建筑业企业设立的管理工作；国务院建设行政主管部门负责外商投资建筑业企业资质的管理工作。省、自治区、直辖市人民政府对外贸易经济行政主管部门在授权范围内负责外商投资建筑业企业设立的管理工作；省、自治区、直辖市人民政府建设行政主管部门按照本规定负责本行政区域内的外商投资建筑业企业资质的管理工作。

Article 5 The foreign trade and economic cooperation administration department of the State Council shall be responsible for the administration of the establishment of foreign-invested construction enterprises. The construction administration department of the State Council shall be responsible for the administration of the qualifications of foreign-invested construction enterprises. The foreign trade and economic cooperation administration departments of the people's government of provinces, autonomous regions or directly administered municipalities shall be responsible for the administration of the establishment of foreign-invested construction enterprises within their authorized jurisdiction; the construction administration departments of the people's government of the provinces, or autonomous regions or directly administered municipalities shall, in accordance with these Regulations, be responsible for the administration of qualifications of foreign-invested construction enterprises within their administrative regions.

第二章　企业设立与资质的申请和审批

Chapter 2 Application for and Examination and Approval of Establishment of Foreign-invested Construction Enterprises and their Qualifications

第六条　外商投资建筑业企业设立与资质的申请和审批，实行分级、分类管理。申请设立施工总承包序列特级和一级、专业承包序列一级资质外商投资建筑业企业的，其设立由国务院对外贸易经济行政主管部门审批，其资质由国务院建设行政主管部门审批；申请设立施工总承包序列和专业承包序列二级及二级以下、劳务分包序列资质的，其设立由省、自治区、直辖市人民政府对外贸易经济行政主管部门审批，其资质由省、自治区、直辖市人民政府建设行政主管部门审批。中外合资经营建筑业企业、中外合作经营建筑业企业的中方投资者为中央管理企业的，其设立由国务院对外贸易经济行政主管部门审批，其资质由国务院建设行政主管部门审批。

Article 6 The application for and the examination and approval of the establishment of foreign-invested construction enterprises and their qualifications shall be managed by a grading and categorization system. Where an applicant is to apply to establish a contractor with Super Grade or Grade A qualifications or to establish a specialized contractor with Grade A qualifications, the establishment of the foreign-invested construction enterprise shall be examined and approved by the foreign trade and economic cooperation administration department of the State Council and its qualifications shall be examined and approved by the construction administration department of the State Council; where an applicant is to apply to establish a contractor or a specialized contractor with Grade B or lower qualifications or any of the subcontractor qualifications, the establishment of the foreign-invested construction enterprise shall be examined and approved by the foreign trade and economic cooperation administration department of the people's government of the province, the autonomous region or the directly administered municipality and its qualifications shall be examined and approved by the construction administration department of the people's government of the province, the autonomous region or the directly administered municipality. Where the Chinese investor to a proposed Sino-foreign equity construction joint venture or a Sino-foreign cooperative construction enterprise is an enterprise administered by the central government, the establishment of the joint venture shall be examined and approved by the foreign trade and economic cooperation administration department of the State Council and its qualifications shall be examined and approved by the construction administration department of the State Council.

第七条 设立外商投资建筑业企业,申请施工总承包序列特级和一级、专业承包序列一级资质的程序:

Article 7 The procedures for the establishment of a foreign-invested construction enterprise as a contractor with Super Grade or Grade A qualifications or a specialized contractor with Grade A qualifications are:

(一)申请者向拟设立企业所在地的省、自治区、直辖市人民政府对外贸易经济行政主管部门提出设立申请。

(1) The applicant shall submit an application to the foreign trade and economic cooperation administration department of the people's government of the province, the autonomous region or the directly administered municipality where the proposed foreign-invested construction enterprise is to be established.

(二)省、自治区、直辖市人民政府对外贸易经济行政主管部门在受理申请之日起30日内完成初审,初审同意后,报国务院对外贸易经济行政主管部门。

(2) The foreign trade and economic cooperation administration department of the people's government of the province, the autonomous region or the directly administered municipality shall complete the preliminary examination within 30 days of receiving the application, and shall, if it grants the preliminary approval, submit the application to the foreign trade and economic cooperation administration department of the State Council for further approval.

(三)国务院对外贸易经济行政主管部门在收到初审材料之日起10日内将申请材料送国务院建设行政主管部门征求意见。国务院建设行政主管部门在收到征求意见函之日起30日内提出意见。国务院对外贸易经济行政主管部门在收到国务院建设行政主管部门书面意见之日起30日内作出批准或者不批准的书面决定。予以批准的,发给外商投资企业批准证书;不予批准的,书面说明理由。

(3) Within 10 days of receiving the application for further approval, the foreign trade

and economic administration department of the State Council shall forward the application to the construction administration department of the State Council for review and comments. The construction administration department of the State Council shall provide its opinion in writing within 30 days of receiving the request. Within 30 days of receiving the response, the foreign trade and economic cooperation administration department of the State Council shall decide whether or not to approve the application and express such a decision in written form. If the application is approved, a foreign-invested enterprise certificate shall be granted; if the application is not approved, reasons for the disapproval shall be given in written form.

（四）取得外商投资企业批准证书的，应当在 30 日内到登记主管机关办理企业登记注册。

(4) Within 30 days of receiving the approval certificate, the applicant shall register with the relevant registration department.

（五）取得企业法人营业执照后，申请建筑业企业资质的，按照建筑业企业资质管理规定办理。

(5) After obtaining the business license for the legal entity, the application by the foreign-invested construction enterprise for qualification approval shall be conducted in accordance with *Regulations on Administration of Construction Enterprise Qualifications*.

第八条　设立外商投资建筑业企业，申请施工总承包序列和专业承包序列二级及二级以下、劳务分包序列资质的程序，由各省、自治区、直辖市人民政府建设行政主管部门和对外贸易经济行政主管部门，结合本地区实际情况，参照本规定第七条以及建筑业企业资质管理规定执行。省、自治区、直辖市人民政府建设行政主管部门审批的外商投资建筑业企业资质，应当在批准之日起 30 日内报国务院建设行政主管部门备案。

Article 8 The procedures for the establishment of a foreign-invested construction enterprise as a contractor or a specialized contractor with Grade B or lower qualifications or any of the subcontractor qualifications shall be administered by the construction administration department and the foreign trade and economic cooperation administration department of the people's government of the province, the autonomous region or the directly administered municipality based on local conditions with reference to Article 7 of these Regulations and Regulations on Administration of Construction Enterprise Qualifications. Examination and approval of qualifications of the foreign-invested construction enterprise by the construction administration department of the people's government of the province, the autonomous region or the directly administered municipality shall be filed with the construction administration department of the State Council within 30 days after the approval is given.

第九条　外商投资建筑业企业申请晋升资质等级或者增加主项以外资质的，应当依照有关规定到建设行政主管部门办理相关手续。

Article 9 The application by a foreign-invested construction enterprise for upgrading its qualifications or adding additional qualifications in addition to major items shall be made to the relevant construction administration department in accordance with relevant regulations.

第十条　申请设立外商投资建筑业企业应当向对外贸易经济行政主管部门提交下列资料：

Article 10　An applicant which intends to establish a foreign-invested construction enterprise shall submit the following documents to the relevant foreign trade and economic cooperation administration department：

（一）投资方法定代表人签署的外商投资建筑业企业设立申请书；

(1) Application forms to establish a foreign-invested construction enterprise signed by the investor's legal representative；

（二）投资方编制或者认可的可行性研究报告；

(2) The feasibility study report prepared or accepted by the investors；

（三）投资方法定代表人签署的外商投资建筑业企业合同和章程（其中，设立外资建筑业企业的只需提供章程）；

(3) The contract for the establishment of a foreign-invested construction enterprise and the articles of association signed by the investor's legal representative (only the articles of association is required for the establishment of a wholly foreign-owned construction enterprise)；

（四）企业名称预先核准通知书；

(4) The notification on pre-verification of the name of the enterprise；

（五）投资方法人登记注册证明、投资方银行资信证明；

(5) Documentary evidence of legal entity registration and bank credential letter of the investor；

（六）投资方拟派出的董事长、董事会成员、经理、工程技术负责人等任职文件及证明文件；

(6) Appointment letters and documentary evidence of the investor's designated chairman and members of the board of directors，managers and technical managers etc；

（七）经注册会计师或者会计事务所审计的投资方最近三年的资产负债表和损益表。

(7) Balance sheets and profit and loss accounts of the investor over the past three years audited by a certified accountant or an accounting firm.

第十一条　申请外商投资建筑业企业资质应当向建设行政主管部门提交下列资料：

Article 11　The applicant applying for foreign-invested construction enterprise qualifications shall submit the following documents to the relevant construction administration department：

（一）外商投资建筑业企业资质申请表；

(1) Application forms for the foreign-invested construction enterprise qualifications；

（二）外商投资企业批准证书；

(2) The approval certificate for the establishment of the foreign-invested construction enterprise；

（三）企业法人营业执照；

(3) The business license for the legal entity;

（四）投资方的银行资信证明；

(4) The bank credential letter of the investor;

（五）投资方拟派出的董事长、董事会成员、企业财务负责人、经营负责人、工程技术负责人等任职文件及证明文件；

(5) Appointment letters and documentary evidence of the investor's designated chairman and members of the board of directors, the enterprise's financial manager, operations managers and technical managers, etc.

（六）经注册会计师或者会计师事务所审计的投资方最近三年的资产负债表和损益表；

(6) Balance sheets and profit and loss accounts of the investor over the past three years audited by a certified accountant or an accounting firm.

（七）建筑业企业资质管理规定要求提交的资料。

(7) Other documents required.

第十二条 中外合资经营建筑业企业、中外合作经营建筑业企业中方合营者的出资总额不得低于注册资本的25％。

Article 12 The total capital contribution of the Chinese party to a Sino-foreign equity construction joint venture or a Sino-foreign cooperative construction enterprise shall not be less than 25％ of the registered capital.

第十三条 本规定实施前，已经设立的中外合资经营建筑业企业、中外合作经营建筑业企业，应当按照本规定和建筑业企业资质管理规定重新核定资质等级。

Article 13 Qualifications of Sino-foreign equity construction joint ventures and Sino-foreign cooperative construction enterprises established prior to the issuance of these Regulations are required to be re-examined and ratified in accordance with these Regulations and Regulations on Administration of Construction Enterprise Qualifications.

第十四条 本规定中要求申请者提交的资料应当使用中文，证明文件原件是外文的，应当提供中文译本。

Article 14 All documents required to be submitted by an applicant under these Regulations shall be in Chinese. If the original documentary evidence is in a foreign language, a Chinese translation shall be provided.

第三章 工程承包范围
Chapter 3 Scope of Contracting

第十五条 外资建筑业企业只允许在其资质等级许可的范围内承包下列工程：

Article 15 Wholly foreign-owned construction enterprises may only undertake the following types of construction projects within the scope of their qualifications:

（一）全部由外国投资、外国赠款、外国投资及赠款建设的工程；

(1) Construction projects funded totally by foreign investments, foreign grants or foreign investments and grants;

（二）由国际金融机构资助并通过根据贷款条款进行的国际招标授予的建设项目；

(2) Construction projects financed by international financial organizations and awarded through international tendering process in accordance with the provisions of the loan agreement;

（三）外资等于或者超过50％的中外联合建设项目；及外资少于50％，但因技术困难而不能由中国建筑企业独立实施，经省、自治区、直辖市人民政府建设行政主管部门批准的中外联合建设项目；

(3) Sino-foreign jointly constructed projects where the foreign investment is equal to or greater than 50％; Sino-foreign jointly constructed projects where the foreign investment is less than 50％ but which Chinese construction enterprises cannot undertake independently due to technical difficulties subject to the approval of the construction administration departments of the people's government of provinces, or autonomous regions or directly administered municipalities;

（四）由中国投资，但因技术困难而不能由中国建筑企业独立实施的建设项目，经省、自治区、直辖市人民政府建设行政主管部门批准，可以由中外建筑企业联合承揽。

(4) China-invested construction projects which Chinese construction enterprises cannot undertake independently due to technical difficulties. Such projects may be jointly undertaken by Chinese and foreign construction enterprises subject to the approval of the construction administration departments of the people's government of provinces, or autonomous regions or directly administered municipalities.

第十六条 中外合资经营建筑业企业、中外合作经营建筑业企业应当在其资质等级许可的范围内承包工程。

Article 16 Sino-foreign equity construction joint ventures and Sino-foreign cooperative construction enterprises shall undertake construction projects within the permitted scope of their grades of qualifications.

第四章 监督管理
Chapter 4 Supervision and Administration

第十七条 外商投资建筑业企业的资质等级标准执行国务院建设行政主管部门颁发的建筑业企业资质等级标准。

Article 17 The criteria of grading of qualifications of foreign-invested construction enterprises shall be in accordance with the criteria of grading of construction enterprise qualifications formulated and issued by the construction administration department of the State Council.

第十八条 承揽施工总承包工程的外商投资建筑业企业，建筑工程主体结构的施工必须由其自行完成。

Article 18 Where a foreign-invested construction enterprise undertakes a construction project as the contractor, it shall itself complete the main structure of the project.

第十九条 外商投资建筑业企业与其他建筑业企业联合承包，应当按照资质等级低的企业的业务许可范围承包工程。

Article 19 Where a foreign-invested construction enterprise contracts for construction projects in the form of a consortium with other construction enterprises, the consortium shall contract for projects within the permitted scope of the lower qualification grade.

第二十条 外资建筑业企业违反本规定第十五条，超越资质许可的业务范围承包工程的，处工程合同价款2%以上4%以下的罚款；可以责令停业整顿，降低资质等级；情节严重的，吊销资质证书；有违法所得的，予以没收。

Article 20 Where a foreign-invested construction enterprise contracts for construction projects beyond the permitted scope of its qualifications in violation of Article 15 of these Regulations, a fine at an amount between 2% to 4% of the construction contract price shall be collected. An order to suspend its business operation and to correct the wrongdoings may also be issued and its qualification certificate may be demoted. In serious situations, the qualification certificate shall be revoked and any proceeds illegally obtained shall be confiscated.

第二十一条 外商投资建筑业企业从事建筑活动，违反《中华人民共和国建筑法》、《中华人民共和国招标投标法》、《建设工程质量管理条例》、《建筑业企业资质管理规定》等有关法律、法规、规章的，依照有关规定处罚。

Article 21 Where a foreign-invested construction enterprise carrying out construction business violates *the Construction Law of the People's Republic of China*, *the Tendering and Bidding Law of the People's Republic of China*, *Regulations on Administration of Engineering Construction Quality and Regulations on Administration of Construction Enterprise Qualifications* and other relevant laws, regulations and rules, it shall be penalized in accordance with relevant provisions.

第五章 附则
Chapter 5 Supplemental Provisions

第二十二条 本规定实施前已经取得《外国企业承包工程资质证》的外国企业投资设立外商投资建筑业企业，可以根据其在中华人民共和国境内承包工程业绩等申请相应等级的建筑业企业资质。根据本条第一款规定已经在中华人民共和国境内设立外商投资建筑业企业的外国企业，设立新的外商投资建筑业企业，其资质等级按照建筑业企业资质管理规定核定。

Article 22 For a foreign enterprise which has already obtained a Foreign Enterprise Qualification Certificate for Contracting for Construction Projects prior to these Regulations come into force, it may apply for a construction enterprise qualification of an appropriate grade based on its track record of project contracting within the territory of the People's Republic of China when establishing a foreign-invested construction enterprise. Where a foreign enterprise which has already established a foreign invested construction enterprise within the territory of the People's Republic of China as stated in Paragraph 1 of this Article is to establish a new foreign-invested construction enterprise, the qualification grade of the new foreign-invested construction enterprise shall be determined in accordance with Regulations on Administration of Construction Enterprise Qualifications.

第二十三条 香港特别行政区、澳门特别行政区和台湾地区投资者在其他省、自治区、直辖市投资设立建筑业企业,从事建筑活动的,参照本规定执行。法律、法规、国务院另有规定的除外。

Article 23 Investors from Hong Kong Special Administrative Region, Macao Special Administrative Region or Taiwan shall establish construction enterprises and carry out construction businesses in other provinces, autonomous regions or directly administered municipalities in accordance with these Regulations, unless it is otherwise provided by laws, regulations or the State Council.

第二十四条 本规定由国务院建设行政主管部门和国务院对外贸易经济行政主管部门按照各自职责负责解释。

Article 24 The construction administration department of the State Council and the foreign trade and economic cooperation administration department of the State Council shall be responsible for interpretation of these Regulations in accordance with their respective functions.

第二十五条 本规定自 2002 年 12 月 1 日起施行。

Article 25 These Regulations shall come into force on 1 December 2002.

第二十六条 自 2003 年 10 月 1 日起,1994 年 3 月 22 日建设部颁布的《在中国境内承包工程的外国企业资质管理暂行办法》(建设部令第 32 号)废止。

Article 26 *The Tentative Measures on Administration of Foreign Enterprise Qualifications for Contracting to Construction Projects Within the Territory of China* issued by the Ministry of Construction on 22 March 1994 (Decree No. 32 of the Ministry of Construction) shall be repealed as of 1 October 2003.

第二十七条 自 2002 年 12 月 1 日起,建设部和对外贸易经济合作部联合颁布的《关于设立外商投资建筑业企业的若干规定》(建建〔1995〕533 号)废止。

Article 27 *Provisions on Establishment of Foreign-invested Construction Enterprises* (*File No.* 533, 1995) jointly issued by the Ministry of Construction and the Ministry of Foreign Trade and Economic Cooperation shall be repealed as of 1 December 2002.

MODULE 12　Construction Testing
模块十二　建筑试验

Learning Objectives 学习目标

In this module, learners should:
- know the Chinese and English names of construction testing.
- master the English conversation techniques of construction testing.

在本模块内，学习者应该能：
- 了解建筑试验相关英文术语。
- 掌握建筑试验的英语会话技巧。

Special Terms 专业词汇

concrete test　混凝土试验
test cube　试块
test piece　试件
vibratory test　振动试验
tensile test　拉力试验
extension test　拉伸试验
destructive test　破坏性试验
pilling test　打桩测试
pile pulling test　拔桩试验
standard penetration test　标准贯入试验
pile redriving test　桩复打试验
magnetic particle inspection　磁粉检验
penetrate inspection　渗透探伤
field identification　现场鉴定
pressure testing record　试压记录
concrete stress　混凝土应力
pile capacity　单桩承载力
pile driving resistance　打桩阻力

concrete design　混凝土设计
test specimen　试样
slump test　坍落度试验
steel reinforcement test　钢筋试验
welding test　焊接试验
bending test　弯曲试验
non-destructive test　无损试验
pile load test　桩荷载试验
penetration test　贯入度试验
field density test　现场密度测试
cold test　冲击试验
bending plastic inspection　弯曲塑性检验
ultrasonic inspection　超声波探伤
field moisture equivalent　现场含水等量
driving record　打桩记录
steel bar strength　钢筋强度
driving stress　打桩应力
depth of penetration　贯入深度

specified penetration　指定贯入度
visual examination　外观检查
final penetration　最终贯入度
lateral pile load test　桩的侧向荷载试验

trial 指为观察、研究某事物以区别其真伪、优劣或效果等而进行较长时间的试验或试用过程；experiment 多指用科学方法在实验室内进行较系统的操作实验以验证、解释或说明某一理论、定理或某一观点等；test 为普通用词，含义广，指用科学方法对某物质进行测试以估价其性质或效能等。

Situational Conversations　情景对话

Oyang: I'd like to have a discussion with you about the steel bar testing. What is the main purpose of doing the steel bar test?

Ridley: The main purpose is to make it clear that whether the physical characters and the chemical components of the steel bars are complied with the specification or not.

Oyang: Can you tell me the procedure of the steel bar test?

Ridley: OK. Before doing the test, you'd better inspect the surface of the steel bar, and check whether the size of the steel bar is complied with the specification, and whether there are any leakages, scars or honeycombs on the surface.

Oyang: What do you test after the surface is accepted then?

Ridley: Then we will do sampling test.

Oyang: What do you mean by sampling test? Is the test physical or chemical?

Ridley: The sampling test we will do for the steel bar in the following is usually the physical one. That is, first we take 6 segments of steel bar from each of 60 tons and cut one piece from each segment, and then divide six pieces into two groups (each group has three pieces) as testing samples.

Oyang: What do you do then?

Ridley: For one group, we will do the tensile test, that is, to test its yield point, tensile strength and the extension rate.

Oyang: Oh, I see. How about the second group?

Ridley: The second group will be tested for its cold bending degree.

Oyang: If brittle leakages or bad welding performance occurred in the test processing, what would you do?

Ridley: In that case, a chemical contentment analysis or other special tests must be done so as to find out the problem.

Oyang: You are right. Now I want to know under what situations you will test the cold tensile processing.

Ridley: The cold tensile processing is tested when the extensile rate of the steel bar is already in excess of the defined maximum extension under the maximum strength.

Oyang: In this case, what tests do you usually do?

Ridley: We usually test the steel bar for its mechanical characteristics. The steel bar is adopted in works according to its actual grade found out in the test.

Oyang: I fully agree with you. I quite understand it too, but can you give me an example?

Ridley: Oh, yeah. If it is a steel bar with a lower grade found out by the test, it cannot be used as the higher grade in the original.

Oyang: I have already known the relationship between the steel bar testing and its application through your patient and detailed explanation. Thank you very much.

Riddley: You are welcome.

Questions

1. What should we do before doing the steel bar test?
2. Under what situations will the cold tensile processing be tested?

Notes 注释

1. the procedure of the steel bar test 钢筋试验的程序。
2. "… check whether the size of the steel bar is complied with the specification, …" 核对钢筋的规格型号是否符合规范要求。"be complied with" 符合，遵守。如 "He complied with the doctor's suggestion that he take a rest." 他听从了医生要他休息的建议。
3. sampling test 抽样检测。

4. "… to test its yield point, tensile strength and the extension rate." 检测钢筋的屈服点、抗拉强度以及延伸率。
5. cold bending degree 冷弯曲程度。
6. "In that case,… so as to find out the problem." 中 "so as to" 意思为 "为了……；以便"，相当于 "in order to"，如 "Speak louder and clearer so as to make everyone hear you." 讲得再响亮点，清楚些，让所有的人都听到。
7. The cold tensile processing is tested when the extensile rate of the steel bar is already in excess of the defined maximum extension under the maximum strength. 在最大力度而钢筋伸展率已经超过规定的最大伸展幅度的情况下才做钢筋冷拉检测。"in excess of" 意思为 "多于，超出"，如 "Luggage in excess of 100 kg will be charged extra." 超过 100 公斤的行李要额外收费。"maximum" 意思为 "最大，最多"，可用作名词、形容词和副词，其反义词为 "minimum"（最小，最少）。

Useful Sentences 必学句型

1. I'd like to have a discussion with you about the steel bar testing. 我想和你讨论一下钢筋试验相关事宜。
2. The main purpose is to make it clear that whether the physical characters and the chemical components of the steel bars are complied with the specification or not. 主要目的是要搞清楚钢筋的物理特性及化学组成成分是否符合规范要求。
3. You'd better inspect the surface of the steel bar, and check whether the size of the steel bar is complied with the specification, and whether there are any leakages, scars or honeycombs on the surface. 在做钢筋试验之前，你最好要检查钢筋的外观，核对钢筋的规格型号是否符合规范要求以及钢筋表面有无坑凹、划痕或麻面缺陷。
4. What do you mean by sampling test? 抽样检测是什么意思？
5. If brittle leakages or bad welding performance occurred in the test processing, what would you do? 如果加工过程中发生脆断或焊接性能不良，你该怎么办？
6. Now I want to know under what situations you will test the cold tensile processing. 现在，我想知道在什么情况下你会做冷拉处理。
7. The steel bar is adopted in works according to its actual grade found out in the test. 根据钢筋试验结果得出钢筋的实际等级再决定钢筋在工程中的使用。

Exercises 练习

1. **Complete the following dialogue in English.**

   A: How many piling tests have you made on the building site?

   B: _____. (到目前为止最少十次。)

   A: What is the most important solution you obtain from your tests?

   B: _____.
   (最重要的结论是，根据桩的设计承载力，得出施打最后 3 阵，每阵 10 次的最大贯入度，以确定桩尖的打入标高。)

   A: That's right. What is the vertical tolerance for the piling?

   B: _____.
   (根据规范，打入后桩的垂直误差不能超过桩长度的 0.5％。)

   A: To speed up the construction progress, can I drive piles by full height for each hammer?

   B: _____.
   (这可不行。开始几次锤击落差必须低，这样才能使桩位更稳固，此后才可把桩锤提升到最大高度。)

   A: Can the hammer of 8 tons be used to drive 350mm * 350mm square piles?

   B: _____.
   (用这么重的桩锤打这种规格的桩是决不允许的。)

   A: Why?

   B: _____.
   (因为 350 毫米乘以 350 毫米桩不能承受 2,000 千牛顿以上的冲击，而 8 吨锤的冲击力超过 3,500 千牛顿。)

   A: What test should you usually do after the pile has been already driven to the position?

   B: _____.
   (为了确保桩的质量，我们通常还要对桩进行应力变化测试。)

   A: Right. Taking it all in all, you know what is what. I am sure you can do your work better in the future.

   B: It is really good of you to say so.

   A: There is no need to thank me.

2. **Read and interpret the following passage.**

   ### Three Modern Pile Driving Methods

   (1) Driven piles: where a prefabricated pile is driven into hard rock, providing a firm base.

   (2) Driven and cast piles: where the vibrator drives a steel tube into the ground, it is reinforced by steel grid and withdrawn after concrete is cast into it.

   (3) Bored and cast piles: where a hole is drilled and a concrete mixture is cast directly

into the hole.

3. Pair work.

A acts as a rebar technician, B acts as a supervising engineer who wants to know something about how to test the steel bar. Use the following expressions:

Can you explain me something about ...?
Yes, I'd like to ...
But what information ...?
It's ...

Supplementary Materials 补充材料

Testing Items of Some Common Building Materials
常用建材的试验项目

Material Name 材料名称	Testing Project 试验项目
Cement 水泥	normal consistency(标准稠度) initial bond(初凝时间) final bond(终凝时间) soundness(定性) mortar strength(胶砂强度) fineness(细度)
Sand 砂	sieving(筛分) mud content(含泥量) clod content(泥块含量) sulfide(硫化物) light component(轻物质) chloride content(氯离子含量) mica content(云母含量) organic matter content(有机物含量) apparent density(表观密度) bulk density(堆积密度) consistency(坚固性)
Stone 碎石	stone crushing index value(压碎指标值) needle-like flaky particle content(针片状颗粒含量) density(密度) sieving(筛分) mud content(含泥量) clod content(泥块含量) consistency(坚固性) void ratio(空隙率)
Water 水	PHvalue(PH值) chloride content(氯离子含量) sulfate content(硫酸盐含量)
Admixtures 外加剂	solid content(固体含量) density(密度) water-reducing rate(减水率) bleeding rate(泌水率) setting time difference(凝结时间差) compressive strength rate(抗压强度比) chloride content(Cl^-含量)
Reinforcing steel 钢筋	ration of elongation(伸长率) yield strength(屈服强度) ultimate tensile strength(抗拉强度) bending test(弯曲试验)
Wood 木材	water content(含水率)
Bricks 砖	bending strength(抗折强度) compressive strength(抗压强度) anti-freezing(抗冻)
Clay and cement tile 粘土和水泥瓦	anti-bending load(抗折荷载) water absorbing capacity(吸水重量)
Plastic drain board 塑料排水板	longitudinal drainage(纵向排水量) filter film infiltration parameter(率膜渗透系数) filter film equivalent aperture(率膜等效孔径) filter film tensile point(率膜抗拉强度) longitudinal moisture-free(纵向干态) lateral wet process(横向湿态)

续表

Material Name 材料名称	Testing Project 试验项目
Geotextile 土工布	unit area(单位面积)　thickness（厚度）　effective pore size（有效孔径）　ultimate tensile strength(抗拉强度)　elongation percentage（延伸率）　CBR puncture strength(CBR顶破强力)　perpendicular infiltration parameter(垂直渗透系数)
PVC civil film PVC土木膜	unit area(单位面积)　film thickness(膜厚)　breaking/rupture strength(断裂强力)　elongation at rupture(断裂延伸率)　tearing strength(撕破强力)　CBR puncture strength(CBR顶破强力)　anti-infiltration strength(抗渗强度)　infiltration parameter(渗透系数)　corrosion resistance(耐蚀性能)
Geogrid 土木格栅	ultimate tensile strength（抗拉强度）　ration of elongation（伸长率）　tensile strength(拉伸力)
Concrete sample 混凝土试件	compressive strength（抗压强度）
Steel pile 钢桩	dynamic load test of pile(桩的动荷载试验)
Masonry mortar 砌筑砂浆	fluidity（流动度）　compressive strength（抗压强度）
Petroleum asphalt 石油沥青	penetration(针入度)　extensibility（延伸度）　softening point（软化点）
Bitumen waterproof roll 沥青防水卷材	impermeability（不透水性）　heat resistance（耐热度）　water absorbency（吸水性）　ultimate tensile strength（抗拉强度）　flexibility（柔度）
Bituminous adhesive 沥青胶	heat resistance(耐热度)　flexibility(柔韧性)　cohesive force(粘结力)

MODULE 13　Construction Surveying
模块十三　建筑测量

Learning Objectives 学习目标

In this module, learners should:
- know the Chinese and English names of instruments and special terms in the field of construction surveying.
- be capable of simply discussing the relevant contents of construction surveying in English.

在本模块内，学习者应该能：
- 掌握建筑施工测量仪器及相关术语的中英文名称。
- 能用英语简单谈论建筑施工测量的有关内容。

Special Terms 专业词汇

types of survey　测量种类
geodetic survey　大地测量
route survey　路线测量
construction survey　施工测量
surveying lines　测量线
broken line　折线
base line　基线
datum line　基准线
axis　轴线
central line　中心线
perpendicular line　垂直线
surveying instruments　测量仪器
high-precision theodolite　高精度经纬
direction theodolite　方向经纬仪
dumpy level　定镜水平仪
automatic level　自动水平仪

plane survey　平面测量
topographic survey　地形测量
hydrographic survey　水文/河道测量
photogrammetric survey　摄影测量
straight line　直线
solid/full line　实线
building line　建筑红线，房基线
datum point　基准点
positioning line　定位线
dimension line　尺寸线
line of level　水平线
theodolite　经纬仪
repetition theodolite　复测经纬仪
leveling instrument　水平仪
quickset level　速调水平仪
microwave ranger finder　微波测距仪

leveling rod　水准标尺	ranging pole　标尺测杆
readjust focusing　调整聚焦	leveler　水准测量员
surveyor　测量员	rod man　标杆员

instrument 是高精密仪器,是 equipment 中的一种,多个 instrument 可以组装成 equipment;equipment 是成套、大型设备或装备;facility 是设施,比如说公共设施 public facility;device 是小元器件,比 instrument 还小一级;appliance 指的是家电之类的东西。

Situational Conversations 情景对话

Edison: It is said that there are many types of surveys, aren't there?

Donna: Yes, indeed there are seven types, namely plane surveys, geodetic surveys, topographic surveys, route surveys, hydrographic surveys, construction surveys and photogrammetric surveys.

Edison: Are they all concerned with construction?

Donna: Not entirely. Only three of them are architecture-related, that is, route surveys, hydrographic surveys and construction surveys.

Edison: Would you mind telling me what route surveys are?

Donna: Of course not. Route surveys are for high-ways, rail-roads, canals, pipelines and other projects which do not close upon the starting points.

Edison: I quite understand it. Why do you say hydrographic survey is also architecture-related?

Donna: That is because hydrographic survey is mainly concerned with construction works of lakes, streams, reservoirs, dams and so on.

Edison: As a student of architecture, I am especially interested in construction survey. Can you tell me something about it?

Donna: No problem. Construction surveys mainly provide locations and elevations of buildings.

Edison: So the first problem to be solved in locating or positing a structure is to do a topographic survey on the construction area, isn't it?

Donna: Yes, it is. We need some reference points to control the construction stakes and to check the work progress.

Edison: Can you explain to me how to do the construction survey well?

Donna: Construction survey is best learned on the job by applying the basic principles to practice, as each work has its own characteristics.

Edison: That is true. Is accuracy absolutely essential in setting out large buildings adopted mainly the prefabricated parts?

Donna: Yes, of course. Precision is absolutely necessary, not err by hair's breadth at all.

Edison: For highly accurate measurements, what should surveyors pay attention to?

Donna: First, he must make sure the measuring tools are of good quality; second, to adjust the instrument accurately, he'd better use a spring balance or a constant-tension handle; third, it is about the surveying and measuring results. The various corrections should be computed and applied to the distance set out.

Edison: All the above mentioned points should be followed, right?

Donna: Certainly. Only following the above can surveyors guarantee accuracy.

Edison: I bear in mind. Thank you for your patient explanation.

Donna: Not at all. Such a trifling thing is hardly worth mentioning.

Questions

1. How many types of surveys are there?
2. In what ways can the construction survey be done well?

Notes 注释

1. namely 即,也就是。如"Only one person can answer the question, namely you."只有一个人能回答这个问题,那就是你。

2. be concerned with 关心;相干。如"A party in power must be concerned with the interest of the mass."执政党必须关心群众的利益。又如"The program for this morning's session will be concerned with earthquake prediction."今天上午的主要议程与地震预报有关。

3. Only three of them are architecture-related, that is, route surveys, hydrographic surveys and construction surveys. 它们中只有三种与建筑相关,也就是,路线测量、水文测量和施工测量。

4. "… other projects which do not close upon the starting points." 不闭合于起始点上的其他工程。
5. "… the first problem to be solved in locating or positing a structure is to do a topographic survey on the construction area …" 在建筑物定位工作中首先要解决的问题就是施工区的地形测量。
6. the construction stakes 施工标桩。
7. Construction survey is best learned on the job by applying the basic principles to practice, as each work has its own characteristics. 施工测量最好是在工作中把测量的基本原理同实践相结合的过程中学习,因为每项工作都有其本身的特点。
8. "… in setting out large buildings adopted mainly the prefabricated parts" 在主要使用预制构件的大型建筑物放样过程中。
9. a spring balance 弹簧秤。
10. a constant-tension handle 拉力稳定的拉力架。
11. The various corrections should be computed and applied to the distance set out. 应当计算各种改正数据并将其运用到所放样的距离上去。"set out"为过去分词短语作定语,修饰"the distance"。

Useful Sentences 必学句型

1. It is said that there are many types of surveys, aren't there? 听说测量有许多种,不是吗?
2. Would you mind telling me what route surveys are? 你不介意的话,可以告诉我什么是路线测量吗?
3. As a student of architecture, I am especially interested in construction survey. 作为建筑专业的学生,我对施工测量特别感兴趣。
4. Can you explain to me how to do the construction survey well? 你能解释一下如何才能做好施工测量这份工作?
5. Precision is absolutely necessary, not err by hair's breadth at all. 精度是绝对必要,决不能有丝毫偏差。
6. For highly accurate measurements, what should surveyors pay attention to? 为确保高精度测量,测量员需要注意什么呢?
7. Only following the above can surveyors guarantee accuracy. 只有遵循上述几点才能保证测量的准确性。
8. I bear the teacher's words in mind. 我记住了老师所说的话。
9. Such a trifling thing is hardly worth mentioning. 区区小事,何足挂齿。

Exercises 练习

1. Complete the following dialogue in English.

A: Can you tell me what surveying is defined as?

B: _____.

（根据字典解释，测量学的定义为对地面上的自然要素和人工地物的相对位置进行量测。）

A: And what does it mean in practice?

B: _____.

（在实践中，测量用来表示那些与测绘平面图有关的操作，即在构成水平面的二维平面上的工作。）

A: I see. What is the purpose of surveying?

B: _____.

（其目的就是将这些测量结果按某种适当比例尺绘制成地图、平面图或断面图。）

A: And what is the meaning of leveling?

B: _____.

（水平测量指在第三维中的工作，即在垂直于水平方向的工作，包括平面和水准测量。）

A: Can you explain them more exactly?

B: _____.

（平面测量就是把地面上的要素表示在平面图上的有关操作；水准测量是与表示地面上各点高度之间相对差数的有关操作。）

A: What are the surveyor's works?

B: _____.

（测量员的工作通常有 4 部分。第 1 部分是在野外进行测量并记录下测量结果；第 2 部分是进行必要的计算，以确定位置、面积和体积；第 3 部分是将测量结果绘制成地图；最后是放样，即定立木桩用于表示边界或指导施工。）

A: Thank you for your explanation. I bet you must be an excellent surveyor.

B: I am most grateful to your praise. Indeed, these are the essential knowledge for any surveyor.

2. Read and interpret the following passage.

The Level

Strictly speaking, the level is an instrument designed primarily to furnish a horizontal line of sight. The line is determined by a telescope with the usual components consisting of object glass, focusing arrangement, diaphragm with cross lines and eyepiece. In practice, the telescope must be capable of rotation about a vertical axis so that it can be pointed in any direction.

The levels in use nowadays can be grouped into three main classes: dumpy levels, automatic levels and tilting levels.

3. Pair work.

A acts as a surveyor of a Construction Engineering Company, B acts as an inspector who wants to know how to do the surveying work well. Use the following expressions:

— Can I help …?
— Yes …
— What should be done to do the surveying well?
— First …; then …; finally …

Supplementary Materials 补充材料

The Standard Translation of Surveying Nouns
测绘名词英汉标准化翻译

engineering survey 工程测量	open traverse 支导线
surveying 测量学	theodolite traverse 经纬仪导线
elementary surveying 普通测量学	subtense traverse 视差导线
topography 地形测量学	stadia traverse 视距导线
surveying control network 测量控制网	plane-table traverse 平板仪导线
horizontal control network 平面控制网	distance measurement 距离测量
vertical control network 高程控制网	electro-magnetic distance measurement 电磁波测距
horizontal control point 平面控制点	
vertical control point 高程控制点	standard field of length 标准检定场
horizontal coordinate 平面坐标	EDM traverse 光电测距导线
control survey 控制测量	minor triangulation 小三角测量
topographic survey 地形测量	linear triangulation chain 线形锁
trilateration network 三边网	linear triangulation network 线形网
triangulateration network 边角网	mapping control 图根控制
traverse network 导线网	traverse leg 导线边
trilateration survey 三边测量	traverse angle 导线折角
triangulateration survey 边角测量	junction point of traverses 导线结点
traverse survey 导线测量	meandering coefficient of traverse 导线曲折系数
horizontal angle 水平角	
vertical angle 垂直角	angle closing error of traverse 导线角度闭合差
description of station 点之记	
station 测站	total length closing error of traverse 导线全长闭合差
station centring 测站归心	
sighting centring 照准点归心	longitudinal error of traverse 导线纵向误差
sighting point 照准点	
closed traverse 闭合导线	lateral error of traverse 导线横向误差
connecting traverse 附合导线	control point 控制点

traverse point	导线点
mapping control point	图根点
elevation point	高程点
detail point	碎部点
graphic mapping control point	图解图根点
analytic mapping control point	解析图根点
increment of coordinate	坐标增量
[forward] intersection	前方交会
side intersection	侧方交会
resection	后方交会
linear-angular intersection	边角交会法
linear intersection	边交会法
Bessel method	贝塞尔法
Lehmann method	莱曼法
subtense method with horizontal staff	横基尺视差法
subtense method with vertical staff	竖基尺视差法
repetition method	复测法
vertical control survey	高程控制测量
leveling	水准测量
annexed leveling line	附合水准路线
closed leveling line	闭合水准路线
elevation of sight	视线高程
polygonal height traverse	多角高程导线
height traverse	高程导线
rigorous adjustment	严密平差
approximate adjustment	近似平差
adjustment of typical figures	典型图形平差
method of equal-weight substitution	等权代替法
adjustment by method of polygon	多边形平差法
adjustment by method of junction point	结点平差
engineering control network	工程控制网
construction control network	施工控制网
three-dimensional network	三维网
construction survey	施工测量
constructioncompletion survey	竣工测量
profile survey	纵断面测量
cross-section survey	横断面测量
profile [diagram]	纵断面图
cross-section profile	横断面图
detail survey	碎部测量
plane-table survey	平板仪测量
mapping method with transit	经纬仪测绘法
rectangular grid	直角坐标网
leveling network	水准网
spur leveling line	支水准路
small scale topographical map	小比例尺地形图
rectangular map-subdivision	矩形分幅
square map-subdivision	正方形分幅
slope distance	斜距
horizontal distance	平距
base map of topography	地形底图
arbitrary axis meridian	任意轴子午线
assumed coordinate system	假定坐标系
independent coordinate system	独立坐标系
deformation observation	变形观测
displacement observation	位移观测
settlement observation	沉降观测
deflection observation	挠度观测
oblique observation, tilt observation	倾斜观测
geological survey	地质测量
prospecting network layout	勘探网测设
prospecting line survey	勘探线测量
prospecting network survey	勘探网测量
prospecting baseline	勘探基线
geological point survey	地质点测量
point for shaft position	井口位置点
bore-hole position survey	钻孔位置测量
geological profile survey	地质剖面测量

fault displacement survey 断层位移测量
regional geological survey 区域地质测量
shaft prospecting engineering survey
　　　　　　　　　　　　井探工程测量
adit prospecting engineering survey
　　　　　　　　　　　　坑探工程测量
prospecting line profile map 勘探线剖面图
adit planimetric map 坑道平面图
geological section map 地质剖面图
map of mineral deposits 矿产图
geological scheme 地质略图
field geological map 野外地质图
geological sketch map 地质草图
geological photomap 影像地质图
geological interpretation of photograph
　　　　　　　　　　　　相片地质判读
regional geological map 区域地质图
title of survey area 测区名称
code of survey area 测区代号
coverage of survey area 测区范围
geostress survey 地应力测量
petroleum pipeline survey 输油管道测量
underground oil depot survey
　　　　　　　　　　　　地下油库测量
petroleum exploration survey
　　　　　　　　　　　　石油勘探测量
mine surveying 矿山测量学
mine survey 矿山测量
mine surface survey 矿山地面测量
control survey of mining area
　　　　　　　　　　　　矿区控制测量
connection survey 联系测量
shaft orientation survey 立井定向测量
geometric orientation 几何定向
physical orientation 物理定向
connection point for orientation
　　　　　　　　　　　　定向连接点
orientation projection 定向投影
projection by suspended plumbing
　　　　　　　　　　　　吊锤投影
laser plumbing 激光投点
damping-bob for shaft plumbing
　　　　　　　　　　　　稳定锤投影
pendulous-bob for shaft plumbing
　　　　　　　　　　　　摆动锤投影
orientation connection survey
　　　　　　　　　　　　定向连接测量
sighting line method 瞄直法
connection triangle method 联系三角形法
straight triangle
　　　　　　　直伸三角形（又称"延伸三角形"）
connection quadrangle method
　　　　　　　　　　　　联系四边形法
orientation error 定向误差
gyrostatic orientation survey
　　　　　　　　　　　　陀螺定向测量
rough orientation 粗略定向
precise orientation 精密定向
reversal points method 逆转点法
tape zero observation 悬挂带零位观测
gyro azimuth 陀螺方位角排
gyro meridian 陀螺仪子午线
gyro orientation error 陀螺定向误差
induction height survey 导入高程测量
underground survey 井下测量
underground closed traverse with overhead crossing 井下交叉闭合导线
gyro EDM traverse
　　　　　　　　　　　陀螺定向光电测距导线
direction-annexed traverse 方向附合导线
roof station 顶板测点
floor station 底板测点
underground height measurement
　　　　　　　　　　　　井下高程测量
centering under point 点下对中
mining panel survey 采区测量
connection survey in mining panel
　　　　　　　　　　　　采区联系测量

detail survey of workings 巷道碎部测量
stop survey 采场测量
underground cavity survey 井下空洞测量
opencast survey 露天矿测量
check-acceptance survey of open pit
　　　　　　　采掘场验收测量
setting-out of technical edge 术境界标定
blasting survey of open pit
　　　　　　　露天矿爆破工作测量
reclamation survey 垦复测量
setting-out of mining yard 矿场标定
setting-out of shaft center 井筒中心标定
setting-out of side plumb-bob 边垂线标定
laser guide of vertical shaft 竖井激光指向
shaft-deepening survey 井筒延伸测量
closure plan of ice wall 冻结壁交圈图
construction survey for shaft drilling
　　　　　　　钻井施工测量
mineral deposits geometry 矿床几何[学]
setting-out of center line of workings
　　　　　　　巷道中线标定
setting-out of workings slope
　　　　　　　巷道坡度线标定
setting-out of junction 交叉点放样
footage measurement of workings
　　　　　　　巷道验收丈量
holing through survey/ breakthrough survey 贯通测量
geometrisation of ore body 矿体几何制图
geometrisation of mineral property
　　　　　　　矿产几何制图
underground prospecting survey
　　　　　　　井下勘探测量
determination of seam elements
　　　　　　　矿层要素测定
reserve management 储量管理
mining subsidence observation
　　　　　　　开采沉陷观测

prediction of mining subsidence
　　　　　　　开采沉陷预计
angle of critical deformation 移动角
boundary angle 边界角
observation of slope stability
　　　　　　　边坡稳定性观测
mining map 矿山测量图
topographic map of mining area
　　　　　　　井田区域地形图
mining yard plan 矿场平面图
shaft bottom plan 井底车场平面图
mining engineering plan 采掘工程平面图
main workings plan 主要巷道平面图
surface-underground contrast plan
　　　　　　　井上下对照图
opencast mining plan 露天矿矿图
striping&mining engineering profile
　　　　　　　采剥工程断面图
plan of striping and mining
　　　　　　　采剥工程平面图
waste dump plan 排土场平面图
water-proof and drainage system plan
　　　　　　　防排水系统图
exchanging map of mining survey
　　　　　　　矿山测量交换图
contour map of seam roof
　　　　　　　矿层顶板等高线图
contour map of seam floor
　　　　　　　矿层底板等高线图
curve diagram of surface movement
　　　　　　　地表移动曲线图
map of mining subsidence 开采沉陷图
urban survey 城市测量
urban control survey 城市控制测量
urban topographic survey 城市地形测量
urban planning survey 城市规划测量
public works survey 市政工程测量
building works survey 建筑工程测量

utility survey 公用事业工程测量
setting-out survey 放样测量
alignment survey 定线测量
pipe survey 管道测量
subway survey 地下铁道测量
surveying for site selection 选厂测量
airport survey 飞机场测量
airfield runway survey 机场跑道测量
square control network 施工方格网
point of square control network 方格网点
setting-out of main axis 主轴线测设
building axis survey 建筑轴线测量
property line survey 建筑红线测量
building subsidence observation
　　　　　　　　建筑物沉降观测
laser alignment 激光准直
optical alignment 光学准直
underground pipeline survey
　　　　　　　　地下管线测量
underground pipe-driving survey 顶管测量
topographic map of urban area 城市地形图
plan of a zone 带状平面图
synthesis chart of pipelines 管道综合图
revision of topographic map 地形图更新
data base for urban survey
　　　　　　　　城市测量数据库
hydrographic engineering survey
　　　　　　　　水利工程测量
exiguous triangle method 微三角形法
checking datum mark 校核基点
starting datum mark 起测基点
method of tension wire alignment
　　　　　　　　引张线法
collimation line method 视准线法
method of laser alignment 激光准直法
minor angle method 小角度法
direct plummet observation 正锤线观测
inverse plummet observation 倒锤线观测
reservoir survey 水库测量

dam site investigation 坝址勘查
dam construction survey 堤坝施工测量
reservoir storage survey 库容测量
setting-out of reservoir flooded line
　　　　　　　　水库淹没线测设
monumental boundary peg 永久界柱
non-monumental boundary peg 临时界桩
catchment area survey 汇水面积测量
canal survey 渠道测量
harbor engineering survey 港口工程测量
drainage map 水系图
road engineering survey 道路工程测量
railroad engineering survey 铁路工程测量
reconnaissance survey 勘测
sketch survey 草测
preliminary survey 初测
location survey 定测
route plan 线路平面图
plane curve location 平面曲线测设
vertical curve location 竖曲线测设
circular curve location 圆曲线测设
spiral curve location 缓和曲线测设
hair-pin curve location 回头曲线测设
center line survey, location of route
　　　　　　　　线路中线测量
method of deflection angle 偏角法
tangent off-set method 切线支距法
chord off-set method 弦线支距法
method of chord deflection distance
　　　　　　　　弦线偏距法
area leveling 面水准测量
route leveling 路线水准测量
profile leveling 中桩水准测量
grade location 坡度测设
slope stake location 边坡桩测设
survey of existing station yard
　　　　　　　　既有线站场测量
turnout survey 道岔测量
construction details 施工详图

construction plan　施工平面图
bridge survey　桥梁测量
tunnel survey　隧道测量
bridge construction control survey　　桥梁控制测量
bridge axis location　桥梁轴线测设
location of pier　桥墩定位
bridge-culvert survey　桥涵洞测量
forest survey　林业测量
forest basic map　林业基本图
stock map，type map　林相图
forest distribution map　森林分布图
compartment survey　林班测量
compass survey　罗盘仪测量
magnetic declination　磁偏角
magnetic dip　磁倾角
magnetic meridian　磁子午线
true meridian　真子午线
magnetic azimuth　磁方位角
magnetic bearings　磁象限角
rural planning survey　乡村规划测量
survey for land smoothing　平整土地测量
land planning survey　土地规划测量
river improvement survey　河道整治测量
irrigation pumping station survey　　灌溉泵站测量
planimeter method　求积仪法
square method　方格法
grid-point method　网点板法
graphical method　图解法
irrigation layout plan　灌区平面布置图
cadastre　地籍
cadastral survey　地籍测量
cadastral survey system　地籍测量系统
cadastral map　地籍图
cadastral lists　地籍册
land register　地籍簿
cadastral management　地籍管理
cadastral survey manual　地籍测量细则

cadastral map series　地籍图册
tax cadastre　征税地籍
multipurpose cadastre　多用途地籍
photogrammetric cadastre　航测地籍
numerical cadastre　数值地籍
coordinate cadastre　坐标地籍
real estates cadastre　房地产地籍
cadastral revision　地籍修测
renewal of the cadastre　地籍更新
cadastral inventory　地籍调查
land consolidation　土地整理
subdivision of land　土地划分
land evaluation　土地评价
land registration　土地登记
statistics of land record　土地统计
land archives　土地档案
certificate of land　土地证
land use　土地利用
present land-use map　土地利用现状图
land boundary survey　地界测量
property boundary survey　地产界测量
natural boundary survey　自然边界测量
land boundary map　地类界图
survey for marking of boundary　标界测量
parcel survey　地块测量
boundary mark，boundary point　界址点
data base of parcel　地块数据库
military engineering survey　军事工程测量
military large scale mapping　　军用大比例尺测图
clearance limit survey　净空区测量
navigation station location survey　　导航台定位测量
military road survey　军用道路测量
military bridge survey　军用桥梁测量
military tunnel survey　军用坑道测量
plane hole survey　飞机洞库测量
ship's hole survey　航艇洞库测量
quarter building survey　营房建筑测量

missile orientation survey 导弹定向测量	precise alignment 精密准直
target road engineering survey 靶道工程测量	precise plumbing 精密垂准
military base survey 军事基地测量	ring control network 环形控制网
precise engineering survey 精密工程测量	particle accelerator survey 粒子加速器测量
precise engineering control network 精密工程控制网	precise survey at seismic station 地震台精密测量
precise ranging 精密测距	

MODULE 14　Construction Plan
模块十四　施工计划

Learning Objectives 学习目标

In this module, learners should:
- know the Chinese and English special terms related to the plan of building constructions.
- be capable of making simple English conversations concerning the plan of building constructions.

在本模块内，学习者应该能：
- 了解与建筑施工计划相关的中英文术语。
- 能够围绕建筑施工计划进行简单的英语会话。

Special Terms 专业词汇

general description of construction　施工说明
construction specifications　施工规格
construction phase　施工阶段
construction error　施工误差
project under construction　施工项目
general conditions of construction　施工总则
detailed schedule　详细计划/进度表
schedule of earthworks　土方工程进度表
schedule of decoration　装修进度
maintain a schedule　保持进度
revise a schedule　修订进度
compliance with a schedule　与计划一致
departure from a schedule　与计划不符
construction steps　施工步骤
preconstruction stage　施工前阶段
work acceptance　施工验收

construction permit　施工许可
construction design　施工设计
construction documents　施工文件
construction worksite　施工现场
construction efficiency　施工效率
construction plan　施工计划
schedule of construction　施工进度表
schedule of material delivery　材料交付计划
be ahead of schedule　超进度
draw up a schedule　制定进度
run on schedule　按进度施工
fulfilment of a schedule　完成计划
be behind of schedule　落后于原计划
preparations for construction　施工准备
construction management　施工组织
inspection of construction　施工检查

supervision of construction 施工监督	construction progress 施工进度
construction period 施工工期	size of construction 施工规模

plan 泛指计划(非具体的);schedule 是时间安排(进度),主要强调时间的分布(how to plan the time);scheme 是系统性的计划(systematic),有阴谋秘密或不正当计划的含义。

Situational Conversations 情景对话

York: As far as I know, your company has succeeded in winning the tender of Queen Mansion. Congratulations!

Heze: Thank you. It is quite an event in our company.

York: Can you tell me your construction plan of Queen Mansion?

Heze: With pleasure. Queen Mansion covers a building area of 57,840 square meters. It is an important project for our company this year.

York: I see. Indeed, it is one of the biggest and also the most important works in our city. How long can it be completed in accordance with the contract?

Heze: It will be completed within twelve months, I suppose.

York: You mean the construction period is twelve months, isn't it?

Heze: That's right. The project will be finished by this time next year.

York: And when are you going to break ground?

Heze: Oh, it is to start on 1st January next year.

York: When are you going to finish the foundation and the main structure, sir?

Heze: They are going to be finished at the end of October, that is, within ten months.

York: How about the installation and decoration works?

Heze: Installation and decoration should be interpenetrated.

York: Good idea. Are you sure you will be able to complete them within the construction period?

Heze: Sure. We plan to finish that ahead of half a month, but we make sure they will be finished by the end of next year. Otherwise, we will be punished.

York: Now through your introduction I can deeply feel your strong determination and confidence. I believe you and your company.

Heze: Thank you for your trust. As you know, credit is a lifeline of our company. Therefore, however great the difficulties may be, we can overcome them.

York: Well said. Is this your progress schedule?

Heze: Yes. It is a more specific schedule with detailed working data clearly marked on. I want to have your comments and advice.

York: Let me read it first and then express my opinions.

(After a few minutes)

York: Your schedule is advanced and practical, leaving me a very deep impression. And I pin my hope on you, sir.

Heze: Thank you for your praise. We will do our best not to let you down.

York: That's all right. And I believe you will be bound to make a satisfactory exam paper to us and to the whole city.

Questions

1. How long is the construction period of Queen Mansion?
2. What does York think of the construction progress schedule of Queen Mansion?

Notes 注释

1. as far as I know 就我所知，as far as sb/sth be concerned 就某人或某事来讲。
2. quite an event 大事。又如 "Driving a car in Central London needs quite an art!" 在伦敦市中心开车可真需要点艺术！
3. "… covers a building area of 57,840 square meters." 占地 57 840 平方米。
4. by this time next year 到明年的这个时候。
5. break ground 破土动工。
6. Installation and decoration should be interpenetrated. 安装与装修应同步穿插进行。
7. ahead of half a month 提前半个月。"ahead of" 意思为"在……之前"，如 "We laboured hard to finish our job ahead of schedule." 我们努力工作，以期把活儿提前干完。

8. "... however great the difficulties may be, we can overcome them." 不管困难有多大，我们一定能够克服。"however great" 等同于 "no matter how great"。

9. "a more specific schedule with detailed working data clearly marked on" 清楚标有详细工作数据的具体的施工进度表。"with detailed working data clearly marked on" 为 with 引导的独立主格结构（the absolute structure）作定语，修饰 "a more specific schedule"。

10. pin my hope on you 对你们寄予厚望。类似的表达还有 "rest my hope on you"。

11. let you down 让您失望，如 "You've let me down once too often and I shall not trust you."你已让我失望多次，我再也不信任你了。

12. be bound to 一定，必定。如 "The new discovery is bound to be of great service to mankind."这项新发现对于人类必定大有用处。

Useful Sentences 必学句型

1. As far as I know, your company has succeeded in winning the tender of Queen Mansion. 据我所知，贵公司成功中标皇后大厦这项工程。
2. It is quite an event in our company. 这可是我们公司的一件大事。
3. Indeed, it is one of the biggest and also the most important works in our city. 事实上，皇后大厦是我市最大也是最重要的工程之一。
4. How long can it be completed in accordance with the contract? 根据合同什么时候能完工？
5. We plan to finish the project ahead of half a month. 我们计划提前半个月完成这项工程。
6. As you know, credit is a lifeline of our company. 正如你所知，信誉是我们公司的生命线。
7. Your schedule is advanced and practical, leaving me a very deep impression. 贵公司的计划很先进，很实际，给我留下了深刻的印象。
8. We will do our best not to let you down. 我们会尽最大努力，决不会让您失望。
9. I believe you will be bound to make a satisfactory exam paper to us and to the whole city. 我相信你们一定会向我们及全市人民交出一份满意答卷的。

Exercises 练习

1. Complete the following dialogue in English.

    A: Can you tell me what the basic construction procedures are?

B：_____.
(施工程序通常根据工种不同进行分类,主要包括现场准备、挖运土方、地基处理、钢结构安装、混凝土浇筑、沥青铺路以及电气和机械安装。)

A：Are the procedures the same in different fields such as buildings, dams and airports?
B：_____.
(每一个工种施工的程序基本相同,但每个工种的相对重要性在各种情况下并不总是相同的。)

A：What preparations should be done on the project site?
B：_____.
(现场准备包括移走和清理拟建场地地表上所有的建筑和生长物。)

A：What does earth moving mainly consist of?
B：_____.(土方包括挖土和土方回填。)

A：When does excavation usually begin? And is there anything especially emphasized in excavations?
B：_____.
(挖土通常在现场准备之后进行。挖土通常从清除表层有机土开始,这是需要强调的第一点。)

A：Sorry to interrupt, but could you give me some reasons for doing that, I just couldn't understand.
B：_____.
(这样做可防止表层土下面用作填方的无机物质受到污染;另外这些表层土可以在后来新建筑物周围景观美化时再次利用。)

A：What about the rest emphasized points?
B：_____.
(第二点需要注意的是,陆地上有效的土方开挖需要干燥的开挖范围,因为很多土体在潮湿状态下不稳定,不能支撑开挖和拖运设备。)

A：I know. What should be paid attention to in filling the earth?
B：_____.
(土方回填后,几乎总要用压路机将其压实以防止后来的沉降,这是挖运土方时需要注意的第三点。)

A：When should the foundation be treated?
B：_____.
(当地质勘察揭示建筑物地基范围内地基土有结构缺陷时,必须进行地基加强处理。)

A：What methods are usually adopted in the foundation treatment?
B：_____.
(通过灌浆的方法将水流、洞穴、裂缝、断层以及其他缺陷进行填塞或加固。)

A：What does grouting mean?
B：_____.

(灌浆就是在压力作用下注入流态混合物，随后这种灌入的浆体在地层空隙中凝固。)

A：What fluid mixtures are usually used in grouting?

B：_____.

(大多数灌浆采用的是水泥和水的混合物，但有些采用沥青、水泥和粘土以及化学沉淀剂的混合物。)

A：What operations does concrete construction consist of?

B：_____.

(混凝土施工包括支模板、混凝土生产、浇注和养护等操作。)

A：What is the form made of? And what is the purpose of forming?

B：_____.

(模板由木材或型钢或两者结合制成，其主要作用是按照所需的最终外形包容和支撑流动的混凝土，直至混凝土拌合物凝固并能支撑自身的重量。)

A：How is concrete placed?

B：_____.

(混凝土浇筑采用斜槽溜浇的方式，可能的话直接从搅拌车上下料，或者从起重机或空中索道悬吊的料斗中下料，也可通过特殊的混凝土泵采用泵送的方式进行浇注。)

A：What is required to be done in concrete curing of exposed surfaces?

B：_____.

(外露表面的混凝土养护需要防止搅拌用水的蒸发或需要补充蒸发的水分。)

A：Today I have learned a lot from your detailed explanation, thank you very much.

B：Not at all.

2. Read and interpret the following passage.

Construction operations

Construction operations are generally classified according to specialized fields. These include preparation of the project site, earth moving, foundation treatment, steel erection, concrete placement, asphalt paving, and electrical and mechanical installations. Procedures for each of these fields are generally the same, even when applied to different projects, such as buildings, dams, or airports. However, the relative importance of each field is not the same in all cases.

3. Pair work.

Work in groups or pairs. Suppose you have won a tender. Ask your partner to tell you what your construction schedule is and how to complete the project on time.

Supplementary Materials 补充材料

The Flow Chart of Housing Construction Engineering
房屋建筑工程施工流程图

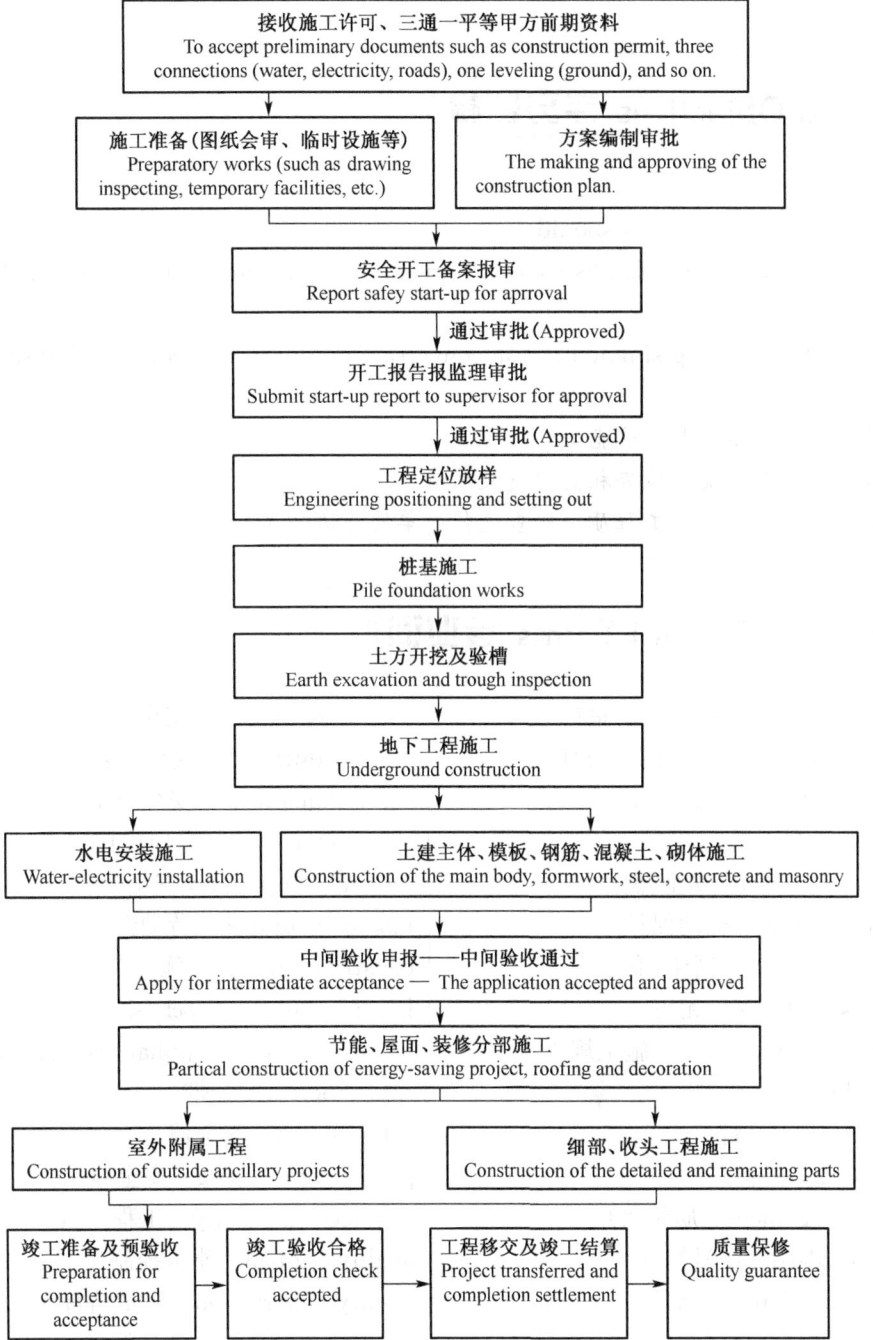

MODULE 15 Construction Inspection
模块十五 施工检查

Learning Objectives 学习目标

In this module, learners should:
- know the Chinese and English special terms related to construction safety and quality control.
- be capable of making simple English conversations concerning construction safety and quality control.

在本模块内,学习者应该能:
- 了解施工安全及质量检查相关中英文术语。
- 能够围绕施工安全及工程质量检查进行简单的英语会话。

Special Terms 专业词汇

safety precautions   安全预防措施
total safety control   全面安全管理
safety inspection   安全检查
safety measures   安全措施
safety in operation   安全操作
labour protection   劳动保护
site security   现场安全措施
safe and sound   安然无恙
construction regulations   施工规则
safety helmet   安全帽
safety lamp   安全灯
safety chain   安全链
quality management   质量管理
quality standard   质量标准
quality inspection   质量检查
site inspection   现场检验

safety regulation   安全规则
safety education   安全教育
safety apparatus   安全设施
safety code   安全操作规程
labour safety   劳动安全
labour insurance   劳动保险
construction sign   施工标志
labour protective supervision   劳动保护监督
labour protection appliances   劳动保护用品
safety belt   安全带
safety catch   安全档
protective clothing   安全服
engineering quality   工程质量
quality control   质量控制
quality supervision   质量监督
site investigation   现场调查

limiting quality 极限质量	acceptable quality 合格质量
defective works 劣质工程	high quality project 优质工程
acceptance test 验收检验	quality certification system 质量保证制度

inspect 和 supervise 都表示对人、工作等进行"监督"的同时起着控制、指导的作用。inspect 侧重表示对质量等进行彻底的"检查"、"审查"，有挑毛病、错误的含义，如"The mayor will inspect our school tomorrow."市长明天要来视察我们学校；supervise 既可表示"监督"一群人（的工作），又可表示"监督"一个人，如"Who is supervising them?"谁在监督他们？

Situational Conversations 情景对话

Mr. Gao: Hello, Mr. Cai. I come here to inspect the project quality that you are in charge of.

Mr. Cai: Welcome! Warmly welcome! Let me show you around.

Mr. Gao: Thanks. First I'd like to check up the size and the location of this building. Where is your theodolite?

Mr. Cai: Here it is. It is a new one.

Mr. Gao: Good. According to the design requirement of the foundation plan, the size, the elevation and the location must be accurate without any error or diviation.

Mr. Cai: I know the importance of the above points you mentioned just now, so we won't be the least bit negligent and not err by a hair's breadth.

Mr. Gao: Well said. Let us go on to check up the sewage and water supply pipes and see whether there is any leak of water or not.

Mr. Cai: Look! There is not any leakage at all.

Mr. Gao: Do you put the concrete aggregate materials accurately?

Mr. Cai: Yes, exactly. The concrete aggregate materials are put in proportion to their weight. These are the concrete testing cubes and their pressure-testing records.

Mr. Gao: Well done. I admire you for having such high responsibility for the project quality.

Mr. Cai: Thanks. That's quite a compliment and encouragement coming from you. Let's go on, sir.

Mr. Gao: There are not any steel bars in the corner between the two walls, so please put them down and redo it. If the same occurs next time, you will be punished.

Mr. Cai: I am extremely sorry for that. I will get to bottom of this matter, and take some remedial measures at once.

Mr. Gao: I am neither intentionally making things difficult for you, nor finding your fault on purpose. But no errors should be treated lightly or shrugged off, am I right?

Mr. Cai: Quite right. It is regulated that without the approval from engineers nothing in the drawings can be modified.

Mr. Gao: This is indisputable, as is mentioned in the contract.

Mr. Cai: Construction projects are to last for generations, therefore, call for good quality above everything else.

Mr. Gao: Right. Any drawing queries on the site should be clarified with the architect. Never act on your own. In future, you should also hold various activities to help your staff workers further improve their quality awareness.

Mr. Cai: OK, you can rest assured that we will do our best to ensure the project quality.

Questions

1. What is the purpose of Mr. Gao's coming to the worksite?
2. How can the concrete aggregate materials be put accurately?

Notes 注释

1. in charge of 主管，负责。如 "I'll be in charge of the whole factory next week when the director is away." 下周厂长不在时，我将负责整个工厂。

2. "... so we won't be the least bit negligent and not err by a hair's breadth." 因此，我们要做到一丝不苟，丝毫不差。"the least bit ＋ adj." 一点点，等同于 "at all" 或 "in the least"，如 "I'm not the least bit interested in what John did." 对约翰做了

什么，我一点儿都不关心。"by a hair's breadth" 几乎，差不多，如 "He escaped death by a hair's breadth. If the other car had been going any faster, he would certainly have been killed". 他简直是死里逃生。要是那辆车开得再快一点，他肯定被撞死了。

3. The concrete aggregate materials are put in proportion to their weight. 按照重量比例投放混凝土骨料。"in proportion to"意思为"按比例"，相当于"at the ratio of, by a ratio of"。如 "A man's vanity is actually in proportion to his ignorance." 一个人的虚荣心实际上和他的愚蠢程度成正比。

4. take some remedial measures 采取一些补救措施。

5. I am neither intentionally making things difficult for you, nor finding your fault on purpose. 我既不是有意为难你，也不是故意挑你刺儿。"neither ... nor ..." 既不……也不……，如 "Neither could theory do without practice, nor could practice do without theory." 理论没有实践不行，实践没有理论也不行。"on purpose"意思为"故意地"，相当于 "intentionally, purposely, deliberately"。

6. Construction projects are to last for generations, therefore, call for good quality above everything else. 建筑工程事关几代人的利益。因此，工程质量高于一切。

7. act on your own 擅自行事。

Useful Sentences 必学句型

1. Let me show you around. 让我带你到处看看。
2. First I'd like to check up the size and the location of this building. 首先，我想检查这幢楼的尺寸和定位。
3. Let us go on to check up the sewage and water supply pipes and see whether there is any leak of water or not. 让我们继续去检查排水管道及给水管子，看看是否有漏水现象。
4. I admire you for having such high responsibility for the project quality. 你对工程质量的这种强烈责任心让我钦佩。
5. That's quite a compliment and encouragement coming from you. 您的话对我来说是莫大的夸奖和鼓励。
6. I will get to bottom of this matter, and take some corrective actions at once. 我将彻查此事，并且立即采取补救措施。
7. No errors should be treated lightly or shrugged off. 对待错误决不可等闲视之。
8. It is regulated that without the approval from engineers nothing in the drawings can be modified. 根据规定，未经工程师同意，设计图不允许有任何修改。
9. You can rest assured that we will do our best to ensure the project quality. 你放心，我们会尽最大努力确保工程质量的。

Exercises 练习

1. Complete the following dialogue in English.

A: Are you the site safety guard?

B: Yes, I am. What is the matter?

A: _____.

(我是主管安全的工程师,你们的安全教育不够,工地上安全隐患随处可见。)

B: It should not be the case. We have had meetings and emphasized the importance of safety construction more than once.

A: _____.

(这固然重要,关键是怎样采取安全措施,以切实有效地消除各种安全隐患。)

B: It looks as if we did not carry them out very well.

A: _____? (请你带我在工地上转一转,行吗?)

B: OK, let us go.

A: _____?

(首先,在建筑工地上干活不戴安全帽是非常危险的,倘若像砖头、木块等东西从高处掉下来,岂不砸到你的头?)

B: Yes, you are right. I will tell the constructors to keep safety in mind all the time.

A: _____.

(看那边!在高空安装灯泡、架电线的那位电工没有采取安全保障措施,这是很危险的。)

B: Yes. It indeed doesn't conform to the construction regulations.

A: _____.

(工人们正在干活的屋顶四周都没有围安全网,请叫他们停止工作,马上下来。)

B: OK. I will stop them right now, and take safety measures as quickly as possible.

A: I am sorry to stop your work. Do you know why?

B: _____.

(知道,是为了我们的安全,我们应树立安全第一的思想。)

A: Safety is for the construction; however, construction must be safe. Be sure to remember what I told you.

B: _____. (一定。防患于未然,因为人命关天。)

A: If we don't speak of our achievements, they won't run away. If we don't keep safety in mind, we'll be in a bad way.

2. Read and interpret the following passage.

Inspecting the quality of welding joints

There are many ways to inspect the quality of welding joints concerning different elements and design requirements. Generally speaking, we take care of the following aspects:

First, we should have an inspection before welding operation. This inspection includes checking of the welding material and electrodes, preparation of welding specification and procedures, the technical skill of the welders and so on.

The second aspect is to inspect the surfaces of welding joints by vision or magnifier (within 20 times magnification) in order to find out the surface defects. The welding joints must be chiseled out and re-welded if any defect which is not allowed by the specification occurs.

For the inspection of the inside welding joints, we usually adopt the extra-sound test, X ray or γ ray test, magnetic test or color test.

3. Pair work.

A is a supervising engineer, B is a resident engineer. They are talking about the quality of the construction works that B and his fellows are building.

Supplementary Materials 补充材料

Record of Construction Inspection (for General Use)
施工检查记录表(通用)

工程名称 Engineering Name		检查项目 Inspection Items	
检查部位 Inspection Parts		检查日期 Inspection Date	

检查依据(Inspection Basis)

检查内容(Inspection Contents)

检查结论(Inspection Conclusions)

复查意见(Reinspection Results)

复查人(Reinspector):   日期(Date):

施工单位 (Construction Unit)		
专业技术负责人 (Technical Director)	专业质检员 (Quality Inspector)	专业工长 (Site Director)

MODULE 16　Building Installation
模块十六　建筑安装

Learning Objectives 学习目标

In this module, learners should:
- know the Chinese and English special terms related to building installation.
- be capable of making simple English conversations concerning building installation.

在本模块内,学习者应该能:
- 了解与建筑安装相关的中英文术语。
- 就建筑安装这一话题进行简单的英语会话。

Special Terms 专业词汇

equipment arrangement　设备布置
sanitary fittings　卫生器具
water supply works　给水工程
water supply pipes　给水管道
water meter　水表
drainage works　排水工程
floor drain　地漏
flange　法兰
heating installation　供暖安装
heating radiator　供暖散热器
ventilating works　通风工程
ventilation facilities　通风设施
air-conditioning equipment　空调设备
electrical works　电气工程
lighting engineering　电气照明工程
circuit installation　线路安装
electric welding works　电焊工程
riveting works　铆接工程
measuring tools　量具

installation drawing　安装图
pipes and fittings　管子与管件
water supply fittings　给水配件
riser water pipe　直立水管
shower and bathtub　淋浴和浴盆
sewerage fittings　排水管件
rain-water pipe　雨水管道
heating works　采暖工程
heating pipe　供暖管道
plumber's tools　水暖工工具
ventilation installation　通风安装
dust keeper　除尘装置
electrical installation　电气安装
electrical construction　电气施工
architectural lighting　建筑照明
electrical materials　电气材料
welding technique　焊接技术
fitter's works　设备安装工程
steel structural works　钢结构工程

erection 由动词 erect 加后缀变化而来，erect 的英文含义是 set upright, fix or place in and upright position, set at right angles，中文是向上装配的意思。因此这个词多用于架子等基础设施的安装；installation 由动词 install 加后缀变化而来，install 的英文译义是 set in position and connect or adjust for use, place or fix (apparatus) in position for use，因此它可以是一种计算机或设备安装，组合到整个系统中去。

Situational Conversations 情景对话

Frank: Is this lift installed by you, young man?

Smith: Yes, sir. I am a fitter, and to install equipments of various kinds is my business.

Frank: Can I start the lift now, Mr. Smith?

Smith: Oh, you cannot start it for the time being, as the installation has just been finished. In order to be perfectly safe, it should be checked up once more.

Frank: I am a layman, so I am very sorry for what I said just now. But to tell you the truth, after your words, a great respect and admiration for your responsibility has naturally risen in my heart.

Smith: Thank you for your encouragement. Anyone in the world who has occupational morality would have done so.

Frank: You are very modest. By the way, can you tell me what works the fitters usually do?

Smith: They mainly mount machines and equipments, such as lathes, cranes, air hammers and so on.

Frank: I'd like to know what tools they usually use.

Smith: Too numerous to mention. They mainly use file, bench vice and hammer.

Frank: What about measuring tools?

Smith: Steel ruler and angle gauge.

Frank: What operative techniques should a fitter master?

Smith: A qualified fitter should be good at setting out the bases, installing and leveling the equipment, cleaning and assembling machine parts, and so on.

Frank: Anything else?

Smith: Besides, he should also know how to adjust and test equipments well so as to make them run smoothly.

Frank: Now, would you mind me trying the lift you mounted?

Smith: Of course not. And if you find any defects, please do not hesitate to tell me.

Frank: Mm. Excellent! You have done a really good job. The base bolts are upright. All the nuts are screwed with collars, and the collars are connected closely with the equipment base.

Smith: Do you think it is OK, sir?

Frank: Certainly. I think the installation of the lift is in perfect accordance with the drawing specifications. Wonderful!

Smith: It's a great relief to hear your approval of my work.

Frank: Fitter is really an indispensible trademen in the building industry, especially in the construction of modern buildings.

Smith: So fitting is also a lofty cause with heavy responsibilities and glorious mission in the modernized constructions.

Frank: Yes, you are right. It is really nice for you to think so.

Questions

1. What works do fitters usually do?
2. What operative techniques should a fitter have?

Notes 注释

1. checked up 检查,如 "I'll reserve my judgement until I've checked up again on the records." 我要再查一查记录之后再作判断。
2. for the time being 暂且,暂时。
3. layman 外行,门外汉。
4. "… a great respect and admiration for your responsibility has naturally risen in my heart." 对您高度负责的敬佩之情油然而生。也可这样表达"Your responsibility for the work filled me with respect and admiration."
5. occupational morality 职业道德。
6. Too numerous to mention. 举不胜举。numerous 很多的,许多的,数不清的;numerable 可数的,可计算的。"too…to" 意思为"太……以至于不能",如"The bridge

is too narrow for two cars to pass."这桥太窄,并排通不过两辆车。

7. operative techniques 操作技能。
8. be good at 擅长,精通。如"A good executive must be good at decision making."优秀的领导者必须善于决策。"be poor at"意思为"在……方面比较差,不擅长"。
9. base bolts 地脚螺栓。
10. All the nuts are screwed with collars, and the collars are connected closely with the equipment base. 螺母与垫圈,垫圈与设备底座都连接得很紧。"be connected with"意思为"与……相连/联系",如"The Internet can be a great help for you to be connected with the world."互联网为你与世界沟通提供了巨大的帮助。
11. in perfect accordance with 完全按照,又如"It is an obvious truism that people act in accordance with their motives."人人都按自己的动机行事是不言而喻的。
12. So fitting is also a lofty cause with heavy responsibilities and glorious mission in the modernized constructions. 因此,在现代化建设中,设备安装也是一项具有高度责任性和光荣使命感的崇高职业。

Useful Sentences 必学句型

1. I am a fitter, and to install equipments of various kinds is my business. 我是一名设备安装工,安装各种设备是我的本职工作。
2. But to tell you the truth, after your words, a great respect and admiration for your responsibility has naturally risen in my heart. 说实话,听完您一席话,对您高度负责的敬佩之情油然而生。
3. A qualified fitter should be good at setting out the bases, installing and leveling the equipment, cleaning and assembling machine parts, and so on. 一个合格的安装工应擅长基础放线、设备安装与找平、机械零部件的清洗与安装等工作。
4. Now, would you mind me trying the lift you mounted? 现在让我试试你安装好的电梯可以吗?
5. And if you find any defects, please do not hesitate to tell me. 如果你发现任何问题,请立刻告诉我。
6. It's a great relief to hear your approval of my work. 听到您对我工作的肯定我就放心多了。

Exercises 练习

1. **Complete the following dialogue in English.**

   A: What is the correct sequence for fixing the steel structures?

B：_____.
（一般来说，我们是按照从低到高，从柱到梁，从主梁到次梁，从中心到周边这样的规范步骤来安装钢结构的。）
A：It seems that you have got much experience in fixing the steel structure.
B：_____.
（过奖了，谈不上经验，但安装钢结构这活已干了十多年。）
A：You are very modest. Anything else to emphasize?
B：_____.
（自然有。在安装过程中最重要的是安排好合理的顺序，同时还应注意每个安装环节。）
A：Right. Do you have any steps to be shown?
B：_____.
（是的。有时为了适应具体情况，还会采取不同的施工方法；安装不同的配件也会有不同的安装顺序。）
A：Can you tell me how to erect the column that is 30m in length and 18t in weight?
B：_____.
（可以。为了确保钢柱不变形，使用两台液压吊车吊装就可以了。）
A：What instruments do you adopt to survey the verticality and position after the steel column is lifted?
B：_____.
（钢柱竖直后，我们通常用两台经纬仪从两个不同方位来检测钢柱的垂直度和水平位置。）
A：And how can you keep the stability of the steel column?
B：_____.
（我们用固定缆绳和预埋螺栓将其固定在精确位置上。）
A：Is there anything else besides the above?
B：_____.
（当然有。把垂直度控制在规定的范围以内后，我们立即垫好垫板并拧紧螺栓。）
A：Do you screw all the high-strength bolts just once for all to keep high quality?
B：_____.
（不。为了把好质量关，我们总是把所有的高强度螺栓至少拧两遍。）
A：Why?
B：_____.
（是为了确保质量。第一次要用规定的扭力矩的一半力度去拧就可以了。）
A：How about the second?
B：_____.
（把所有的螺栓全都拧完第一遍后，方可再拧第二遍，而且还要把扭力矩的力度误差控制在5%以内。）
A：Every step is done very carefully. Only in this way, can you guarantee the installation quality.

B: Right. You know every trade has its own operating rules.

2. Read and interpret the following passage.

Electrical inspectors

Electrical inspectors examine the installation of electrical systems and equipment to ensure that they function properly and comply with electrical codes and standards. They visit worksites to inspect new and existing sound and security system, wiring, lighting, motors, and generating equipment. They also inspect the installation of the electrical wiring for heating and air conditioning systems, appliances and other components.

3. Pair work.

You are a fitter of ×××Construction Installation Company, mounting a large and tall bridge crane on a material yard. Try to say how to mount, adjust and test it, and then see whether it runs well after you finish mounting.

Supplementary Materials 补充材料

Installation of Electric Appliance
电气器具安装

一、开关插座安装　The installation of switch and socket

1. 工艺流程　Technological process

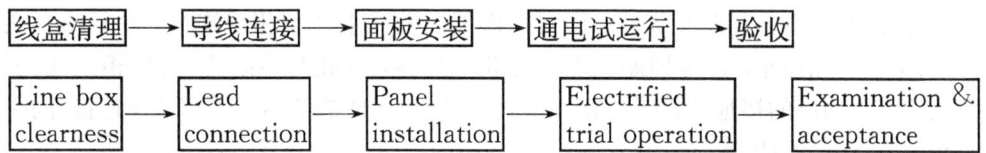

2. 开关、插座安装基本要求 Basic requirements on installation of switch and socket

（1）开关、插座的面板及接线盒盒体完整、无碎裂、零件齐全。

The panel of switch and socket and the body of terminal box are integrated without any break and all parts are complete.

（2）暗装的开关、插座面板应紧贴墙面,四周无缝隙,安装牢固,表面光滑整洁、无碎裂、划伤,装饰帽齐全。

The hidden switch and socket panel should be close to the wall compactly without any seam around. They are installed firmly and the surface is smooth and neat without any crack or scrape. The decorative nuts are complete.

（3）开关位置应与灯位相对应,同一单元内开关方向应一致;开关边缘至门框边缘的距离为150 mm～200 mm;不得置于单扇门后。

The position of switch should correspond to that of lamp. The direction of switch in the same unit should be consistent. The distance from the edge of switch to that of doorframe is about 150 mm～200 mm. They should not be put at the back of single door.

（4）在卫生间、大堂等墙面上贴石材瓷砖的地方,开关、插座的面板布置在瓷砖的几何中心，并紧贴墙面，安装端正，参见下图：

At the place stuck with stone ceramic tile on the wall in toilet and hall, the panel of switch and socket should be arranged at the geometrical center and stuck to the wall closely as while as installed correctly. It may refer to the following figure.

开关面板在墙上的做法
Installation of Switch Panel on Wall

（5）相同型号并列安装及同一室内开关安装高度一致，且控制有序不错位。暗装插座距地面要符合图纸要求；同一室内安装的插座安装高度一致。

The same MODULE should be installed in parallel. The installing height of switch at the same room should be consistent and controlled in order without any dislocation. The distance of hidden socket to the surface should accord with requirements in drawings. The installing height of sockets at the same room should be consistent.

3. 开关、插座安装 Installation of switch and socket

（1）开关、插座接线：同一建筑物内的开关的通断位置一致，操作灵活、接触可靠，灯具的相线应经开关控制；单相两孔插座，面对插座的右孔或上孔与相线连接，左孔或下孔与零线连接；单相三孔插座，面对插座的右孔与相线连接，左孔与零线连接；单相三孔、三相四孔及三相五孔插座的接地或接零线接在上孔；插座的接地端子不与零线端子连接；同一场所的三相插座，接线的相序应一致。

Wiring on switch and socket: The on-off positions of switches in the same building should be consistent. They operate flexibly and touch reliably. The phase line of lamp should be controlled through switches. To socket with single-phase-two-hole, the right or upper hole facing to socket is connected with the phase line, and the right or lower hole is connected with the null line. To socket with single-phase-three-hole, the right hole facing to socket is connected with the phase line, and the left hole is connected with the null line. To socket with single-phase-three-hole, three-phase-four-hole, or three-phase-five-hole, the ground line or null line is connected with the upper hole. The grounding terminal of socket is not connected with that of null line. To three-phase socket at the same spot, the phase sequence of wiring should be consistent.

（2）暗装开关、插座：先用錾子轻轻地将盒子内杂物清出盒外，将盒内清理干净，然后按接线要求，将盒内甩出的导线与开关、插座的面板连接好，将开关或插座推入盒内（如果盒子较深，大于2.5 cm时，应加装套盒），对正盒眼，用机螺丝固定牢固。固定时要使面板端正，并与墙面平齐。

Hidden switch and socket: firstly, use a cold chisel clean out the mess in box lightly.

Clean the box, and connect the conducting wire out of box with the panel of switch and socket. Push the switch or socket into box (if the box is deeper more than 2.5cm, add a sleeve box). Aim at the hole of box, and use screws to fix firmly. When fixing, correct the panel and make it level with wall space.

（3）明装开关、插座：先将从盒内甩出的导线由绝缘台的出线孔中穿出，再将绝缘台紧贴于墙面用螺丝固定在盒子或砖上，绝缘台固定后，将甩出的相线、地（零）线按各自的位置从开关、插座的线孔中穿出，按接线要求将导线压牢。然后将开关或插座贴于绝缘台上，对中找正，用螺丝固定牢。最后再把开关、插座的盖板上好。

Open switch and socket: firstly, pass the conducting wire out of box through the outlet hole of insulating plate. Then, stick the insulating plate to wall space closely, and use screws to fix on the box or brick. After fixing the insulating plate, pass the phase line and null line out of box through the outlet hole of switch and socket according to each position. Press the conducting wire firmly according to the connecting requirement. Then, stick the switch or socket on the insulating plate, center to aim at. Use screws to fix firmly. Finally, put the cover of switch and socket well again.

二、灯具安装 The installation of lamps

1. 工艺流程 Technological process

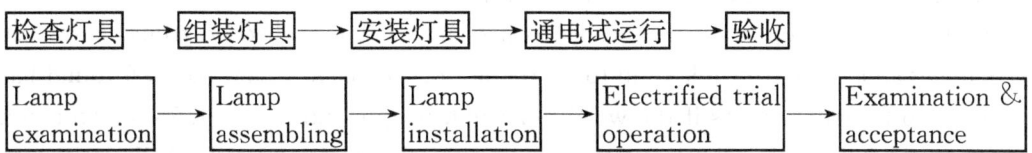

2. 灯具安装基本要求 Basic requirement of installing lamps

穿入灯具的导线在分支连接处不得承受额外应力和磨损，多股软线的端头需盘圈、涮锡；灯具内的导线不应过于靠近热光源，并应采取隔热措施，当灯具距地面高度小于 2.4 m 时，灯具的可接近裸露导体必须使用专用接地螺栓接地并有明显标识。

The conducting wire through lamps must not endure additional stresses and wears at the joint of branch. The terminals of multiple flexible cords need windings and rinsing tins. The conducting wire in lamp should not near light sources too much and adopt some heat-insulating measures. When the distance from lamps to the ground level is less than 2.4 m, the exposed conductor that lamps may near must use the special grounding bolt to ground and have obvious marks.

3. 灯具安装 Installation of lamps

（1）嵌入式灯具安装 Installation of embedded lamps

本工程办公区使用嵌入式荧光灯，嵌入式安装的荧光灯用 Φ9 的圆钢做灯具的吊杆，嵌入式荧光灯安装见下图：

The office area in the project uses embedded fluorescent lamps. The embedded fluorescent lamp that is installed uses Φ9 round bar steel as a boom of lamp. The installation on embedded fluorescent lamp is shown as in the following figure.

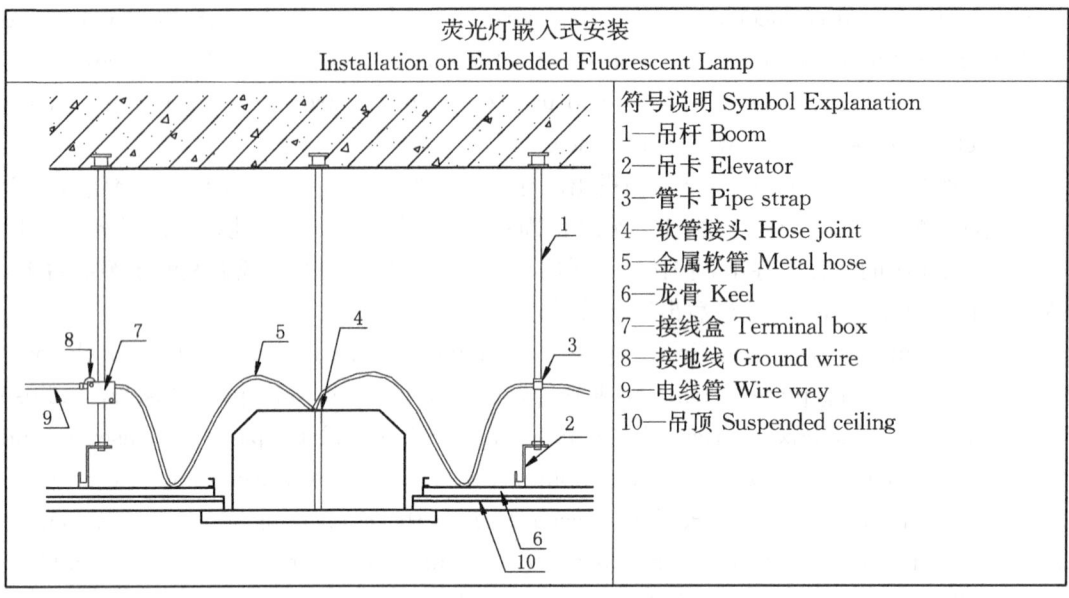

本工程 F01 大堂区域使用嵌入式筒灯，嵌入式筒灯用筒灯的卡具在装饰龙骨上固定，如果筒灯的重量超过 1.5KG，则需用 Φ6 圆钢吊杆固定筒灯，镇流器与灯具的本体分开的筒灯，镇流器需要单独固定，嵌入式筒灯安装见下图：

F01 hall in the project uses embedded trunk lamps. The embedded trunk lamps use the clamping apparatus of trunk lamp to fix on decorative keels. They need Φ6 round bar steel boom to fix trunk lamps if the weight of trunk lamp is more than 1.5KG. To trunk lamps that the ballast resistor is separated with the body of lamp, the ballast resistor needs to be fixed individually. The installation of embedded trunk lamps is shown as in the following figure.

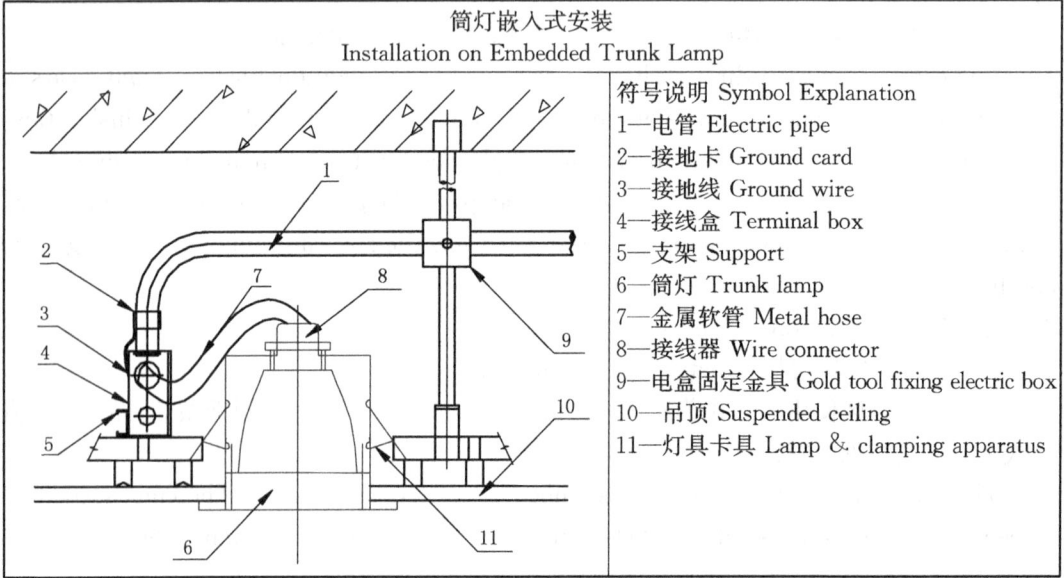

(2) 壁灯安装　Installation of Wall Lamp

墙内嵌入式安装的灯具，在结构施工阶段预留灯具孔洞，装饰施工阶段安装灯具，安全出口指示灯安装见下图：

To the lamp installed and embedded in wall, pre-leave holes for lamps in the phase of structure construction. Install lamps at the phase of decoration and construction. The installation of indicator at safety outlet is shown in the following figure.

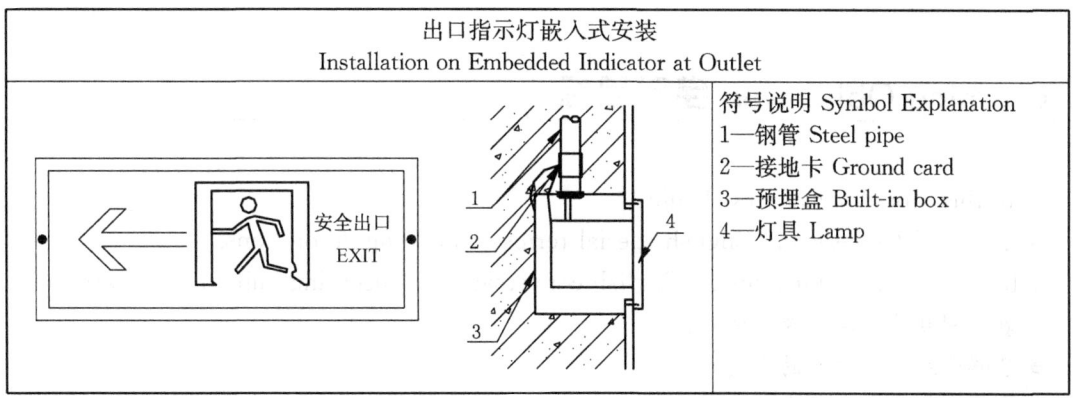

MODULE 17   Building Decoration
模块十七   建筑装饰

Learning Objectives 学习目标

In this module, learners should:
- know the Chinese and English special terms of building decorations.
- be capable of making simple English conversations concerning building decorations.

在本模块内，学习者应该能：
- 了解建筑装饰方面的中英文术语。
- 能进行与建筑装饰有关的英语对话。

Special Terms 专业词汇

wall decoration   墙面装饰
interior decoration   室内装饰
folding screen   屏风
mural   壁画
embossing   雕刻凸饰
decorative materials   装饰材料
hemp cut   麻刀
straw pulp   纸筋
aluminium alloy   铝合金
mosaic   马赛克
ceramic ware   陶瓷制品
dolomite   白云石
face brick   面砖
adhesive   胶黏剂
marble   大理石
glass cutter   玻璃刀
working bench   工作台
plastering tools   粉刷工具
chalk line case   粉线盒

decorative arts   装饰艺术
exterior decoration   室外装饰
folding partition   折壁
fiber board ceiling   纤维板顶棚
carved figures   雕刻画像
white cement   白水泥
lime putty   白灰膏
granite   花岗石
non-fading coloured paint   不褪色面漆
quarry tile   缸砖
glazed brick   釉面砖
brocatelle   彩色大理石
terrazzo tile   水磨石
plastic steel   塑钢
stainless steel   不锈钢
putty knife   油灰刀
wooden decoration materials   木装饰材料
scratching board   刮板
wood-working machines   木工机械

在建筑陶瓷中,porcelain tile 一般指的是抛光砖,瓷底,吸水率(ABSORPTION)在 1%以下;ceramic tile 一般指的是瓷片(内墙砖,陶底,也有可能是部分的仿古砖),吸水率国家规定在 17%以下。

Situational Conversations 情景对话

Wendel: I am the chief inspector of this project. Can you tell me something about the decorative works?

Li Hua: With pleasure. Decorative works are of vital importance to the building engineering. In the meantime, good decorators are especially important to such works.

Wendel: Right. It is just as important as the person's beautiful clothes or the horse's suitable saddle.

Li Hua: A large number of skilled decorators are the prerequisite for the high-quality project. With the development of the times, decoration will gradually show its own value.

Wendel: How magnificent the marble-decorated hall is! It pleases not only my eyes but also my mind.

Li Hua: Yes, I feel just the same as you.

Wendel: By the way, how do you treat the surface of the aluminum alloy?

Li Hua: All the surfaces of the aluminum alloy are first thoroughly cleaned, and then painted with a coating of clear, non-fading, coloured or colourless paint.

Wendel: But why to do so, I really do not understand?

Li Hua: What we did to the surface of the aluminum alloy is just a precaution and protection against damages from alkaline cement plaster and similar materials.

Wendel: Is it necessary?

Li Hua: Absolutely. Please look at the aluminum alloy windows that have been treated in the above mentioned way. How do you think of them?

Wendel: They are really very nice. But the marble floor is not polished well, I think.

Li Hua: Sorry, I will send someone to repolish it at once.
Wendel: Besides, I have to remind you that you must do the wall decoration well: brush the paints evenly, glue the wallpapers well and inlay the wallboards neatly.
Li Hua: Why do you say so?
Wendel: Because wall decoration shows the main part of the decorative works, thus easily leaving people a first visual sense and impression, which is vitally important to the judgment of the decoration quality.
Li Hua: What you've said is reasonable. Decorative works are to embellish the buildings, beautify the environment and bring endless enjoyment to the mankind, so every decorator must have a high sense of responsibility and do his own work well.
Wendel: Right. Only in this way can the quality of the whole decorative works be guaranteed, can your company hold its ground and establish itself in an unassailable position.

Questions

1. What roles do decorative works play in the building engineering?
2. How is the surface of the aluminum alloy usually treated? And why?

Notes 注释

1. the chief inspector of this project 项目总监。
2. Decorative works are of vital importance to the building engineering. 装修工作对建筑工程有着至关重要的作用。"be of ＋n. ＋to sth. /sb."等同于"be ＋adj. ＋to sth. /sb.",此句可改写为"Decorative works are vitally important to the building engineering."
3. "in the meantime"意思为"在……期间,同时;与此同时",相当于"meanwhile"。
4. A large number of skilled decorators are the prerequisite for the high-quality project. 大批能工巧匠是保证精品工程的前提。"a large number of"意思为"许多,大量的"。
5. How magnificent the marble-decorated hall is! 大理石装饰的大厅多么宏伟壮观啊! "how＋adj. /adv. ＋主语＋谓语"以及"what＋a/an＋adj. ＋n. ＋主语＋谓语"为感叹句式,此句可改写为"What a magnificent marble-decorated hall (it is)."
6. All the surfaces of the aluminum alloy are first thoroughly cleaned, and then painted

with a coating of clear, non-fading, coloured or colourless paint. 所有的铝合金表面彻底清理干净后再涂上一层清晰的不褪色或无色面漆。

7. What we did to the surface of the aluminum alloy is just a precaution and protection against damages from alkaline cement plaster and similar materials. 我们对铝合金表面这样处理是为了避免铝合金受到水泥浆类带有碱性的涂饰物腐蚀而采取的一种防范保护措施。

8. "I have to remind you that ..." 我必须要提醒你……。又如" I always remind myself that time and tide wait for no man." 我总是提醒自己岁月不待人。

9. a first visual sense and impression 第一视觉和第一印象。

10. Decorative works are to embellish the buildings, beautify the environment and bring endless enjoyment to the mankind, so every decorator must have a high sense of responsibility and do his own work well. 装饰工程是为美化建筑物，美化环境，带给人类无穷无尽的享受，因此，每个装饰工人都应具有较高的责任感，做好自己的本职工作。

Useful Sentences 必学句型

1. It is just as important as the person's beautiful clothes or the horse's suitable saddle." 装饰工程就像人的衣服马的鞍一样重要。
2. With the development of the times, decoration will gradually show its own value. 随着时代的发展，装饰工程逐渐显现出自身的价值。
3. It pleases not only my eyes but also my mind. 它让我赏心悦目。
4. I have to remind you that you must do the wall decoration well. 我不得不提醒你，你必须把墙面装饰工作做好。
5. Only in this way can the quality of the whole decorative works be guaranteed, can your company hold its ground and establish itself in an unassailable position. 只有这样，整个装饰工程的质量才有保证，你的公司才能站住脚，永远立于不败之地。

Exercises 练习

1. **Complete the following dialogue in English.**

   A: Frankly speaking, I am not satisfied with the works performed by your decoration teams.

   B: _____? （你能否指出你不满意装修工程的哪部分工作？）

   A: Please see the timbers. They are quite different from the samples you have submitted before decoration.

B: _____.
(让我看看。这些材料看起来与我们交的样品并无两样。)
A: _____.
(这些木材等级似乎没变,但据我们测试,湿度大大超出不低于10%不高于20%的规定。)
B: We will make a test for the timber. And we will not do the assembling and installation until the materials reach the required wet condition.
A: _____.
(请记住如果任何装修在保质期内出现卷缩、弯曲、松弛和其他任何缺陷,受到工程师投诉,你们必须自费重装,直到合格为止。)
B: We will do our best to avoid any such things from happening. Are there any other problems?
A: _____?
(现在我想看一下抹灰和砂浆找平,你们从哪里运来工程用砂?砂源离海近吗?)
B: The sea sand is strictly forbidden to be used for screeds, backing to tiles, rendering, plastering or other finishes externally even if it is thoroughly washed.
A: What kind of sand do you use for backing coat and pointing of tiles?
B: _____.
(所有外用陶瓷制品、砖瓦、玻璃马赛克等的衬垫和打底,我们都是采用碎花岗岩砂粒。)
A: Concerning the quarry tiles you should pay more attention to it, especially in the office building area.
B: _____.
(是的,我们会的。我们已经训练了我们的工人。每一个步骤都必须严格遵守施工程序。)
A: What are the steps for laying the quarry titles 194 mm×194 mm×11 mm, for example?
B: _____.
(首先,混凝土地板在铺砖之前都必须打扫并彻底清洗,而且此区域在铺砖之前必须测量好以避免不必要的切割。)
A: Are there any treatment to the titles before being laid?
B: _____.
(是的。先要将地板砖完全浸泡在水中,然后按要求的模式铺设。要注意伸缩缝、角落和圆边瓷砖的铺砌。)
A: What protective measures should be taken after the paving of the floor?
B: _____.
(待铺设工作完成后,地面要盖上厚聚乙烯或防水帆布,且在边缘部位妥善搭接并且铺砌后7天内不能扰动。)

2. Read and interpret the following passage.

Ceramic bricks

Ceramic bricks are divided into wall bricks and floor bricks. They are sturdy and durable, bright in colour, easy to clean, fire retarding, anti-water, wear- and corrosive-resisting. Now there are also glaze tiles with dural color and stereo vision. Ceramic bricks are widely used in the decorative works of modern buildings.

3. Pair work.

Suppose you are decorating a new hotel. Ask your partners to tell you what types of exterior and interior decorations are adopted, how to do the hotel decorative works well, and how to conform to the design requirements.

Supplementary Materials 补充材料

Table of Common Wood in Chinese and English
常用木材中英文对照表

编号 No.	英文名称 English Name	中文名称 Chinese Name	编号 No.	英文名称 English Name	中文名称 Chinese Name
1	FIGURED ANEGRE	红影	20	SYCAMORE	白影（欧洲）
2	FIGURED MAKORE	麦哥利	21	LACEWOODBURL	尼丝木树根
3	ASPEN	亚士宾	22	LARCH	松木直纹
4	FIGURED AVIGA	亚米加虎影	23	LAUROPRETO	普利托月桂
5	BEECH	红榉直纹	24	LAUELBURL	月桂树根
6	BIRCH	桦木	25	MADRONABURL	麦当娜树根
7	BIRCH BURL	桦木树根	26	MAHOGANYPOMELE	球纹桃花芯
8	BIRD'S EYE MAPLE	雀眼枫木	27	MAKOREPOMELE	麦哥利保美利
9	BUBINGA POMELE	花梨保美利	28	MAPLE	枫木
10	BUBINGA	花梨直纹	29	MAPLEBURL	枫木树根
11	CHERRY	樱桃	30	MAPLEPOMELE	枫木保美利
12	FIGURED CURLY MAPLE	卷纹枫影	31	MAPPABURL	白杨树根
13	EBONY	乌木（黑檀木）	32	MOUVINGUE	金影
14	FIGURED EUCALYPTUS	有影尤加利	33	PERO	美洲梨木
15	FIGURED MAPLE	有影枫木	34	REDOAK	红橡直纹
16	INDIAN ROSEWOOD	印度酸枝	35	SANTOSROSEWOOD	山度士酸枝
17	KAYA	桃花芯	36	ASH	栓木直纹
18	LACEWOOD	尼丝木	37	SAPELE	沙比利
19	SWISSPEAR	瑞士梨木	38	TEAKWOOD	柚木

续表

编号 No.	英文名称 English Name	中文名称 Chinese Name	编号 No.	英文名称 English Name	中文名称 Chinese Name
39	VAVONABURL	苇云娜树根	56	GOLDTAU	金檀木
40	WALNUT	黑胡桃	57	SILKYOAK	丝绸橡木
41	WENGE	乌班木	58	GOLDENACER	金枫影
42	WHITEASH	白栓木	59	GRAYWOOD	灰栓木
43	WHITEOAK	白橡直纹	60	GREENWOOD	格兰木
44	ZEBRANO	斑马木	61	GREYERABLE	灰雀眼
45	BLISSWOOD	碧灰木	62	HAZELWOOD	紫粟木
46	BOXWOOD	盒木	63	LAND CROCODILE	灰鳄木
47	BRASSWOOD	巴式木	64	LAND TAU	地檀木
48	BRONZEWOOD	铜木	65	LEMONPOPLAR	柠檬杨
49	BROWNWOOD	咖啡木	66	SILVERACER	银枫影
50	CHARCOALWOOD	炭木	67	SILVERFRISE	银影
51	COPPERACER	铜板影	68	SKYTAU	天檀木
52	COPPERFRISE	灰影木	69	SUNTAU	太檀木
53	CREAMYCROCODILE	乳鳄木	70	SEATAU	海檀木
54	DARKCROCODILE	黑鳄木	71	WHITECROCODILE	白鳄木
55	DARKERABLE	黑雀眼	72	XENON FRISE	式龙影木

MODULE 18　Building Cost
模块十八　建筑造价

Learning Objectives 学习目标

In this module, learners should:
- know the Chinese and English special terms related to building cost.
- be capable of making simple English conversations concerning building cost.

在本模块内，学习者应该能：
- 了解建筑造价方面的中英文术语。
- 能进行与建筑造价有关的英语对话。

Special Terms 专业词汇

estimate/cost estimate　估算/费用估算	types of estimate　估算类型
equipment estimate　设备估算	control estimate　控制估算
analysis estimate　分析估算	proposal estimate　报价估算
initial control estimate　初期控制估算	check estimate　核定估算
direct material cost　直接材料费用	equipment cost　设备费用
bulk material cost　散装材料费用	construction cost　施工费用
labor cost　施工人工费用	standard hours　标准工时
labor productivity　劳动生产率	manhours rate　人工时单价
cost of construction supervision　施工监督费	indirect cost of construction　施工间接费
subcontract cost　分包合同费用	non payroll　非工资费用
profit/expected profit　利润/预期利润	service gains　服务酬金
risk analysis　风险分析	risk memorandum　风险备忘录
contingency　未可预见费	client change　用户变更
approved client change　认可的用户变更	pending client change　待定的用户变更
project change　项目变更	contract change　合同变更
internal change　内部变更	authorised change　批准的变更
mandatory change　强制性变更	optional change　选择性变更
internal transfer　内部费用转换	escalation　涨价值
lump sum contract　总价合同	reimbursible contract　偿付合同

"cost"通常表示与主营业务相关的支出,可以直接归结到产品中去的生产耗用,一般包括直接人工、直接材料等;"expense"主要指与主营业务没有直接联系的费用支出,不可以直接归结到某个产品中去,因为它的耗用是在产品生产过程中因为管理等等产生的消耗。

Situational Conversations 情景对话

Mr. Wang: I know cost estimating is one of the most important steps in project management. Can you tell me something about it?

Mr. Zhao: OK. The importance of cost estimating lies in the fact that it establishes the base line of the project cost at different stages of the project development. And a cost estimate at a given stage of project development represents a prediction provided by the cost engineer or estimator on the basis of available data.

Mr. Wang: How is the cost estimation performed? In other words, what are the basic approaches adopted to estimate the construction cost?

Mr. Zhao: Virtually all cost estimation is performed according to one or some combination of the following basic approaches: production function, empirical cost inference, unit costs for bill of quantities, allocation of joint costs.

Mr. Wang: What does production function mean in construction?

Mr. Zhao: In construction, the production function refers to the relationship between the construction volumes and production factors such as labor or capital. It relates the output amount or volume to the various inputs of labor, material and equipment.

Mr. Wang: Can you give me an example?

Mr. Zhao: The relationship between the size of a building project (expressed in square feet) to the input labor (expressed in labor hours per square foot) is a typical example of the production function in construction.

Mr. Wang: I understand it now. How is the empirical cost inferred?

Mr. Zhao: In the empirical cost inference, the regression analysis techniques are required, the role of which is to estimate the best parameter values or constants in an assumed cost function.

Mr. Wang: Is the unit cost method the simplest among the four approaches? Does it mean the total cost is the summation of the product quantities multiplied by the corresponding unit cost?

Mr. Zhao: Yes, you are right. The unit cost method is straightforward in principle but quite laborious in application. First the whole construction process is disaggregated into a number of tasks. Once these tasks are defined and quantities representing these tasks are assessed, a unit cost is assigned to each and then the total cost is determined by summing the costs incurred in each task. The level of detail in decomposing into tasks will vary considerably from one estimate to another.

Mr. Wang: What is the category of basic costs in an allocation process?

Mr. Zhao: In construction projects, the accounts for basic costs can be classified according to labor, material, construction equipment, construction supervision and general office overhead. These basic costs are then allocated proportionally to various tasks which are subdivisions of a project.

Questions

1. How is the construction cost estimation performed?
2. What is the category of basic costs in an allocation process?

Notes 注释

1. cost estimating 造价估算。在工程项目的不同阶段,项目投资有估算、概算、预算、结算和决算等不同称呼,这些"算"的依据和作用不同,其准确性也"渐进明细",一个比一个更真实地反映项目的实际投资。
2. What are the basic approaches adopted to estimate the construction cost? 建筑成本估算采用哪些基本方法？"adopted to estimate the construction cost" 作定语,修饰"approaches"。adopt 采用,采纳；adapt 适应,改编。
3. production function 生产函数。
4. empirical cost inference 成本经验推断。
5. unit costs for bill of quantities 工程量清单单价。

6. allocation of joint costs 联合费用的分摊。
7. It relates the output amount or volume to the various inputs of labor, material and equipment. 生产函数建立了生产量与各种劳动力、材料和设备投入量之间的关系。"relate ... to/with ..."将……与……联系起来,如"It is difficult *to relate* these results with/to any known cause." 很难把结果与任何已知原因联系起来。
8. the regression analysis techniques 回归分析法。
9. the best parameter values or constants 最佳参数值或常数。
10. "... will vary considerably from one estimate to another"将会因估价项目的不同而有很大不同。"vary from ... to ..."……在范围变……,如"Soccer formation can vary from time to time or team to team." 足球队形的排列随各个时间不同而不同,或队与队之间不同。"vary with ..." 随……而变化,如"The prices of some goods vary with the season." 某些货物的价格随着季节的变化而变动。
11. general office overhead 普通的办公管理费。

Useful Sentences 必学句型

1. The importance of cost estimating lies in the fact that it establishes the base line of the project cost at different stages of the project development. 造价估算的重要性在于它设立了项目发展不同阶段项目成本的底线。
2. Virtually all cost estimation is performed according to one or some combination of the following basic approaches. 事实上,所有的成本估算都是根据如下基本方法中的一种或多种结合来进行的。
3. In construction, the production function refers to the relationship between the construction volumes and production factors such as labor or capital. 在建筑中,生产函数指施工量与生产因素如劳动力或资金之间的关系。
4. The total cost is the summation of the product quantities multiplied by the corresponding unit cost. 总造价为工程量与相应单价的乘积之和。
5. The unit cost method is straightforward in principle but quite laborious in application. 单价法原则上简单易懂,但应用时相当繁琐。
6. The level of detail in decomposing into tasks will vary considerably from one estimate to another. 分解作业的细目程度对于不同的估价项目有很大不同。
7. In construction projects, the accounts for basic costs can be classified according to labor, material, construction equipment, construction supervision and general office overhead. 在施工项目中,可根据劳动力、材料、施工设备、施工监理和普通的办公管理费对基本成本的账目进行分类。

Exercises 练习

1. **Complete the following dialogue in English.**

   A: What is the main purpose of control estimates?

   B: _____.

   (为了在施工期间对项目进行监督,根据可利用资料做出造价控制从而确定融资概算、签约后施工前的预算成本以及施工过程中完成部分的预算价值。)

   A: Both the owner and the contractor must adopt some basic line for cost control during the construction, am I right?

   B: _____.

   (是的。对于业主而言,为了做项目长期的投资计划,必须尽可能早地采用概算。)

   A: Is it necessary for the owner to revise the budgeted cost?

   B: _____.

   (是的,无论是由于业主提出变更单或由于意外的费用超支或节约,修正预算成本是非常有必要的。)

   A: How about the control estimates for the contractor?

   B: _____.

   (对于承包商而言,投标报价通常被认作概算,用于控制投资的目的以及规划建设资金。)

   A: Should the budgeted cost be also updated periodically?

   B: _____.

   (是的。概算定期修正的目的是反映完成的预算价值以及确保项目完成有足够的现金流转。)

2. **Read and interpret the following passage.**

   ### Bid estimates

   For the contractor, a bid estimate submitted to the owner either for competitive bidding or for negotiation consists of direct construction cost including field supervision, plus a markup to cover general overhead and profits. The direct cost of construction for bid estimates is usually derived from a combination of the following approaches: subcontractor quotations, quantity take-offs and construction procedures.

3. **Pair work.**

   You are a cost engineer of ×××Construction Company. Try to say something about your specific duties in stages of the overall design, the initial design, the construction drawing design and the competition.

Supplementary Materials 补充材料

Table of Engineering Budget Analysis
工程预算分析表

序号 No.	定额编号 Ration No.	工程项目名称 Project Name	计量单位 Measurement Unit	数量 Quantity	预算总价 Total Estimated Cost	其中 Including		
						人工费 Labor Cost	材料费 Material Cost	机械费 Mechanical Cost
		实体项目(一般建筑) Real project (common buildings)						
		土石方工程 Earth-rock works						
		砌筑工程 Masonry works						
		M5.0 水泥砂浆砖基础 M5.0 cement mortar brick foundation						
		M7.5 水泥砂浆砖基础 M7.5 cement mortar brick foundation						
		混凝土及钢筋混凝土工程 Concrete and reinforced concrete works						
		……						
		直接工程费合计 (土石方除外)Sum of DCC excluding earth-rock works						
		措施性项目费 Step item cost						
		……						
		可竞争措施费(土建) Competitive measure cost (civil engineering)						
		不可竞争措施费(土建) Non-competitive measure cost (civil engineering)						

续表

序号 No.	定额编号 Ration No.	工程项目名称 Project Name	计量单位 Measurement Unit	数量 Quantity	预算总价 Total Estimated Cost	其中 Including		
						人工费 Labor Cost	材料费 Material Cost	机械费 Mechanical Cost
		土石方、垂运等合计 Sum of earth-rock and transport cost						
		实体项目(装饰工程) Real project (decorative works)						
		门窗工程 Door and window works						
		……						
		装饰工程费合计 Sum of decoration cost						
		措施性项目费 Step item cost						
		……						
		可竞争措施费(装饰) Competitive measure cost (decorative works)						
		不可竞争措施费(装饰) Non-competitive measure cost (decorative works)						

MODULE 19　Claims of Construction Works
模块十九　工程索赔

Learning Objectives 学习目标

In this module, learners should:
- know the Chinese and English special terms related to construction claims.
- be capable of making simple English conversations concerning construction claims.

在本模块内，学习者应该能：
- 了解与工程索赔相关的中英文术语。
- 能够围绕工程索赔进行简单的英语会话。

Special Terms 专业词汇

abide by the contract　遵守合同	accept a claim　接受索赔
refuse a claim　拒绝索赔	waive a claim　放弃索赔
satisfy a claim　满足索赔	clear up a claim　清理索赔
act of god　天灾，不可抗力	amicable settlement　友好解决
amount of claim　索赔额	cause for claim　索赔原因
claim for quantity　数量索赔	claim for quality　质量索赔
claim for construction period　工期索赔	procedure for claims　索赔程序
claim sheet　索赔清单	claims agent　索赔代理
notice of claim　索赔通知	claim adjuster　索赔理算人
claimer　索赔人	compensator　赔偿人
blanket claim　一揽子索赔	claim right　索赔权
claim management　索赔管理	assessment of claims　索赔评定
detailed claim　详细索赔	interim claim　中间索赔
final claim　最终索赔	payment of claims　索赔的支付
unreasonable claim　不合理的索赔	valid period of claim　索赔时效
claim for additional payment　索赔额外费用	contractual claims　合同规定的索赔
arbitration agreement　仲裁协议	arbitration award　仲裁解决
place of arbitration　仲裁地点	rules for arbitration　仲裁规则
notice of default　违约通知	substantiation of claim　索赔证明

| conflict of interest 利益冲突 | potential dispute 潜在争议 |
| defect liability 缺陷责任 | default party 违约方 |

waive 常用来表示权利、规则、条款的放弃；而 abandon 则多用来表示对地点、事物、观点或是人的放弃或抛弃，如放弃条款时用 waive，而不用 abandon 或 give up，而弃船则用 abandon。

Situational Conversations 情景对话

David: Will you explain me something about claims in the construction field?

Smith: Surely. First of all, we should make it clear that claims are quite normal in the construction field. Just like a person, he unavoidably makes some mistakes and walks up to the perfection in the process of correcting mistakes from time to time.

David: So claim is the charge of expenses arising from the correction of mistakes, isn't it?

Smith: Yes, your comprehension is basically right.

David: What items does the claim include?

Smith: Let me see. It mainly includes technical issues, financial problems, cost disagreements of materials, machines, manpower and so on.

David: Can you exemplify claims for technical issues?

Smith: Of course, I can. The technical claims are mainly caused either by delays of issuing construction drawings or by no timely reply to the technical clarification request or by non-conformance between drawing and specification.

David: What about the financial claims?

Smith: They are arised from the delay of progress payment and the fluctuation of exchange rates between U.S. Dollars and the local currency.

David: What are the claim procedures?

Smith: The procedures are quite complex, which usually consist of three steps. The first is the time period, that is, the claim has to be submitted within 14 days regulated in the condition of the contract. The second is the claimed amount, that is, the bill for the claim cost should be submitted within 30 days after the claim notice. And the third is the further analysis of the claim, which must be submitted within 14 days.

David: Now I have already known the procedures and time period of the claim, thank you very much.

Smith: Not at all. But I have one more thing to point out. All the records and reports should be with signatures by both sides.

David: I see. That must be the final decision, which will take a long time, perhaps two or three months.

Smith: Yes, it is the maximum time period of the claim in normal procedures.

David: Oh. What a complicated procedure it is! When can the total compensation of the claim be entitled to be received?

Smith: In accordance with the condition of the contract, within 60 days after the receipt of the further convincing materials of the claim, the engineer will inform the contractor of the final decision of the claim after his consulting with the employer. If the claim is reasonable, a full settlement will be effected.

David: I see. Thank you for telling me so much claim knowledge.

Smith: Don't mention it!

Questions

1. What items does the claim include?
2. What are the claim procedures?

Notes 注释

1. "… walks up to the perfection in the process of correcting mistakes from time to time." 在不断改进错误的进程中走向完美。from time to time 不时地，时而，如 "Good ideas swim into my mind from time to time." 我的脑海里不时地会浮现出一些好主意。

2. So claim is the charge of expenses arising from the correction of mistakes, isn't it? 因此，索赔就是对纠正过失产生费用的索取，不是吗？"charge"在此表示"索要，要求支付（常与 for 连用）"，如 "Is there an extra charge for baggage in excess of my weight allowance?" 超重的行李需要额外付费吗？"arise from" 意思为"起因于，来源于"，如 "Great inventions arise from the inspiration of daily life." 伟大的发明来源于日常生活中的灵感。

3. "either...or..."或者，要么。如"Some college courses are graded in terms of either a pass or a fail."有些大学课程按及格或不及格评分。
4. The procedures are quite complex, which usually consist of three steps. 索赔程序相当复杂，它一般包括三步。"consist of"的意思为"由……组成；包括"。如"Matters consist of molecules, and molecules of atoms."物质由分子构成，而分子由原子构成。
5. time period 索赔期限。
6. the claimed amount 索赔金额。
7. the maximum time period of the claim 索赔的最长期限。
8. When can the total compensation of the claim be entitled to be received? 什么时候才能收到索赔的总金额？"be entitled to"有权做……，如"If the employer delays the start, then the Contractor will be entitled to financial compensation."如果业主延误开始，承包商有权得到财务补偿。
9. "...will inform the contractor of the final decision of the claim after his consulting with the employer." 同业主协商后将索赔的最终决定通知承包商。"inform sb. of sth."告诉/通知某人某事，如"Please inform me of your arrival time beforehand."请事先通知我你抵达的时间。"consult with sb."意思为"与某人商量"，如"If she had had a plan, she would consult with an expert."如果她以前有这样的计划，她当时也就会找专家商量。

Useful Sentences 必学句型

1. Will you explain me something about claims in the construction field? 你能给我解释一下建筑领域的索赔吗？
2. First of all, we should make it clear that claims are quite normal in the construction field. 首先，我们应清楚索赔在建筑行业是一件很正常的事情。
3. Can you exemplify claims for technical issues? 你能举例说明下技术索赔吗？
4. The technical claims are mainly caused either by delays of issuing construction drawings or by no timely reply to the technical clarification request or by non-conformance between drawing and specification. 技术索赔主要是由延误颁发施工图纸，没有及时回答技术核校单，或是图纸和规范相矛盾等问题引起。
5. All the records and reports should be with signatures by both sides. 所有的记录和报告都应该经双方人员验收签字。
6. What a complicated procedure it is! 多么复杂的索赔程序啊！
7. In accordance with the condition of the contract, within 60 days after the receipt of

the further convincing materials of the claim, the engineer will inform the contractor of the final decision of the claim after his consulting with the employer. 根据合同条款,在收到索赔的进一步证明材料后的 60 天内,工程师同业主协商后将索赔的最终决定通知承包商。

Exercises 练习

1. **Complete the following dialogue in English.**

    A: _____.
    (到目前为止,我们已从贵公司收到 145 份索赔要求,但多数索赔并没有多少理由。)
    B: We think they are reasonable. As we know, the claims are quite normal things in construction field.
    A: _____.
    (只要合同条款有索赔这一条,我们不会对根据合同提出的索赔权置之不理的,但索赔的提出和解决应根据事实并通过一定的程序来进行。)
    B: Yes, of course. All claims are submitted to you on the basis of what has happened during the execution of the construction works and strictly following the procedure step by step.
    A: _____.
    (那好,请你对这些索赔做出说明。然后,我们将把我们认为理由充足并且有效的索赔提交给我们的董事会,由他们做出最终决定。)
    B: _____.
    (总起来看,在 145 项索赔中,大多数属于技术问题,诸如延误颁发施工图纸、不及时回答技术核校单、图纸和技术规范相矛盾等等。)
    A: How many items do you think belong to technical issues?
    B: _____.
    (根据我们的统计,属于技术问题的有 85 项,其次有 50 项属于承包商与业主之间的协调问题。)
    A: These two kinds account for 135 items of the claims. What about the remaining 10 claims?
    B: _____.
    (其中有 4 项属于财务问题,这其中有 2 项是因为工程进度款拨付延误而引起的索赔,2 项是由于美元和当地货币的汇率差浮动引起的索赔,剩下的 6 项归为"其他"。)
    A: What do "others" mean? Can you give me an example?
    B: _____.
    (对于那些无法指定属于哪一类的,我们将其归为"其他"。如由于政府官员要来参观工地,贵方通知我们要进行彻底的大清理,这样的特殊清理当然是会增加开支的。)
    A: Now I'd like to discuss these claims with you one by one.

B: OK. Let us start from ...

2. Read and interpret the following passages.

(1) In international construction contracting, the contractor often makes claims against the owner for a variety of reasons, among which are different understanding of the contract documents, delay by the owner in issuing drawings and instructions, differing site conditions and events of force majeure.

(2) 合同是工程索赔的依据，它明确或暗示地规定了承包商在何种情况下进行索赔的权力以及索赔的程序。因此，认真研究和掌握合同文件的规定，认真地管理工程实施中的一切来往函件和现场资料是索赔成功的基础。

3. Pair work.

Suppose A is a supervising engineer, B is a resident engineer. They are talking about how to solve the problem of manpower and material claims.

Supplementary Materials 补充材料

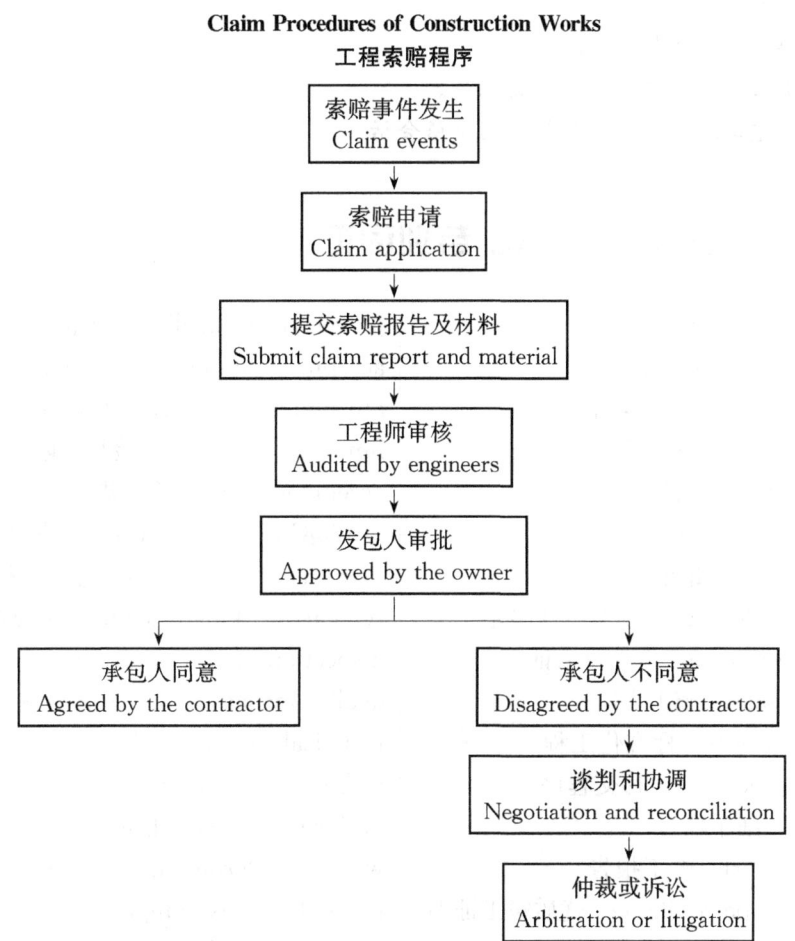

Claim Procedures of Construction Works
工程索赔程序

MODULE 20 Acceptance of Construction Works
模块二十 工程验收

Learning Objectives 学习目标

In this module, learners should:
- know the Chinese and English special terms related to the acceptance of construction works.
- be capable of making simple English conversations concerning the acceptance of construction works.

在本模块内，学习者应该能：
- 了解建筑工程验收相关的中英文术语。
- 能够围绕建筑工程验收进行简单的英语会话。

Special Terms 专业词汇

building appraisement　工程评价
acceptance check　验收检查
acceptance procedure　验收程序
function of acceptance　验收函数
acceptance lot　验收批量
completion certificate　完工证书
survey records　测量记录
construction tolerance　施工允许误差
inspection certificate　检验合格证
construction plan　施工方案
standardized works　标准化工程
taking-over procedure　移交程序
minor items　细小项目
completion report　竣工报告
excellent execution certificate　优质竣工证书
substantial completion　实质性竣工

judgement of quality　质量评定
acceptance standard　验收标准
acceptance certificate　验收证书
limit of acceptance　验收界限
acceptance code　验收规范
QA/QC inspection forms　质保/质控文件
execution-tracing files　隐蔽工程记录
refer to working drawing　参见施工图
inspection of works progress　工序检查
quality management　质量管理
technical sampling　抽样法
as-built drawing　竣工图纸
performance test　性能试验
written undertaking　书面承诺，书面保证
bonus for early completion　提前竣工奖
practical completion　基本竣工

complete 除表示一般性的"完成"外,还强调一切完备、没有欠缺的地方,尤其指通过填补失掉或缺陷的部分来配齐或完成。finish 与 complete 基本同义,着重指圆满地结束或完成已着手的事,或者表示对已经做完的事进行精密加工。

Situational Conversations 情景对话

Jordan: Now, the whole works have reached substantial completion under the contract. We are looking forward to your issuing the taking-over certificate as early as possible.

Mr. Lin: That's great news! But we need a careful plan for the acceptance inspection and tests, which includes a timetable for the taking-over procedure, as-built drawings and a list of all the parts to be inspected and tested.

Jordan: Yes, you are right. The works cannot be deemed to be substantially completed until we have presented these documents to you.

Mr. Lin: Is there any work which you think is still outstanding?

Jordan: Yes, but they are minor items, such as the surface reinstating.

Mr. Lin: In my opinion, the taking-over process can be divided into two phases: first, our expert panel, accompanied by your technical staff, will inspect the completed works and see whether they are satisfactory. If everything is all right, we will enter into the second phase, that is, to carry out the performance tests of the equipment and instruments as specified in the contract.

Jordan: I agree. When can we start the acceptance inspection and tests?

Mr. Lin: We need about 3 days to make some preparations. Shall we start on 19th of this month?

Jordan: No problem.

(*The whole acceptance process goes smoothly and lasts 5 days. Now, they are having a discussion about the completion report and the taking-over certificate.*)

Mr. Lin: Congratulations! The whole works have passed all the tests and our engineers are quite satisfied with the test results. However, a few minor defects have been found and there are still some outstanding works.

What do you plan to do with these items?

Jordan: It is true that a few minor defects remain to be rectified and some items of the work need to be completed, but they don't affect the normal operation of the whole works. This means, according to the contract, the substantial completion has been achieved and we should receive a taking-over certificate from you.

Mr. Lin: We can issue a taking-over certificate to you provided that you give us a written undertaking that you will finish the outstanding work and make good the defects with due expedition during the maintenance period.

Jordan: No problem.

Mr. Lin: Now, we can acknowledge that the works are substantially completed on November 24th, 2011. Now that the whole works have been accepted, why don't you have some relaxations?

Jordan: We still have two things to do: first, to apply for an excellent execution certificate for this project; second, to ask for the bonus for our early completion.

Mr. Lin: You are entitled to have the certificate and the bonus.

Questions

1. Will Mr. Lin issue a taking-over certificate to Jordan? Why?
2. What are the two phases of the taking-over process?

Notes 注释

1. Now, the whole works have reached substantial completion under the contract. 现在，整个工程按合同已经达到实质性竣工。"substantial completion"实质性竣工，指工程已基本竣工，可以投入运行，允许在验收时存在部分未完成的扫尾工作和一些小缺陷，但不能影响工程的正常运行。
2. the acceptance inspection and tests 验收检查与试验。
3. "be deemed to"意思为"被认为"，如"This date will be deemed to be the date of shipment."该日期将被视为发运日期。
4. outstanding 未完成的，如"The outstanding bill must be paid next week."这笔未偿还的账下周必须还清。
5. the surface reinstating 地表面恢复。
6. expert panel 专家组。

7. "satisfied"是一个主观性形容词,是自身感觉到的,表示对某事/某人感觉到满意。一般组成的短语是:be satisfied with sb. /sth."对某人/某物感觉满意",如"One shouldn't be satisfied with only a little success."一个人不应该只因一点小成就而感到满足;"satisfactory"是一个客观性形容词,是事物/情况给人的感觉,表示事物/情况本身具有的性质或特点,是"令人满意的"意思。如"To be plain with you, we do not consider your work entirely satisfactory."老实告诉你,我认为你的工作并不完全令人满意。
8. "... provided that you give us a written undertaking..."假定你给我们一个书面承诺……,"provided that"假设,如"Provided that we get support from them, we will win the match."假如我们能取得他们的支持,我们就能赢得比赛。
9. with due expedition 迅速地办理。"expedition"意思为"迅速(办理)",如"They carried out the captain's orders with all possible expedition."他们毫不迟疑地迅速执行船长的命令。
10. "... to apply for an excellent execution certificate for this project" 申请优质工程奖。
11. "... to ask for the bonus for our early completion." 要求提前竣工奖。

Useful Sentences 必学句型

1. We are looking forward to your issuing the taking-over certificate as early as possible. 我们期盼着您尽早颁发移交证书。
2. The works cannot be deemed to be substantially completed until we have presented these documents to you. 这些资料不提交给你们,工程还不能被认为已基本竣工。
3. If everything is all right, we will enter into the second phase. 如果一切正常,我们将进入到第二阶段。
4. The whole works have passed all the tests and our engineers are quite satisfied with the test results. 整个工程已经通过了验收,我们的工程师对试验结果相当满意。
5. What do you plan to do with these items? 你打算如何处理这些细小项目?
6. Now that the whole works have been accepted, why don't you have some relaxations? 既然整个工程已验收,为什么不放松一下呢?
7. You are entitled to have the certificate and the bonus. 你们有权拥有这个(优质工程)证书和(提前竣工)奖金。

Exercises 练习

1. Complete the following dialogue in English.

    A: When will you issue the completion certificate of the project?

B：_____.（我认为,颁发该证书为时尚早。）

A：Why not? But I am afraid I could not agree with you at this point, since we have finished 95% of the total works.

B：_____.
（可是从统计报表上看,你们仅完成了这项工程的 90%。）

A：What should we do in you opinion?

B：_____.
（我建议你们尽最大努力在 20 天内完成整个工程,届时我们将为你们颁发完工证书。）

A：I see, sir. But does the retention period begin from the day of issuing the completion certificate?

B：Yes, you are right. But there is one important thing you should keep in mind during this period.

A：_____.
（你指的是施工图吧？我们会在 5 天内彻底收集完施工图。）

B：That's all right. In addition to this, all the necessary information, such as QA/QC inspection forms, survey records, executing tracing files should be ready for submission.

A：_____.
（没有问题。在验收过程中通常会发现一些不足之处,我们会在一定的时间内修复完好。）

B：Yes, all the defects will be repaired very soon and the works will be kept perfect even after the final handing over.

A：_____.
（那是肯定的,你们一定会对我们的工程满意的。顺便问一下,验收小组由哪些部门的人员组成？）

B：_____.
（应该由业主、承包商和政府有关部门联合组成验收小组。）

A：What will the inspection group do then?

B：_____.
（在随后的 10 天内,验收小组就合同范围内所有工程项目进行检查。在对所有必要方面检查过后,将提出一份报告。）

A：I see. The final completion certificate is issued after all the procedures are fulfilled in accordance with the condition of the contract, right?

B：Right.

2. Read and interpret the following passages.

(1) On the completion of every stage of the project, A and B sides should form an acceptance group to sign an acceptance certificate according to the drawings and specifications for the qualified works. If the works-done are not conformable to the drawings, B side should remedy it up so as to reach the drawings, and all the expenditures are up to B

side. The defects liability period of the project is one year from the date of the signing of taking over documents of the completion, the poor quality causing from the construction, B side will maintain it up to drawings at his own cost.

(2) 在工程达到实质性竣工或基本竣工时，组织工程的验收对承包商来说是十分重要的一项工作，因为工程一旦移交给业主，工程的照管责任即从承包商转到业主一方，承包商并且能获得相应的权益。由于每一项工程的性质与所签订的合同类型不尽相同，工程的移交程序也有差异，但其程序大致如下：

① 承包商通知业主工程已达到实质性竣工，并按业主要求提交一份移交计划。计划中应包括：要求业主进行检查与试验的时间表；竣工时应提交给业主的各类资料；未完成的扫尾工作等。

② 制定记录验收检查与试验结果的各种表格。

③ 起草验收报告。这一报告应该是对工程项目的公正性评价，在其中说明工程于某日期竣工和维修开始日期，以及指出承包商应在维修期完成的扫尾工作及小缺陷。

④ 颁发移交证书。一旦承包商收到了移交证书，承包商要催促业主按合同规定退还保留金，同时组织维修期的维修工作。

3. Pair work.

A acts as an inspector, B acts as a representative from a construction company who wants A to issue the completion certificate. Make up a dialogue by using the following expressions:

A: Can I ... ?
B: Certainly. But ...
A: Please show ...
B: OK. It is ...

Supplementary Materials 补充材料

Works Completion Inspection Request
工程竣工报验单

SH/T 3903-A.10	工程竣工报验单 Works Completion Inspection Request	工程名称 Work Titles:
		编号 Item No.:

致　　　　　（监理单位）
To　　　　　（CS/CMC）

我方已按合同要求完成了工程，经自检合格，请予以检查和验收。
We have completed the works according to the requirements of the contract, after the self-check, it is on spec, please inspect and accept.

附 Attached:

续表

承包单位（章） Contractor（chop）	项目经理 Project manager 日期 Date

审查意见 Review comments

经初步验收，该工程：
After the preliminary inspection and acceptance, this works:

1. ☐ 符合 ☐ 不符合我国现行法律、法规要求；
   ☐ meet ☐ not meet the requirements of the current state laws and regulations;

2. ☐ 符合 ☐ 不符合我国现行工程建设标准；
   ☐ meet ☐ not meet the requirements of the current national construction standards;

3. ☐ 符合 ☐ 不符合设计文件要求；
   ☐ meet ☐ not meet the requirements of the design documents;

4. ☐ 符合 ☐ 不符合施工合同要求。
   ☐ meet ☐ not meet the requirements of the construction contract.

综上所述，该工程初步验收☐合格☐不合格，☐可以☐不可以组织正式验收。

Based on the above points, the preliminary inspection and acceptance of this works is ☐ on spec/☐ off spec, the formal inspection and acceptance ☐ can be/☐ cannot be organized.

监理机构： CS/CMC：	总监理工程师： Chief supervision engineer： 日期： Date：

APPENDIX Ⅰ Answers to Questions of SC
附录1　情景对话问题答案

MODULE 1　Architectural Majors and Courses(模块一　建筑专业和课程)

1. What major is Xiaoli studying?

   He is studying civil and industrial architecture.

2. Why is Xiaoli determined to be a builder?

   He is moved by the greatness of the hard-working and bright builders who have been setting up buildings from ancient times to the present. Being a builder, he can build up high buildings and large mansions with his own hands.

MODULE 2　Architectural Job Interview(模块二　建筑求职面试)

1. What was Zhang Jie's ideal job? Why?

   Zhang Jie's ideal job is to be a civil engineer. There are two reasons: first, the job of being a civil engineer makes what he has learnt in college useful; second, the workplace is located very near his home, which would bring him a lot of convenience.

2. How did Zhang Jie say about his technical ability and practical skills?

   He said that in the first three years he had been working mainly on theoretical aspects so that he could have a firm foundation, and in the last two years he had been asked to work on a practical project of some kind or other. What he said meant as an engineering student of higher vocational college the study focus of the first three years was on theory and that of the last two years was on practice.

MODULE 3　Architectural Workers(模块三　建筑工程人员)

1. What kinds of tradesmen are there on Mr. Wang's worksite?

   There are bricklayers, carpenters and plasterers. As the main structures are going to be finished, some civil construction workers are leaving while installers and decorators are coming soon.

2. What are the advantages of employing some local people?

   Employing local people to take part in construction not only solves their employment problems but also picks up the construction speed.

MODULE 4　Construction Enterprises(模块四　建筑施工企业)

1. What is CCEC mainly concerned about?

   CCEC is mainly concerned about contracting various kinds of civil and industrial construction works and providing labor service.

2. Does CCEC have a high competition in the world? Why?

Yes. First, CCEC is a historic and well-known company with abundant capital funds; second there are many dab hands and galaxy talents in CCEC.

MODULE 5　Kinds of Buildings(模块五　建筑物类型)

1. What does high-rise building mean?
   According to the Code for Design of Civil Buildings GB 50352—2005, for dwellings, buildings of more than 10 storeys are high-rise; for public buildings, the high-rise ones are more than 24 meters.
2. What are the differences between ancient and modern architecture?
   According to the conversation, the difference between ancient and modern architecture first lies in whether there is an overhanging roof; besides, there are many other differences in aspects of materials, structures, etc.

MODULE 6　Building Materials(模块六　建筑材料)

1. What and how much building materials did Li Lu want to buy?
   Li Lu wanted to buy 200 tons of cement, 1,000 tons of steel bars and 1,000 cubic meters of timber.
2. What is the total cost for the three building materials bought by Li Lu?
   As the respective unit prices of the three building materials are: 1 dollar per kilogram of cement, 500 dollars per ton of steel bars, and 650 dollars per cubic meter of timber; the quantities Li Lu intended to buy are: 200 tons of cement, 1,000 tons of steel bars and 1,000 cubic meters of timber; and the final discount for the order is 15%, so the total cost is 202,500 dollars, which is calculated by the following equation: $(200 \times 1,000 \times 1 + 1,000 \times 500 + 1,000 \times 650) \times 15\% = 202,500$.

MODULE 7　Building Machinery(模块七　建筑机械)

1. What does a mechanized building site mean?
   A mechanized building site means every procedure on the site is completely done by machines.
2. What suggestions did James offer to Li Qin?
   He suggested that before operation the driver should carefully test the machine's performance and in driving the driver should concentrate efforts without slackening any vigilance.

MODULE 8　Architectural Drawings(模块八　建筑图纸)

1. What is an essential prerequisite for construction well?
   Reading and studying drawing carefully is an essential prerequisite for construction well.
2. What does "Construction is the translation of design into reality" mean?
   As every drawing is meticulously designed, the sizes and figures on the drawing are also calculated exactly, constructors should regard it as the norm and the guide of the construction works. In this sense, construction is the translation of design into reality.

MODULE 9　Construction Tendering(模块九　建筑招投标)

1. What does Mr. Wu's company have to do before sending the tender?

   Normally, the company has to submit the relevant materials on cost, construction time and the volume of works concerning some already constructed big projects before.

2. When is the last tendering day of the pavilion constructions of the 2010 Shanghai World Expo according to the conversation?

   Ten days before Jan. 1st, 2007.

MODULE 10　Construction Contract(模块十　建筑合同)

1. How does Mr. Wang think of the performance bond in Clause 10?

   He thinks in Clause 10, 15% of the performance bond is higher than the usual practice, so he wonders whether it can be modified to 10% or not.

2. Does Mr. Green agree with Mr. Wang's modification of the liquidated damages for delay? Why or why not?

   No. Because any delay of such a large project is a very heavy loss for the owner, it is definitely necessary to have such a high amount of liquidated damages.

3. What are the final proposals to Clause 61?

   The final proposals are to add a sub-clause like that in case the contractor suffers delay of drawings supply he is entitled to have an extension of time to the contract period and obtain an amount of compensation for the cost on catching up the progress. But the time extension and cost increase must be determined by the engineer after due consultation with the employer and the contractor.

MODULE 11　Construction Laws and Regulations(模块十一　建筑法律法规)

1. What is the main purpose of the Construction Law?

   The Construction Law is enacted with a view to enhancing supervision and administration over building operations, maintaining order in the construction market, ensuring the quality and safety of construction projects and promoting the sound development of the building industry.

2. What do building operations refer to in the Construction Law?

   The building operations referred to in the Construction Law mean the construction of all types of housing and the construction of their ancillary facilities as well as their matching installation operations of wiring, piping and equipment.

MODULE 12　Construction Testing(模块十二　建筑试验)

1. What should we do before doing the steel bar test?

   Before doing the test, we should inspect the surface of the steel bar, and check whether the size of the steel bar is complied with the specification, and whether there are any leakages, scars or honeycombs on the surface.

2. Under what situations will the cold tensile processing be tested?

   The cold tensile processing is tested when the extensile rate of the steel bar is already in excess of the defined maximum extension under the maximum strength.

MODULE 13　Construction Surveying(模块十三　建筑测量)

1. How many types of surveys are there?
   There are seven types of surveys, namely plane surveys, geodetic surveys, topographic surveys, route surveys, hydrographic surveys, construction surveys and photogrammetric surveys.
2. In what ways can the construction survey be done well?
   Construction survey is best learned on the job by applying the basic principles to practice.

MODULE 14　Construction Plan(模块十四　施工计划)

1. How long is the construction period of Queen Mansion?
   The construction period is twelve months.
2. What does York think of the construction progress schedule of Queen Mansion?
   The schedule is advanced and practical, leaving him a very deep impression.

MODULE 15　Construction Inspection(模块十五　施工检查)

1. What is the purpose of Mr. Gao's coming to the worksite?
   Mr. Gao came to the worksite with the purpose of inspecting the project quality charged by Mr. Cai.
2. How can the concrete aggregate materials be put accurately?
   The concrete aggregate materials are put in proportion to their weight.

MODULE 16　Building Installation(模块十六　建筑安装)

1. What works do fitters usually do?
   They mainly mount machines and equipments, such as lathes, cranes, air hammers and so on.
2. What operative techniques should a fitter have?
   A qualified fitter should be good at setting out the bases, installing and leveling the equipment, cleaning and assembling machine parts, and so on. Besides, he should also know how to adjust and test equipments well so as to make them run smoothly.

MODULE 17　Building Decoration(模块十七　建筑装饰)

1. What roles do decorative works play in the building engineering?
   Decorative works are of vital importance to the building engineering, just like beautiful clothes to the person and suitable saddle to the horse.
2. How is the surface of the aluminum alloy usually treated? And why?
   All the surfaces of the aluminum alloy are first thoroughly cleaned, and then painted with a coating of clear, non-fading, colored or colorless paint. They are treated in this way just for a precaution and protection against damages from alkaline cement plaster and similar materials.

MODULE 18 Building Cost(模块十八 建筑造价)

1. How is construction cost estimation performed?

   Virtually all cost estimation is performed according to one or some combination of the following basic approaches: production function, empirical cost inference, unit costs for bill of quantities, allocation of joint costs.

2. What is the category of basic costs in an allocation process?

   In construction projects, the accounts for basic costs can be classified according to labor, material, construction equipment, construction supervision and general office overhead.

MODULE 19 Claims of Construction Works(模块十九 工程索赔)

1. What items does the claim include?

   It mainly includes technical issues, financial problems, cost disagreements of materials, machines, manpower and so on.

2. What are the claim procedures?

   The procedures are quite complex, which usually consist of three steps. The first is the time period, that is, the claim has to be submitted within 14 days regulated in the condition of the contract. The second is the claimed amount, that is, the bill for the claim cost should be submitted within 30 days after the claim notice. And the third is the further analysis of the claim, which must be submitted within 14 days.

MODULE 20 Acceptance of Construction Works(模块二十 工程验收)

1. Will Mr. Lin issue a taking-over certificate to Jordan? Why?

   Yes, Mr. Lin will issue a taking-over certificate to Jordan, but Jordan should guarantee in the written form that he will finish the outstanding work and make good the defects with due expedition during the maintenance period.

2. What are the two phases of the taking-over process?

   The first phase is that the expert panel will inspect the completed works and see whether they are satisfactory. If everything is all right, they will enter into the second phase, that is, to carry out the performance tests of the equipment and instruments as specified in the contract.

APPENDIX Ⅱ　Key to the Exercises
附录 2　练习答案

MODULE 1　Architectural Majors and Courses(模块一　建筑专业和课程)

1. Complete the following dialogue in English.
    A：How do you do?
    A：Of course. /Certainly.
    A：I am a student in this university.
    A：Engineering cost.
    A：It's a hot/promising major these years, and I like it.
    A：There are more than ten courses, which are compulsory/mandatory/required and basic/ fundamental courses.
    A：Construction Techniques. Because the teacher can clarify the lesson from the shallower to the deeper and from the easier to the more advanced, and integrate theory with practice.
    A：You are welcome.
2. Read and interpret the following passage.

数　　学

　　在大学，整个工科课程体系都非常强调数学的重要性。现在，数学包括统计学，其主要进行数据或信息资料的收集、分类和使用工作。统计数学的一个重要部分是概率论，它研究的是当影响某个事件结果的不同因素或变量存在时，某种结果出现的可能性。例如，在建造一座桥梁之前，要对该桥预期承受的交通流量进行统计研究。在设计这座桥梁时，必须考虑诸如基础上的水压力、冲击力、不同风力作用等变量以及很多其他因素。

MODULE 2　Architectural Job Interview(模块二　建筑求职面试)

1. Complete the following dialogue in English.
    A：I am studying in Jiangsu Jianzhu Institute.
    A：In July this year.
    A：I am a student in this institute.
    A：Civil and industrial architecture.
    A：I have good grades, and I'm one of the top students in the class.
    A：I have obtained CET4, the National Certification of Construction Cost Estimator Qualification and the Driving License.
    A：I have rich experience with computers and I am good at operations of Windows, Word and Excel.
    A：My background and experience make me perfectly suitable for the job, and I am

very interested in it. Besides, your company is the leading one in this field.

A: The school education and practices and the practical work experience should qualify me to be competent for the job, and I think I will be successful.

A: Your company is very reputed in this city; I heard much praise for your company.

A: Thank you, sir. I expect to hear good news from you as soon as possible.

B: Would you please let the next applicant come in on your way out?

2. Read and interpret the following passage.

求 职 信

先生/女士：

　　您好。阅读了今天《新华日报》招聘广告栏目，得知贵公司招聘建筑工程技术人员，特冒昧自荐。本人简历如下：

　　出生地：中国上海

　　年龄：22 岁

　　薪酬期望：5 000 元/月

　　文化程度：上海电视大学毕业，专业是工业与民用建筑。

　　工作经验：在南通三建公司拥有两年建筑从业经历。

　　如上述条件尚能符合贵公司的要求，请约期面谈。我每天下午 3 点至 5 点都可以接受面试，请至少提前一周通知我。

　　盼能早日回复，不胜感激。

李　华

MODULE 3 Architectural Workers(模块三　建筑工程人员)

1. Complete the following dialogue in English.

Peter: Certainly. But what do you want to know?

Peter: I am a resident engineer, and also a site director in charge of this worksite.

Peter: I am fully responsible for the safe construction on the worksite. Specifically speaking, I mainly do the safety supervision and guidance for the construction projects.

Peter: At present, there are more than 1,000 workers.

Peter: Yes. About 10% among them are the engineering technicians and administrative staff. Others are the civil construction workers such as bricklayers, carpenters, plasterers and so on.

Peter: Yes, we will employ several hundred local workers during the construction peak period.

Peter: Employing local workers can firstly solve their employment problems and secondly maximally speed up the construction.

Peter: We will offer some timely architectural training to the newly engaged local workers.

2. Read and interpret the following passage.

建筑生产工种

建筑生产中有四大工种,这四大工种是土建工人、建筑安装工人、建筑机械工人和建筑装饰工人。当然,每一大工种都包括八种以上的工种。例如:建筑安装工人可分为水暖工、电工、焊工、起重工、通风工、铆工、安装钳工等工种。各工种之间密切配合,缺一不可。每一工种都在建筑施工中起着重要的作用。

MODULE 4　Construction Enterprises（模块四　建筑施工企业）

1. Complete the following dialogue in English.

　　B: Sure.

　　B: It is headquartered in Nantong, a city in Jiangsu Province known as a land of architecture.

　　B: No. Established in 1952, it is a private economic entity, operating independently, assuming sole responsibility for its own profits and losses, seeking self-development and self-reliance.

　　B: At present, the group-corporation has a registered capital of 360 million *yuan*, a total assets of 1.7 billion *yuan*.

　　B: The group-corporation administers 29 civil construction and professional subsidiary companies, which are distributed in six regional markets of North, East, South, Northwest, Northeast China and the overseas. With 34 member companies and over 20 thousand workers, the annual business scale reaches nearly one hundred billion *yuan*.

　　B: At present, in our group-corporation there are almost two thousand economic, technical and managerial personnel. Hundreds of staff and workers have middle or senior class professional titles and qualifications. Among them, there are 7 professor-grade senior engineers, 48 senior and 109 middle class workers, 117 constructors, 154 associate constructors and 18 other certificated staff.

　　B: Too numerous to mention. Domestically there are the architectural complex of Tian'anmen Square, the Capital Nationalities Cultural Palace, the Nanjing Yangtse River Bridge and so on; at abroad there are the Palace Basement in Kuwait, the National Stadium in Barbados and the office building of the Ministry of Education in Mozambique.

　　B: It should be said that our group-corporation has a strong competitiveness, as for six years on end, it has been selected for the top 60 Chinese constructors, the top 30 Jiangsu provincial comprehensive construction enterprises and the top 10 outward construction enterprises in Jiangsu; for four times, it has topped on the chart of the top 225 contractors and the top 225 international contractors of ENR; and for three times, it has been short-listed for the top 500 Chinese private enterprises.

　　B: A period of time of aftertime, we will make great efforts to develop the new integrated operation mode of research, design, construction and service, transform the concept of being a famous building constructor into that of being an outstanding architectural service provider, and stride forward towards the great goals of creating the first-class trans-regional, trans-industry (inter-trade) and trans-national construction enterprise in China, with the scientific organization system, the diversified market structure, the intensified construction and the modernized business management.

2. Read and interpret the following passage.

公　司

公司是一个法律实体,与其业主分离而独立存在。公司的资产属于公司,而不属于公司个人。公司的业主称之为股东,他们的所有权是通过可转让的股份得到确认的。公司为其债务负责的同时,还必须为其盈利支付所得税。作为一个独立的法律实体,公司可以签订合同,在法庭上同自然人一样起诉和应诉。

MODULE 5　Kinds of Buildings (模块五　建筑物类型)

1. Complete the following dialogue in English.
   B: Generally speaking, buildings can be classified into three general types according to usage, namely the civil buildings, the industrial buildings and the agricultural buildings.
   B: The civil buildings include the residential as well as the public buildings.
   B: Examples of public buildings are too numerous to list, such as buildings of offices, hotels, shops, schools, airports, stations.
   B: Of course you can, the National Stadium is not only spectacular but also strong, with the main structure designed for working life up to 100 years.
   B: Yes, due to the need of a wider span, the roofs of the National Stadium are steel-structured, and the other load-bearing members use the reinforced concrete.
   B: Yes, for public buildings, those with more than 2 storeys and over 24 meters high are high-rise buildings.
   B: Residential buildings of more than 10 storeys can be regarded as the high-rise ones.

2. Read and interpret the following passage.

住　宅

世界上有许多不同类型的住宅。它们可能是大的或小的、古代的或是现代的、中式的或是西式的。绝大多数住宅都是方形的,极少数住宅是圆形的。有些住宅仅有一层,而另外的一些住宅却有两层或几层,甚至还有不少多层的建筑。

许多住宅的设计都是相似的,楼上设有两三个卧室和浴室,而楼下设有餐厅、厨房和客厅,在房前屋后还拥有一个小花园。

绝大多数住宅都是由混凝土、钢材、木材、石块或砖建造而成的。

MODULE 6　Building Materials (模块六　建筑材料)

1. Complete the following dialogue in English.
   B: Yes. I plan to order a large stock of stone materials from you.

B: Mainly for housing decoration.

B: I am very interested in the marbles here. If the price is reasonable, I can place the order with you right away.

B: What is the lowest price for the pure white marble?

A: I am afraid not. 700 *yuan* per square meter is our bottom price. Moreover, these are purely natural marbles, and each has its unique pattern and color.

A: Those at low prices are artificial marbles, with no good transparency or becoming lusterless.

A: The easiest way is simply to dip a few drops of diluted hydrochloric acid on the marbles, the natural ones will be effervescing vigorously, while the artificial ones will be effervescing weakly or will not be effervescing at all.

A: Of course, you can. As the saying goes, pure gold does not fear furnace.

A: Very good! It's a pleasure to do business with you.

A: No problem at all. We will not delay your business.

2. Read and interpret the following passages.

1) 窑制砖在发达国家广泛应用于房屋建筑。它们的尺寸和式样是由各个国家标准规定的，现在有动议要建立国际标准。砖的尺寸和比例可以广泛地选择，这样，泥瓦工就能单手持砖，把砖块平行和垂直于墙面地砌筑在一起。

大多数砖是以粘土或板岩为原料在砖窑里烧制成的。然而，也有些砖是由硅砂和石灰制成的，这一类砖称为硅钙砖。建筑砌块要比砖稍大一些，而且通常是由混凝土浇筑而成的。

2) As a high-grade product for building decorations, the stone can be classified into the natural as well as the man-made one (also known as the artificial stone). The natural stone includes granite, marble, sandstone, limestone, lava and so on. With the incremental development of science and technology, products of the artificial stone are also continuously multiplied and changing with each passing day and month, and the quality and aesthetics of the the artificial stone have no longer been short of the natural stone. Along with the development of the economy, stones have already been one of the most important materials used in building, decoration, roads and bridge construction.

MODULE 7　Building Machinery（模块七　建筑机械）

1. Complete the following dialogue in English.

B: There is something wrong with the concrete mixer and it doesn't work normally.

B: Look! The motor is running well. What is the problem on earth?

B: If the concrete mixer can't work, most builders on the site have to stop and wait for materials and the construction must be delayed, so I want to know how long it will take to repair the machine well.

B: I am worried to death about it. Why does not the drum move while the motor is in normal state?

B: Is the belt too slack to use?

A: The slack belt has been replaced by a new one. Please start it again.

A: Don't mention it. My duty is to serve the construction in order to assure that machines run normally and constructions proceed smoothly.

C: Excuse me, the brake of my dumper doesn't hold well and I also have some troubles in shifting the gears. Could you please check the brake and the gears for me?

C: Very good. Thank you for showing due respect for my feelings. Let's go.

2. Read and interpret the following passage.

铲运机和平地机

建房用地的平整以及现代公路的修筑,采用专用的铲运机和平地机。铲运机可以是自驱动的或是由牵引机拖动。它有刀形刮片,能切除一层表土并收集到内部的拖斗中,并能一次性挖掘 1 400 立方英尺(40 立方米)土方并运到附近的地点倾倒。

一般在铺设道路混凝土之前要用平地机精确地整修路基。平地机有 2～4 米宽的可调角度的刮板,由液压控制并悬挂在轮子之间,大多数平地机是自驱动式的。

MODULE 8 Architectural Drawings (模块八 建筑图纸)

1. Complete the following dialogue in English.

B: Certainly. What do you want to know about building drawings?

B: The so-called building drawings are the designs drawn minutely and accurately by the method of orthogonal projection in accordance with the relevant regulations for the proposed buildings in the content of the internal and external shape and size, the structure, construction, decoration and equipment of different parts, and so on.

B: You are right. Buildings drawings have always been regarded as the norm and the guide of our construction works.

B: According to the professional content and functions, a complete set of building drawings generally include the catalogue, the general design specification, the building construction drawing, the structural working drawing and the equipment construction drawing.

B: The building construction drawing specifies the inside layout, the external shape and the requirements of decoration, structure and construction.

B: The structural working drawing specifies the layout, the type, the size and the construction of the load-bearing parts of a building.

B: Yes. The commonly used instruments are the drawing pen, the drawing-compasses, the T-square, the French curve, and so on.

B: Right. At present the architectural drawings are mainly finished by the computer AutoCAD software, the advantages of which are self-evident in contrast to the manual drawing.

B: AutoCAD is an automated computer-aided design software developed by the American Autodesk Corporation for two-dimensional and three-dimensional design and graphing.

B: Of course not. If necessary, you can give me a call, and I will do my best to

help you.
2. Read and interpret the following passage.

建筑图纸

建筑图纸有许多种，例如：平面图、立面图、剖面图、平面布置图、鸟瞰图、仰视图、标准图、施工图……。图纸在建筑施工中起着至关重要的作用。因此，图纸被视为施工的准则和指南，也就是说，施工就是把设计转化为现实。

MODULE 9: Construction Tendering(模块九：建筑招投标)

1. Complete the following dialogue in English.

B: Good afternoon! Nice meeting you too. Firstly, I would like to congratulate that after our examination of your prequalification your company has been accepted to enter the stage for tendering of the Da Long power station project.

B: Certainly not! It belongs to our commercial secrets.

B: Now let us return to the tender document. You see there are so many volumes. Volume 1 is the contract conditions worked out on the basis of FIDIC, which is fair to both contractor and client. We hope you will agree with these conditions.

B: OK. Let's go on to the tender document. Volume 2 is the bill of quantities, in which there are 18 sections with 989 items of rates.

B: This is a rate-based contract which means the total amount of the contract will depend on the actual quantities performed by the contractor. As the structure of the power plant is quite complicated and quantities of the works involve a great deal, there must be some changes during the construction.

B: Volume 3 is the scope of works. You should provide the detailed construction schedules for each building in accordance with our general guiding schedule shown in this volume.

B: No, you can't. The key dates for the most important part of the works are fixed, and there is no leeway to adjust. There are penalties in different grades for the liquidated damages caused by the delay of the key dates.

B: Volume 4 and 5 are the technical specifications. As the power station is designed by a British engineering company, the British standard is adopted for all the works. In these two volumes there is a list of British standard used in the project.

B: Volume 6 is the quality assurance. For this project there are 3 grades of quality assurance defined.

B: The first grade QA1 applied in the structures is directly connected with the power generating such as the boiler frame, etc.; the second grade QA2 is applied to the structures which play an important role in the power plant such as the main power building, etc.; the third grade is QANC which is the same as the structures of the normal civil works.

B: Volume 7 is the drawings. All the drawings are stamped by "for Tender Use Only". In case you win the tender for the project, you will be issued the drawings stamped by "for Construction Use Only".

B: That depends on the fulfilling degrees of Volume 8 of the bidding document. If there is no strong competitive power, you will not obtain the drawings stamped by " for Construction Use Only".

B: Volume 8 is the bidding document which includes letter of agreement, construction method statement, quality and safety programs and bill of quantities.

B: We will make our decision in accordance with our comprehensive analysis and judgment to your tender document. We hope you will do your best to fulfil all the parts of the tender document and hand over to us before 12 o'clock p.m. on 30 calender days later from today.

2. Read and interpret the following passage.

发函投标

敬启者：
　　我们研究了贵方筹建处提供的法定方式和条件，现随函附上在塞百路兴建泰来宾馆的标书，并有信心能中标。

谨上

附件：如文

MODULE 10　Construction Contract(模块十　建筑合同)

1. Complete the following dialogue in English.

    B: Right. This contract is made out in two originals, and each is written in both Chinese and English languages, bearing the same legal status. The two originals are separately held by each party.

    B: Yes. The contract includes basically all we have agreed upon during the negotiation. This is a copy of the contract. Would you please read it again before signing?

    B: Good. If any problems arise in the work, we will deal with them at any time.

    A: OK. But I think we'd better add one sentence into the contract: if one side fails to meet the contractual conditions, the other side has the right to terminate the contract.

    A: Some main points, upon mutual agreement, can be included in the supplementary document of the contract.

    B: We will strictly abide by the contract, guarantee high quality, have close coordination and increase friendship.

2. Read and interpret the following passage.

承建友谊宾馆合同

　　华夏旅行社(以下简称甲方)和天山建筑总公司(以下简称乙方)就承建友谊宾馆一事订立合同。双方同意下列事项：

　　1. 甲方委托乙方承建一座宾馆，其设计图纸由甲方提供。

　　2. 双方同意承建费用定为 600 万美元整。甲方在合同签订后 10 天内支付给乙方 30% 的承建费，其余部分应在宾馆建成后 2 周之内全部付清。

3. 承建宾馆的所有建筑材料由甲方提供,并且必须符合一致同意的标准和规格。

4. 该宾馆限定在本合同签订后 12 个月内建成。1995 年 10 月 1 日交工。

5. 所承建的宾馆保证 50 年不倒不漏,如果出现倒漏现象,应由乙方负责免费修理。

6. 本合同书于 1994 年 10 月 1 日在伦敦签订,共 2 份,每份均用中文和英文写成,两种文本具有同等的法律效力。

  杨明   大卫·史密斯

  (签名)   (签名)

华夏旅行社代表   天山建筑总公司代表

附件略

MODULE 11　Construction Laws and Regulations(模块十一　建筑法律法规)

1. Complete the following dialogue in English.

 B: Before the start of construction projects, construction units shall, in accordance with the relevant provisions of the State, apply to the competent construction administrative departments under the prefecture-county governments or above for construction licenses.

 B: No, except for small projects below the threshold value set by the competent construction administrative department under the State Council. And construction projects which have obtained approval of work start reports in accordance with the power limits and procedure stipulated by the State Council are no longer required to apply for construction licenses.

 B: The following conditions are required for the application of construction licenses: (1) Having gone through the approval formalities for construction project land use; (2) Constructing enterprises for the projects have been chosen; (3) Working drawings and technical data are available to meet the need of construction; (4) Specific measures are available for ensuring the quality and security of construction; (5) Funds of construction are available.

 B: Construction projects within urban planned districts should obtain licenses of planning.

 B: Yes, where demolition and relocation are necessary, the progress of demolition and relocation should comply with the requirements of construction.

 B: The competent construction administrative departments shall issue construction licenses to qualified applicants within 15 days from the date of receipt of applications.

 B: Units in charge of construction should start to build the projects within three months since obtaining construction licenses.

 B: If the work cannot start on schedule, applications should be filed to the license issuing agencies for delay, which shall only be permitted twice in maximum for each case, each permission of delay covering a maximum period of three months. In cases of those projects that neither start on schedule nor apply for delay or exceed the period of permitted delay, the validity of the working licenses automatically expires.

B: The constructing units should report to the license issuing agencies within one month from the stoppage of construction and should also well maintain and manage the construction projects in accordance with provisions.

B: Yes, of course. Before the resumption of work on construction projects which have stopped for over one year, units in charge of construction shall apply to the license issuing agencies for verification of their working licenses.

2. Read and interpret the following passage.

施工准备阶段分为工程建设项目报建、委托建设监理、招标投标、施工合同签订;施工阶段分为建设工程施工许可证领取、施工;竣工阶段分为竣工验收及期内保修。

工程建设项目报建表示项目前期工作结束,施工准备阶段开始;取得工程建设项目施工许可证表示施工准备阶段结束,施工阶段开始;竣工验收表示施工阶段结束,竣工阶段开始;保修期限届满,全部工程建设项目实施阶段程序结束。

MODULE 12　Construction Testing(模块十二　建筑试验)

1. Complete the following dialogue in English.

    B: At least ten piling tests till now.

    B: The most important solution is that the maximum penetration to the last 3 groups with each 10 nos hammering and the bottom level of the piling can be fixed according to the designed loading capacity of the piles.

    B: In accordance with the specification, the vertical error cannot be more than 0.5% of the pile length after the driving operation.

    B: No, you can't. The first several hammerings must be in low height to fix the piles in stable position, after that, the hammer can be lifted to its full height.

    B: No, it is not allowed to drive piles of this size by such a heavy hammer.

    B: Because 350mm * 350mm piles cannot stand a stroke of more than 2,000 kn (kilogram newtons). But the hammer of 8 tons will produce stroke force of more than 3,500 kn.

    B: We should carry out the strength variation test to the piles to make sure that the piles are driven in good situation.

2. Read and interpret the following passage.

三种现代打桩方法

(1) 打入桩:将预制桩打入基岩中,就可以提供坚固的基座。

(2) 沉管灌注桩:用振动锤将钢管打入地下后,在钢管里放入钢筋,浇完混凝土后再把钢管拔出。

(3) 钻孔灌注桩:先进行钻孔再把混凝土直接灌入桩孔中。

MODULE 13　Construction Surveying(模块十三　建筑测量)

1. Complete the following dialogue in English.

    B: According to the dictionary, surveying is defined as the art of making measurements for the relative positions of the natural and man-made features on the earth's surface.

B: In practice, the term "surveying" is often used to refer to those operations dealing with the making of plans, namely, the works in the two dimensions which form the horizontal place.

B: It is to plot these measurements to a map, plan or section by some suitable scale.

B: The term "leveling" covers work in the third dimension, namely the dimension normal to the horizontal, thus we have leveling and surveying.

B: Surveying refers to operations connected with representation of ground features in a plan; while leveling refers to operations connected with representation of relative difference in altitude between various points on the earth's surface.

B: A surveyor's work is usually divided into four parts: the first part is to make and record measurements in the field; the second part is to make the necessary calculations so as to determine locations, areas and volumes; the third part is to plot these measurements and draw a map; the last part is to set stakes to delineate boundaries or to guide construction works.

2. Read and interpret the following passage.

水 准 仪

严格地说，水准仪主要是为提供一条水平视线而设计的一种仪器，这条视线是由具备物镜、调焦装置、十字丝环和目镜这些常规部件组成的望远镜所决定的。在使用中，望远镜应能绕竖轴旋转，使它能瞄准任何方向。

目前所使用的水准仪可归纳为定镜水准仪、自动安平水准仪和微倾水准仪等三种。

MODULE 14 Construction Plan(模块十四　施工计划)

1. Complete the following dialogue in English.

B: Construction operations, according to different specialized fields, can be generally classified into preparation of the project site, earth moving, foundation treatment, steel erection, concrete placement, asphalt paving, electrical and mechanical installations, etc.

B: Procedures for each of these fields are generally the same, but the relative importance of each field is not the same in all cases.

B: Preparation of the project site consists of the removal and clearing of all surface structures and the growth from the site of the proposed structure.

B: Earth moving includes the excavation and placement of the earth fill.

B: Excavation usually follows the preparation of the project site. And it generally starts with the separate stripping of the organic topsoil, which is the first point to be especially emphasized.

B: Doing this can prevent the contamination of the inorganic materials which are below the topsoil and may be required for fill. Besides, the topsoil can be later reused for landscaping around the new structure.

B: The second emphasized point is that a dry excavation area is required for an effective excavation on land. That is because many soils are unstable when wet and cannot support the excavating and hauling equipment.

B: After the placement of the earth fill, it is almost always compacted to prevent subsequent settlement, which is the thrid point to be particularly stressed.

B: When the subsurface investigation reveals the structural defects in the foundation area to be used for a structure, the foundation must be strengthened.

B: Water passages, cavities, fissures, faults and other defects are filled or strengthened by grouting.

B: Grouting means the injection of the fluid mixtures under pressure, and the fluids subsequently solidify in the voids of the strata.

B: Most grouting is done with mixtures of cement and water, but some with mixtures of asphalt, cement and clay, and precipitating chemicals.

B: Concrete construction consists of several operations including forming, concrete production, placement and curing.

B: The form is made of timber or steel sections or a combination of the both, and the function is to contain and support the fluid concrete within its desired final outline until it solidifies and can support itself.

B: The concrete is placed by chuting directly from the concrete mixer, where possible, or from buckets handled by means of cranes or cableways, or it can be pumped into place by special concrete pumps.

B: The curing of exposed surfaces is required to prevent the evaporation of water for mix or to replace the moisture that does evaporate.

2. Read and interpret the following passage.

施工程序

施工程序通常根据工种不同来分类，包括现场准备、挖运土方、地基处理、钢结构安装、混凝土浇筑、沥青铺路以及电气和机械安装。每一个工种施工的程序基本相同，即使对于不同项目如建筑物、堤坝或机场等也是如此。但是，每个工种的相对重要性在各种情况下并不总是相同的。

MODULE 15　Construction Inspection(模块十五　施工检查)

1. Complete the following dialogue in English.

    A: I am an engineer in charge of safety. Your safety education is not enough, and the hidden dangers can be seen everywhere on the site.

    A: That is important, but the key is how to take measures to remove the hidden dangers effectively.

    A: Will you take me to have a look around your site?

    A: First, it is very dangerous to work on the site without a safety helmet. If some things like brick, timber are dropping down from a height, don't you be afraid of their hitting you on the head?

A: Look over there! Without taking any safety measures, it is very dangerous for the electrician to fix the bulbs and wires in the height.

A: There is no safety net round the roof where the builders are doing their work, so please tell them to stop working and come down at once.

B: Yes, it is for our safety, and we should establish the thinking of safety first.

B: Be sure. As an event bearing on human life, we will take preventive measures to guard against possible dangers.

2. Read and interpret the following passage.

焊接质量的检测

根据不同的构件和设计要求我们有很多检测焊接质量的方式。一般来说我们特别注意以下几个方面：

首先，在焊接作业前我们要进行检测。这种检测包括检查焊接材料和电焊条，检查必须做的工艺评定，制定焊接细则、程序，以及焊工的操作技巧等。

第二个方面是用肉眼或放大镜（扩大20倍）检查焊缝表面以找出表面瑕疵。发现不符合规范的焊缝必须凿除重焊。

对于焊缝内部的检查，我们通常采用超声波检测法、X射线或γ射线检测法、放大镜检测法或色彩检测法。

MODULE 16　Building Installation（模块十六　建筑安装）

1. Complete the following dialogue in English.

B: Generally speaking, we start to fix the steel structures in the regular sequence, from low to high, from column to beam, from main beam to secondary beam, and from center to the outer sides.

B: You are just flattering me. I am far from being experienced, but I have done the work of fixing steel structures for more than ten years.

B: Of course. During the fixing, the most important is to arrange reasonable sequences and every fixing step should also be cared at the same time.

B: Yes. Sometimes different sequences should be adopted depending on the specific conditions. And each component should be fixed by its own sequence.

B: OK. To ensure no deformation of the column, it is out of question to use two hydraulic cranes for lifting operations.

B: After the steel column is lifted, we usually adopt two theodolites to check up its verticality and horizontal position from two different directions.

B: We use moored cables and embedded bolts to keep it in accurate position.

B: Yes. After the verticality is within the specified scope, we will fix the wedging plate at once and tight the bolts.

B: No. We always screw all the high strength bolts at least twice so as to guarantee the quality.

B: For the sake of high quality. The bolts are screwed by half torque force for the first time.

B: After all bolts are screwed once, the second screwing can be done, and the error of torque force must be controlled within 5%.

2. Read and interpret the following passage.

电气监理人员

电气监理人员检查电气系统和设备的安装,以保证它们功能正常,符合电气规范和标准。他们到现场检查新的和已有的声控和安全系统、配线、照明、电动装置和发电设备。他们还要检查用于供热与空调系统的配线、仪器和其他组成部分的安装。

MODULE 17　Building Decoration(模块十七　建筑装饰)

1. Complete the following dialogue in English.

B: Can you show me which part of the works you are not satisfied with?

B: Let me see. The materials seem to be of the same quality as the samples we have submitted.

A: The grades of the timber seem of no difference, but the moisture content is much higher than the specification of being no less than 10% and no more than 20%.

A: Please remember that if any joinery works shrink, warp, wind, or show any other defects within the maintenance period and are condemned by the engineer, they shall be removed and redecorated at your own expenses until the joinery works are qualified.

A: Now I'd like to see the plastering and the paving works. Where do you bring the sand for the works? Is the sand source close to the sea?

B: We use the crushed granite fines for backing coat and pointing in all external ceramic tile, quarry tile, glass mosaic and so on.

B: Yes, we will. We have trained our workers to strictly follow the work procedures in every step.

B: First of all, the concrete sub-floors should be well swept and washed before the tiling is laid and the areas should be set out with tiles before bedding to avoid unnecessary cuttings.

B: Yes. The quarry tiles should be thoroughly soaked in the water and then be laid in the stretcher bond pattern, with special attention paid to the paving of the expansion joints, corner fittings, round edge tiles, etc.

B: After the paving is finished, the floor will be covered with heavy polythene sheet or tarpaulins and well lapped at edges. And it will be left to set without disturbing for not less than seven days.

2. Read and interpret the following passage.

陶 瓷 砖

陶瓷砖分为墙砖和地砖,这种材料具有坚固耐用,而色彩鲜艳、易于清洗、防火、抗水、耐磨、耐腐蚀等诸多优点。现在还有双色立体感釉面砖、彩釉地砖等。陶瓷砖现被广泛应用于现代建筑的装饰工程。

MODULE 18　Building Cost(模块十八　建筑造价)

1. Complete the following dialogue in English.

    B: To monitor the project during the construction process, a control estimate is derived from available information to establish the budget estimate for financing, the budgeted cost after contracting but prior to construction, and the estimated cost of the completed parts in the construction process.

    B: Yes, you are right. For the owner, a budget estimate must be adopted early enough for planning long term financing of the facility.

    B: Yes. A revised estimated cost is necessary either because of the order changes initiated by the owner or due to the unexpected cost overruns or savings.

    B: For the contractor, the bid estimate is usually regarded as the budget estimate, which will be used for controlling investment as well as for planning construction funds.

    B: Yes. The purpose of updating the budgeted cost periodically is to reflect the completed estimated cost as well as to ensure adequate cash flows for the completion of the project.

2. Read and interpret the following passage.

投标报价

对于承包人,为竞标或谈判而递交给业主的投标报价的组成有包括现场管理费用在内的直接施工成本,加上包含常规企业管理费用和利润在内的上涨幅度。投标报价中的直接施工成本通常结合下述方法而得出:转包商报价单、工程量清单和施工程序。

MODULE 19　Claims of Construction Works(模块十九　工程索赔)

1. Complete the following dialogue in English.

    A: Up to now we have received 145 nos. of claims from you. But it is hard to convince us that there are no reasons for most of your claims.

    A: As long as it is mentioned in the conditions of the contract, we will not ignore your right to claim in accordance with the contract. But it should be raised on the basis of facts and solved through certain procedures.

    A: OK, now please make your explanations to these claims. After understanding your reasons for the claims, then the claims, which we consider are reasonable and effective, will be submitted to the board of directors, who will make the final decisions.

    B: Generally speaking, within the total 145 nos. of claims, we can see most items belong to the technical issues, such as the delay of issuing construction drawings, the delay of reply to the technical clarification request, the non-conformance between drawing and specification, and so on.

    B: According to our statistical results, there are 85 items that belong to the technical issues, 50 items belonging to the coordination between the client and the contractor.

    B: There are 4 items belonging to the financial problems, in which 2 items belong to the delay of progress payment and the other 2 items belong to the fluctuation of exchange rates between US dollars and the local currency. The remaining 6 items belong to "others".

B: Those items, which cannot be catalogued into the above areas, are put in "others". For instance, we are instructed to clean the site thoroughly because of the government officials' visit of the site. As you know, this particular cleaning will certainly increase the cost.

2. Read and interpret the following passages.

(1) 在国际工程施工承包中，有许多因素可导致承包商向业主索赔，其中有对合同文件的不同的理解；业主颁发图纸与指示的拖延；现场条件的变化以及不可抗力事件。

(2) The contract is the base of the construction claim, which expressly or impliedly stipulates under what conditions the contractor can have the right to file a claim and what the claim procedure is. Therefore, to seriously study and master the requirements of the contract terms and conditions, and to carefully manage all correspondence and site materials in construction constitute the foundation of successful claims.

MODULE 20 Acceptance of Construction Works(模块二十　工程验收)

1. Complete the following dialogue in English.

B: I think it is too early to issue the certificate.

B: According to the statistical statements, you have only finished 90% of the whole works.

B: I suggest that you try your best to finish all the works within 20 days. After the acceptance of a further inspection to the whole works, we will issue you the certificate.

A: You mean the working drawings? We will have a thorough collection of all the drawings within 5 days.

A: No problem. Usually some defects will be found during the inspections, and we will repair them well within a period of time.

A: Surely. You must be satisfied with our works. By the way, by whom do you set up jointly an inspection group?

B: The inspection group should be set up by the employer, the contractor and representatives from relevant government departments.

B: The group will inspect all the works within the scope of the contract in the following 10 days, and after the inspection, they will issue a report for the results.

2. Read and interpret the following passages.

(1) 工程每一阶段完工后，由甲、乙双方人员组成验收小组，按照工程设计要求和规范进行验收。在验收过程中，如发现施工不符合设计要求，应由乙方采取必要补救措施，使之达到图纸设计的质量标准，但所产生的费用应由乙方承担。工程保修期应为每阶段的竣工移交书签字之日起一年。在此期间，如发现因施工原因造成的质量问题，应由乙方无偿修复，直到达到施工图的标准。

(2) When the works have reached substantial or practical completion, it is very important for the contractor to organize the acceptance inspection and test. Because once the works have been taken over to the owner, the responsibility for the care of the works is shifted from the contractor to the owner, and the contractor will get the corresponding rights and benefits. Due to differences in the nature of the works and in the types of the contracts, the taking-over procedures are also different, but roughly as follows:

① The contractor will inform the owner of the substantial completion of the works, and submit a taking-over plan as is required by the owner. The plan should include a timetable for the inspection and test, various documents submitted to the owner when completion, some outstanding minor works, etc.

② To make various recording forms for the acceptance inspection and test.

③ To draw up the completion report, which should be the fair evaluations of the works. The report should state the completion date of the works, the starting date of the maintenance, and the outstanding work and some minor defects the contractor should do during the maintenance period.

④ To issue the taking-over certificate. Once the contractor has received the taking-over certificate, he should according to the contract urge the owner to release the retention money and organize the maintenance works within the maintenance period.

APPENDIX Ⅲ　Chinese Translation of SC
附录3　情景对话中文译文

MODULE 1　Architectural Majors and Courses(模块一　建筑专业和课程)

海伦：你是一名学生，对吗？
小李：对，不过你是怎么知道的？
海伦：我是从你的言语和外表看出来的，因为你戴着一副眼镜，温文尔雅。
小李：您可真有眼力，就连我做什么的都能看出来。
海伦：是吗？请告诉我你学的是什么专业好吗？
小李：工业与民用建筑。
海伦：你认为你的专业怎么样？
小李：我认为挺好！我很喜欢。
海伦：为什么如此喜欢，年轻人？
小李：正如您所知，从古到今所有的建筑物都是由勤劳而又聪明的建筑者们建立起来的，他们真伟大！所以我立志学建筑，毕业后就要成为一名建筑者，也能亲手建起高楼大厦。
海伦：建成广厦千万栋，兴邦立国为人民。你的梦想一定能实现，年轻人。我知道你喜爱你的专业，我也相信你一定是你们学校的好学生，更希望你成为一名造福于民的建设者。
小李：多谢你的鼓励。我一定珍惜这一良机，刻苦学习，实现梦想。
海伦：我很高兴听到你这样说。你能告诉我，你的专业设有多少门课程？
小李：我想有10多门吧。例如，建筑材料、房屋建筑学、施工技术、施工组织、力学等多门必修课程，英语和政治经济学等属于基础课。
海伦：这么多课程。老师们怎样讲授？
小李：由浅入深、由易到难地认真讲解书本知识，并用通俗易懂的语言解释深奥的理论。
海伦：这就是所谓的循序渐进式教学。顺便问一下，你们学校的教学设施怎样？
小李：很好。建筑学的基本理论知识主要是在教室内讲授，而操作技能则是在现代化的建筑实验室以及拥有合作关系的建筑工地上予以训练和实践。
海伦：对高职院校而言，理论联系实际和对口实习是一种有效和实用的教学方法。你们的学校大吗？
小李：不是很大。
海伦：知道了。你能带我看看你们学校吗？
小李：好啊，请这边走！
海伦：非常感谢。

MODULE 2　Architectural Job Interview（模块二　建筑求职面试）

经理：上午好！请坐！
张洁：上午好，先生！谢谢！
经理：首先，我想了解一下你建筑方面的资格条件，你能给我讲讲吗？
张洁：好的。作为土木工程专业的五年制学生，我将于今年7月从江苏城市职业学院毕业。在这5年时间里，我收获颇多。英语方面，我拿到了高等学校英语应用能力考试的A级，全国英语等级考试的3级以及全国大学英语等级考试的4级证书。此外，我还考取了造价工程师、建造师等职业资格证书。
经理：非常好。你能把你的证书给我看一下吗？
张洁：当然可以！这正是我所想的，请看吧。
经理：我看一看。我们集团公司是中国建筑企业100强，世界建筑企业500强。因目前海内外市场业务的发展壮大，我们需要扩大工程技术人员队伍。你想从事这种职业的哪一岗位？
张洁：我想成为一名土木工程师。
经理：你为什么应聘我们公司的这个岗位呢？
张洁：首先，土木工程师是我梦寐以求的职业，它能使我学有所用；其次，贵公司离我家很近，我在贵公司上班很方便。
经理：我明白你的意思。此次招聘我们看中的是技术能力和实操技能。许多大学毕业生持有职业资格证书，但是他们能把书本知识转化为实际能力吗？对此，你是怎么看的？
张洁：作为职业院校的工科学生，在前三年里，我们主要学习理论知识，以便打下坚实基础。但是，到了后两年，我们的学习重心从理论转向了实践。后两年的每个学期我们都要做一些工程方面的实践练习。
经理：你能举个例子吗？
张洁：可以。在上学期，我绘制了许多现代建筑方面的技术图纸。学期期末时，我就我所绘制的最好的图纸向大家做了一场非常精彩的展示。
经理：我知道了，很有抱负。今天我们就谈到这儿吧。我们决定后，我会尽快把结果告诉你的。
张洁：谢谢。我期待着您的好消息。

MODULE 3　Architectural Workers（模块三　建筑工程人员）

怀特：喂，年轻人，你在这家建筑工地工作，不是吗？
林强：是的，先生，我毕业于一所建筑技术学院。
怀特：可否介意告诉我你在建筑工地上是做什么工作的？
林强：当然不介意，我是一名电工，负责这家工地的电气安装工作。
怀特：啊！一名电工，不错，你的工作关系到千家万户的用电安全，所以容不得半点疏忽，我说的对吗？
林强：是啊，责任重于泰山。

怀特：没错。我想知道那边的那位女工是谁？
林强：她是我们公司的一名焊工兼技师。
怀特：我知道啦。她的技术一定很棒，是吧？
林强：是的，这是无可置疑的。她在公司是一流的焊工，无人可比。去年，她还获得了全国"三八红旗手"称号。
怀特：对于这样一位年轻女孩来讲，确实了不起！那一帮男男女女也是你的工友，对吗？
林强：是啊！他们都是刚招聘来的安装工，有管道工、钳工、铆工、通风工等工种。
怀特：他们都很年轻，有活力。站在他们前面的那位长者是谁？
林强：他是我们的工地主任，王主任。
怀特：他在那里干什么？
林强：他在给他们上安全课。需要我把他介绍给您吗？
怀特：那是当然的，谢谢你。
老王：您好。
怀特：您好，王主任。
老王：请问先生想了解哪方面的情况？
怀特：我对你们工地的招聘和用工很感兴趣。你知道，这是一个超大工地，而且施工紧张有序，捷报频传。我想知道这里有多少建筑施工人员。
老王：有1 000多人，其中约10%是工程技术和管理人员。
怀特：现在有哪些工种？
老王：有瓦工、木工和粉刷工。由于主体工程即将结束，一些土建工人即将离开此地，而安装工和装饰工很快就要进驻工地。
怀特：我知道啦。也许你们有足够的技术工人来完成你们的建设任务。不过你们怎么没有考虑培训一些当地人呢？
老王：好主意。我们在施工高峰期间会招聘几百名当地人。
怀特：雇佣当地人参与施工不仅解决了他们的就业问题，而且加快了你们的施工进度。
老王：这是件两全其美的好事。
怀特：是件好事。但怎样保证施工质量不受影响呢？
老王：根据不同施工阶段的要求，我们会尽早分类培训他们的工作技能，提高他们的质量和安全意识。
怀特：对呀！这样做会使当地工人极大地帮助你们提高工作效率，确保你们的施工如期完成。
老王：对啊，你说得对。

MODULE 4　Construction Enterprises（模块四　建筑施工企业）

布朗：先生，你能给我简单地介绍一下土木建筑工程总公司吗？
张寅：作为土木建筑工程总公司的总经理，我很乐意给您介绍。
布朗：土木建筑工程总公司是国有还是私有？
张寅：是一家国有企业，已创建了二十多年，主要承包海外各种工业与民用建筑工程施工并提供劳务。

布朗：贵公司历史悠久，名扬海内外。那贵公司目前拥有多少注册资金呢？
张寅：海外经营注册资金5亿美元。
布朗：拥有如此雄厚的资金，贵公司确实是一家大型的实力派企业。
张寅：那是无可置疑的，先生。
布朗：我想知道贵公司有多少名职工？
张寅：60多万名。
布朗：公司的配置结构怎样？
张寅：相当不错。其中拥有1 000多名高级工程师、高级经济师和各类专家，5 000名工程师、经济师以及相关的专业管理人才。
布朗：那你们的技术工人怎样？
张寅：我们拥有从事土建、安装、机械、装饰、实验、测量与维修的各种技术工人。
布朗：他们都具有较高的施工技能吗？
张寅：是的，工人们大都较好地掌握了中国传统的以及世界一流的施工技术。
布朗：有这么多能工巧匠和优秀人才，我敢打赌，贵公司在世界上一定很有竞争力。
张寅：对，这是不争的事实。
布朗：那贵公司有多少个施工公司和技术服务单位？
张寅：拥有40个施工公司和16个技术服务单位，主要参加国际投标与承包成套工程项目。
布朗：好极了！贵公司一定承建了世界上许多国家的各种建筑工程，对吗？
张寅：那当然啦！请看这些画册上的各式各样的建筑，全都是我们公司近年来承建的。
布朗：我来看看吧！
张寅：你觉得怎么样？漂亮吗？
布朗：啊，好极了！漂亮！土木建筑工程总公司确实名不虚传。

MODULE 5　Kinds of Buildings（模块五　建筑物类型）

皮特：劳驾，你能告诉我在这里你们要建什么楼房？
李雅：要建一栋多层楼房。
皮特：多层楼房？这栋楼有多少层？
李雅：有5层左右。
皮特：多层楼房是什么意思？高层建筑和低层建筑有什么不同？
李雅：根据《民用建筑设计通则》(GB 50352-2005)，10层（包括10层）以上的为高层建筑，7~9层为中高层，4~6层为多层，不足4层（1~3层）的为低层建筑。
皮特：哦，我明白了。这种分类只限于住宅建筑，那公共建筑呢？
李雅：对公共建筑而言，24米以下为单层或多层，大于24米为高层，100米以上的则称之为超高层。
皮特：我清楚了。那在建的这栋楼预期高度是多少？
李雅：可能是在20米以上，但在24米以下。
皮特：那这栋楼有什么用途呢？

李雅：有几层作为商业用，剩下的则用作住宅。
皮特：哪几层作为商业店铺？
李雅：低层，也就是一层和二层。
皮特：你为什么这样安排呢？
李雅：因为这两层隔墙少，大房间常用作办公室和店铺。
皮特：其他楼层的房间呢？
李雅：其他楼层的房间则有很多隔墙，常用作卧室、客厅、浴室等。
皮特：对的。这栋建筑物属于中式建筑还是西式建筑？
李雅：我想它属于西式建筑，而有大屋顶的通常属于中式或古代建筑。
皮特：因此，现代建筑和古代建筑的区别就是是否有大屋顶，对吗？
李雅：我认为应该是。不过现代建筑和古代建筑在用料、结构等方面还有许多其他不同之处。
皮特：我还是不很清楚，请给我举几个古代建筑的例子好吗？
李雅：好的。如北京的紫禁城（也称之为故宫），西安的钟鼓楼都是古代建筑的突出实例。
皮特：再举几个现代建筑的实例可以吗？
李雅：举不胜举，比如北京的人民大会堂，上海的东方明珠都属于现代建筑。
皮特：我明白了。谢谢你详细的解释。
李雅：不客气。

MODULE 6 Building Materials（模块六 建筑材料）

马克：我们好久没见了，李女士。我能为你做些什么吗？
李璐：好久不见！我来这里是想买些建材。
马克：你打算买什么建材呢？
李璐：主要是些普通材料，像水泥、钢筋、木材等。你能告诉我目前的市价吗？
马克：哦，让我看一看。水泥每公斤1美元，钢筋每吨500美元，木材每立方米650美元……
李璐：能给我一份价目单看看吗？
马克：好的，给你。我们店里的建材不贵，但质量上乘，你可以放心。
李璐：老实说，现在的建材价格比1年以前要贵多了。对于像我这样的老主顾有优惠吗？
马克：给你说实话，最近建筑材料的价格一直在飞涨，这使得我们很难有好的利润。但是，对于像您这样的老主顾，我们可以根据购货量的大小提供不同程度的折扣。
李璐：我想知道，购买200吨水泥，1 000吨钢筋和1 000立方米木材，你能给我的最大优惠是多少？
马克：考虑到这三种建筑材料的购买量，我们可以给你10%的折扣。
李璐：10%？太低了！你能想办法把折扣提到20%吗？
马克：什么？你想让我破产？你不能让我做如此大的降价。

李璐：哦，眼前有如此大的一笔订单，你没必要担心。请好好想想，我的老朋友。
马克：考虑到我们长期的生意关系，我才给你10%折扣。你也知道，我们做生意是建立在平等互利的基础上的。此外，建筑材料的价格有上涨趋势，其市场需求巨大。
李璐：我知道目前的市场行情。不管怎样，让我们折中一下，15%怎样？
马克：你真是一位了不起的女商人！好吧，我同意给你15%的折扣。
李璐：成交！请说话算数，要按时发货！
马克：请放心。我们会尽最大努力保证供货，并运送到工地，不会误事的。
李璐：谢谢！

MODULE 7 Building Machinery（模块七 建筑机械）

詹姆斯：这是机械化的建筑工地吗，李女士？
李琴：是的，你需要帮助吗？
詹姆斯：是的。工地上有这么多的机器，就像是建筑机械的展览。我想知道工地上的每道工序都完全是机械作业吗？
李琴：哦，对的。我猜你一定是第一次来机械化的建筑工地吧。
詹姆斯：你说的没错。尽管我以前听说过，但从未亲眼见过。今天能够大开眼界，我真的是很幸运。
李琴：从过去繁重的手工操作到今天的机械化施工，建筑业经历了巨大的变化。
詹姆斯：所以你们也在与时俱进啊。能告诉我你的工地上都有什么建筑机械吗？
李琴：很高兴回答你的问题。工地上有起重机、输送机、混凝土机械、土石方机械等。
詹姆斯：这么多。你在建筑工地上做什么工作呢？
李琴：我是一名翻斗车司机。
詹姆斯：很好。你有驾驶执照吗？
李琴：当然有了。工地上的每个机械工必须持证上岗。
詹姆斯：意思就是说你是通过竞争上岗的，对吗？
李琴：你说得对。首先，我们必须要接受至少1年的训练，然后参加机械操作规程的严格测试。只有通过考试，我们才能拿到操作机械的执照。
詹姆斯：这些规定和我们国家一样严格。顺便问一下，除了翻斗车，你还会操作其他机械吗？
李琴：是的，我还可以操作许多其他机械，比如说，混凝土搅拌车、提升机等。
詹姆斯：你真是一个万能的机械手。让我看一看你是如何驾驶翻斗车的，可以吗？
李琴：万能机械手不敢当。不过我很高兴展示一下我驾驶翻斗车的技术。
詹姆斯：嘿，真了不起！操作很熟练，技术很过硬。不过我建议你在操作机械之前必须仔细检查机械的性能；开车时要集中精力，不可胡思乱想。
李琴：多谢。我不会忘记的，今后一定按照你说的做。

MODULE 8 Architectural Drawings（模块八 建筑图纸）

乔丹：嗨，李工，能帮我个忙吗？
李灿：愿为您效劳。

乔丹：我不清楚配电控制板安装的具体位置，可以在墙上给我画出来吗？
李灿：要根据图纸的尺寸来画。图纸在哪里？
乔丹：这就是，李工。
李灿：抱歉，图纸拿错了。
乔丹：有问题吗？
李灿：这是一张平面图，而我需要的是立面图，上面清楚地标有配电控制板的位置，现在可以帮我拿来吗？
乔丹：好的，给你。
李灿：谢谢。（过了一会儿）看，配电控制板就在靠近两道墙角处。
乔丹：你观察得很仔细，我非常佩服你。
李灿：我相信如果你处在我的位置，你也会这样做。
乔丹：那是肯定的。但配电控制板距离地面有多高？
李灿：1.5米高。
乔丹：你是怎么知道具体尺寸的？
李灿：因为你第二次给我的是一张标有尺寸的图纸。如果你不相信的话，你可以拿把比例尺亲自量一下。
乔丹：事实上没有这个必要了。看来识图并认真钻研图纸是搞好施工的前提，不是吗？
李灿：绝对是这样。因为每一张图纸都是精心设计出来的，图纸上的尺寸和数据也是精确计算出来的，所以我们应该把图纸看做我们施工的指南和准则。
乔丹：对，也就是说，施工就是把设计变成现实。
李灿：太对了。看上去你不是很擅长识图啊。
乔丹：哦，一般般了。
李灿：我个人认为你应该努力识好图。只有这样才能做好你的本职工作。你难道不这样认为吗？
乔丹：当然。我会听从您的建议，加倍努力来补习建筑制图方面的知识。
李灿：若是以后的工作和学习上遇到了建筑图纸方面的问题，请只管给我打电话，我会尽最大努力来帮你的。
乔丹：你太好啦！谢谢你。
李灿：不客气。能够做一些对你有益的事，我也倍感荣幸。

MODULE 9　Construction Tendering（模块九　建筑招投标）

乔治：吴先生，有好几家公司都参与了2010年上海世博会场馆建设的投标。难道贵公司不想参加投标吗？
吴林：我们当然想了。但是，首先我们想了解一下在投标之前我们应做哪些准备工作。
乔治：通常的做法是，你们应该把所承建的一些大工程项目的造价、工期及工程量等相关资料都寄来。
吴林：我明白了，我们会尽快寄来。此外，你能告诉我投标委员会的一些要求吗？
乔治：好的。你们怎样确定工程项目的工程量？

吴林：根据已经积累的相关资料来确定。何时能给我们公司办理投标注册手续？
乔治：我认为等我们收到你们寄来的相关资料后会尽快办理的。
吴林：什么时候是投标的截止日期？
乔治：开标前10天。
吴林：那何时计划开标？
乔治：2007年1月1日。
吴林：我记住了。你看我们成功的可能性有多大？
乔治：很难说，这要取决于你们的标书和诚意。你们在这一方面富有经验，实力很强，因此，我认为你们中标的几率很高。
吴林：但愿如此。
乔治：祝你及贵公司好运，能够中标。
吴林：多谢。我们肯定会抓住机遇的。

MODULE 10　Construction Contract（模块十　建筑合同）

格林先生：今天我们讨论一下合同条件，好吗？
王先生：有机会讨论合同条件太好了。我们以为合同条件已经定下，不容讨论。
格林先生：没有，现在敞开谈。首先，我想说明一下该合同条件是符合FIDIC基本原则的。
王先生：我们非常赞成采用FIDIC，因为它对业主和承包商都是比较公平的。
格林先生：我想你们一定仔细研究过这些特殊条件了，现在可以提出你们的意见。
王先生：坦率地讲，如果你们不介意的话，我们对这个合同条件确实有不同的看法。首先，在条款10中，15％的履约担保金比通常情况要高，因此我想知道能否将其调整为10％。
格林先生：我们会考虑你们对此条款的提议。
王先生：对于条款41，我们认为承包商在签订合同后的10天内必须开工有点紧。
格林先生：我们并不这样认为。在10天内调遣人员和施工设备进场开始施工已足够。对工期如此紧张的施工项目，我们不能允许延长进场时间。
王先生：既然这样，我们撤回对此条款的建议。在条款47中，违约罚金的数目远远高于通常水平，因此我们不能同意。
格林先生：你能告诉我通常是多少吗？
王先生：例如，去年我们完成了一项同样的工程。而违约罚金的支付只有这个数目的一半。
格林先生：该工程的规模有多大？我推测也许只有本工程的一半。因为这样庞大工程的任何延期对业主来说都是非常巨大的损失，所以采用高额的违约罚金是绝对有必要的。对其他的条款还有意见吗？
王先生：第61条款提到工程师将根据图纸提供时间表中规定的工程进度提供所有的图纸。问题是当图纸提供推迟确实发生了，我们该怎么办？
格林先生：我们将尽力不让其发生。
王先生：因此，我们建议加上1条副条款，若承包商因图纸提供延误受到损失，他有权得到合同工期的顺延及因赶工而增加费用的补偿金。

格林先生：我们原则上同意你的提议。但是工程的延期以及费用的增加应在与业主和承包商适当协商后由工程师决定。这一点必须加在副条款中。

王先生：好的。我们同意你对此副条款的修改。

格林先生：对合同条件还有其他的建议吗？

王先生：目前没有了。

格林先生：好的，现在让我们结束对合同条件的讨论。如果还有什么要说的，你可以在你们的信中说明，如有必要的话，我们再安排讨论。

王先生：好的。

MODULE 11　Construction Laws and Regulations（模块十一　建筑法律法规）

史密斯先生：我对中华人民共和国建筑法了解甚少，你能大略地介绍一下吗？

张先生：好的。你想了解什么，史密斯先生？

史密斯先生：建筑法总共有几部分？

张先生：总共有8章，分别是总则、建筑许可、建筑工程发包与承包、建筑工程监理、建筑安全生产管理、建筑工程质量管理、法律责任和附则。

史密斯先生：哦，我明白了。那建筑法的主要目的是什么？

张先生：制定建筑法的主要目的是为了加强对建筑活动的监督管理，维护建筑市场秩序，保证建筑工程的质量和安全，促进建筑业健康发展。因此，在中华人民共和国境内从事建筑活动，实施对建筑活动的监督管理，应当遵守本法。

史密斯先生：你能详细地解释一下此法中建筑活动指的是什么吗？

张先生：本法所称建筑活动，是指各类房屋建筑及其附属设施的建造和与其配套的线路、管道、设备的安装活动。

史密斯先生：因此，建筑活动应当确保建筑工程质量和安全，符合国家的建筑工程安全标准。我说的对吗？

张先生：很对。任何单位和个人都不得妨碍和阻挠依法进行的建筑活动。也就是说，从事建筑活动应当遵守法律、法规，不得损害社会公共利益和他人的合法权益。

史密斯先生：哪个部门应对全国的建筑活动负责？

张先生：国务院建设行政主管部门对全国的建筑活动实施统一监督管理。

史密斯先生：这部法律所体现的国家对建筑行业的总体政策是什么？

张先生：国家扶持建筑业的发展，支持建筑科学技术研究，提高房屋建筑设计水平，鼓励节约能源和保护环境，提倡采用先进技术、先进设备、先进工艺、新型建筑材料和现代管理方式。

MODULE 12　Construction Testing（模块十二　建筑试验）

欧阳：我想同你讨论一下钢筋试验相关事宜。钢筋试验的主要目的是什么？

里德里：主要目的是要搞清楚钢筋的物理特性及化学组成成分是否符合规范要求。

欧阳：你能告诉我钢筋试验的程序吗？

里德里：好的。在做钢筋试验之前，你最好要检查钢筋的外观，核对钢筋的规格型号是否符合规范要求以及钢筋表面有无坑凹、划痕或麻面缺陷。

欧阳：如果表面合格的话，还要做哪些试验？
里德里：然后我们对钢筋进行抽样试验。
欧阳：你所说的抽样试验是什么意思？它是物理试验还是化学试验？
里德里：我们接下来要做的钢筋抽样试验通常是物理试验。也就是说，我们首先从60吨钢筋中抽出6根，再从每根截取一小段，并把它们分成两组（每组三根）作为试验样品。
欧阳：接下来做什么？
里德里：其中一组做拉力试验，也就是检测钢筋的屈服点、抗拉强度以及延伸率。
欧阳：哦，我明白了。那第二组呢？
里德里：第二组将做冷弯曲试验。
欧阳：如果加工过程中发生脆断或焊接性能不良，你该怎么办？
里德里：如果那样的话，就一定要做化学成分分析或其他特殊试验来找出问题之所在。
欧阳：你说得对。现在，我想知道在什么情况下你会做冷拉处理。
里德里：在最大力度而钢筋伸展率已经超过规定的最大伸展幅度的情况下才做钢筋冷拉检测。
欧阳：在这种情况下，你们通常做些什么试验？
里德里：我们通常做钢筋机械性能的试验。根据钢筋试验结果得出钢筋的实际等级后，再决定钢筋在工程中的使用。
欧阳：我完全赞同你的做法，也基本明白了相关试验，不过你能给我举个例子吗？
里德里：哦，可以。如果试验结果表明钢筋的等级较低，那就不能按照厂家所表示的高等级来使用。
欧阳：通过你耐心和详细的讲解，我已经了解了钢筋试验与应用的关系。非常感谢。
里德里：不客气。

MODULE 13 Construction Surveying（模块十三 建筑测量）

爱迪生：听说测量有许多种，不是吗？
唐娜：是的，事实上有7种，分别是平面测量、大地测量、地形测量、路线测量、水文/河道测量、施工测量和摄影测量。
爱迪生：它们都与建筑有关吗？
唐娜：不完全是。只有三种与建筑有关，即路线测量、水文测量和施工测量。
爱迪生：你介意告诉我什么是路线测量吗？
唐娜：当然不介意。路线测量是为兴建公路、铁路、开挖河道、铺设管道和其他不闭合于起始点上的工程而进行的测量工作。
爱迪生：我很清楚了。为什么说水文测量也与建筑有关呢？
唐娜：那是因为水文测量主要与湖泊、溪流、水库、水坝等的建设工作有关。
爱迪生：作为建筑专业的学生，我对施工测量更感兴趣。你能给我讲讲吗？
唐娜：没问题。施工测量主要提供建筑物的位置和高度。
爱迪生：因此，施工区的地形测量是在建筑物定位工作中首先要解决的问题，对吗？

唐娜：是的。我们需要一些用于控制施工标桩并依据其检查施工进度的参考点。
爱迪生：你能给我解释一下如何才能做好施工测量工作吗？
唐娜：施工测量最好是在工作中把测量的基本原理同实践相结合的过程中学习，因为每项工作都有其本身的特点。
爱迪生：你说得对。在主要使用预制构件的大型建筑物放样过程中，精度是绝对必要的吗？
唐娜：那当然啦。精度是绝对必要，决不能有丝毫偏差。
爱迪生：为确保高精度的测量，测量员应注意些什么呢？
唐娜：首先，他必须保证所使用的测量工具质量高；其次，为便于校准仪器，他最好使用弹簧秤或拉力稳定的拉力架；最后是有关测量结果的，测量员应当计算各种改正数据并将其运用到所放样的距离上去。
爱迪生：上述几点都必须遵守，对吗？
唐娜：当然。只有这样才能保证准确性。
爱迪生：我记住了。谢谢你不厌其烦的讲解。
唐娜：不客气。区区小事，何足挂齿。

MODULE 14　Construction Plan（模块十四　施工计划）

约克：据我所知，贵公司中了皇后大厦的标。祝贺你们！
何泽：谢谢。这可是我们公司的一件大事。
约克：你能告诉我皇后大厦的施工计划吗？
何泽：很乐意。皇后大厦占地 57 840 平方米，是我们公司本年度的一项重点工程。
约克：我知道了。事实上，它也是我市最大、最重要的工程之一。依照合同，多长时间能竣工？
何泽：我觉得 12 个月就能竣工。
约克：你的意思是说这项工程的工期为 12 个月，不是吗？
何泽：对。这项工程将于明年这个时候完工。
约克：你们计划何时破土动工？
何泽：哦，明年元月 1 日开始。
约克：先生，计划何时完成基础和主体工程？
何泽：计划在 10 月底，也就是说基础和主体工程于 10 个月内完成。
约克：那安装和装修工程呢？
何泽：安装和装修工程应同步穿插进行。
约克：好主意。你能肯定在施工期内完工吗？
何泽：当然。我们计划提前半个月完工，但是我们相信明年年底一定能完成。否则我们会受罚的。
约克：通过你的介绍，我此时能深刻地感受到你的决心和信心。我相信你及你的公司。
何泽：谢谢你的信任。你也知道，信誉是我们公司的生命线，因此，不管遇到多大困难，我们必须要克服。

约克：说得好。这是你们的施工进度表吗？
何泽：是的。这是一份具体的施工进度表，上面清楚地标有详细的工作数据。我想听听您的意见和建议。
约克：我先看看再说。
（几分钟后）
约克：你们的施工进度很先进、很实际，给我留下了深刻的印象。我对你们寄予厚望。
何泽：谢谢您的夸奖。我们会尽最大努力，绝不会让你们失望的。
约克：不客气。我相信你们一定会向我们及全市人民交出一份满意答卷的。

MODULE 15　Construction Inspection（模块十五　施工检查）

高先生：蔡先生，我前来贵地检查你所负责的工程质量。
蔡先生：欢迎！热烈欢迎！让我带你到处看看。
高先生：谢谢。首先，我想检查一下这幢楼的尺寸和定位。你们的经纬仪在哪里？
蔡先生：给你，这是一台新的。
高先生：很好。根据基础平面图的设计要求，尺寸、标高和定位都必须准确无误，不能有偏差。
蔡先生：我知道你刚才所说的几点内容的重要性，因此我们要做到一丝不苟，丝毫不差。
高先生：说得好。让我们继续检查一下排水管道和给水管子，看看是否有漏水现象。
蔡先生：请看！一点都不漏水。
高先生：你们把混凝土骨料投放准确了吗？
蔡先生：是的，绝对准确。混凝土骨料是按重量比投放的。这些是混凝土试块和试压记录。
高先生：做得好。你对工程质量有高度的责任心，这让我很钦佩。
蔡先生：谢谢。你的话对我是莫大的夸奖和鼓励。我们继续吧，先生。
高先生：这两道墙的拐角处没放钢筋，请推倒重砌。下次再发生类似情况，你就得受罚。
蔡先生：非常抱歉。我会彻查此事，并立即采取补救措施。
高先生：我并非有意在刁难你，更不是挑你刺儿。对于错误决不能等闲视之，我说得对吗？
蔡先生：对。根据规定，未经工程师同意，设计图不允许有任何修改。
高先生：这在合同中已标明，对此无可争辩。
蔡先生：建筑工程事关几代人的利益。因此，工程质量高于一切。
高先生：对。现场的任何图纸问题均应与建筑设计师协商解决，决不能自作主张。今后，你也应该举办各种活动帮助你的员工进一步提高质量意识。
蔡先生：好的，你放心，我们会尽最大努力保证工程质量的。

MODULE 16　Building Installation（模块十六　建筑安装）

弗兰克：小伙子，这部电梯是你安装的吗？
史密斯：是的，先生。我是一名设备安装工，安装各种设备是我的本职工作。
弗兰克：史密斯先生。现在我能启动电梯吗？

史密斯：哦，暂时还不能，因为这只是基本安装完毕。为确保万无一失，电梯还需要再进一步检查。
弗兰克：我是外行，因此对我刚才所说的话表示歉意。但是，说实话，听完你的一番话，对你高度负责的敬佩之情油然而生。
史密斯：多谢你的鼓励。世界上任何有职业道德的人都会这样做的。
弗兰克：你很谦虚。顺便问一下，安装工通常都做些什么工作？
史密斯：主要安装各种车床、起重机、气锤等机械和设备。
弗兰克：我想知道他们通常都用什么工具。
史密斯：举不胜举，主要是锉刀、台钳和锤子。
弗兰克：那量具呢？
史密斯：钢尺和角规。
弗兰克：一名钳工应当掌握什么样的操作技能？
史密斯：一名合格的安装工应擅长基础放线、设备安装与找平、机械零部件的清洗与安装等多项技能。
弗兰克：还有其他的吗？
史密斯：此外，他也应该知道如何调试和检测设备以保证这些设备正常运转。
弗兰克：现在介意我试试你安装的电梯吗？
史密斯：当然不介意了。如果发现问题，请尽管说。
弗兰克：嗯。好极了！做得不错。地脚螺栓垂直，螺母与垫圈，垫圈与设备底座都连接得很紧。
史密斯：先生，你觉得我安装得还行吧？
弗兰克：当然。我认为电梯的安装非常符合图纸的设计要求。了不起！
史密斯：听到你对我工作的肯定我放心多了。
弗兰克：钳工的确是建筑业中不可缺少的工种，特别是在现代建筑的施工中。
史密斯：因此，在现代化建设中，设备安装也是一项具有高度责任性和光荣使命感的崇高职业。
弗兰克：是的，你说得对。你能这样认为真的是太好了。

MODULE 17　Building Decoration（模块十七　建筑装饰）

温德尔：我是负责这个项目的总监。你能告诉我关于装饰工程的一些情况吗？
李　华：很乐意为您效劳。装修工作对建筑工程有着至关重要的作用。同时，好的装饰工人对于装饰工程显得特别重要。
温德尔：对的。装饰工程就像人的衣服马的鞍一样重要。
李华：大批能工巧匠是保证精品工程的前提。随着时代的发展，装饰工程逐渐显现出自身的价值。
温德尔：大理石装饰的大厅多么宏伟壮观啊！它真让我赏心悦目。
李华：是的，我也有同感。
温德尔：顺便问一下，你们是怎么处理铝合金表面的？

李华：所有的铝合金表面都要彻底清理干净，然后再涂上一层清晰的不褪色或无色面漆。

温德尔：我并不是很明白，你们为什么要这样做呢？

李华：我们对铝合金表面这样处理是为了避免铝合金受到水泥浆类带有碱性的涂饰物腐蚀而采取的一种防范保护措施。

温德尔：有这个必要吗？

李华：绝对有必要。请看这些按上述方法处理过的铝合金窗户，你认为怎样？

温德尔：真的不错。不过我认为大理石地面打磨得不够光滑。

李华：抱歉，我会立即派人再打磨的。

温德尔：此外，我必须要提醒你，墙面装饰一定要做好，比如涂料要刷匀，壁纸要贴牢，墙板要镶紧。

李华：为什么这样说呢？

温德尔：因为墙面装饰展现的是装饰工作的主要部分，极易给人留下第一视觉和第一印象，这对装饰质量的判断是至关重要的。

李华：言之有理。装饰工程是为美化建筑物，美化环境，带给人类无穷无尽的享受，因此，每个装饰工人都应具有较高的责任感，做好自己的本职工作。

温德尔：对的。只有这样，整个装饰工程的质量才有保证，你的公司才能站住脚，永远立于不败之地。

MODULE 18　Building Cost（模块十八　建筑造价）

王先生：我知道造价估算是项目管理中最为重要的步骤之一。你能给我讲讲吗？

赵先生：好的。造价估算的重要性在于它设立了项目发展不同阶段项目成本的底线。在项目发展的不同阶段所作出的成本估算表现了造价工程师或预算员以可利用资料为基础所作的预算。

王先生：成本估算是怎样进行的？换句话说，成本估算都采用了哪些基本方法？

赵先生：事实上，所有的成本估算都是根据如下基本方法中的一种或多种结合来进行的：生产函数、成本经验推断、工程量清单单价和联合费用的分摊。

王先生：在建筑中，生产函数是什么意思？

赵先生：在建筑中，生产函数指施工量与生产因素如劳动力或资金之间的关系。它建立了生产量与各种劳动力、材料和设备投入量之间的关系。

王先生：能给我举个例子吗？

赵先生：建筑工程的规模（用平方英尺表示）与投入的劳动量（用每平方英尺所消耗的劳动时间来表示）的关系就是生产函数在建筑工程中表现出的一个典型实例。

王先生：我现在明白了。经验成本是如何推断的呢？

赵先生：成本函数的经验估算需要回归分析法来完成，其作用为在假定的成本函数中估计最佳参数值或常数。

王先生：单价法是四种方法中最简单的吗？它是否意味着总造价为工程量与相应单价的乘积之和？

赵先生：是的，你说得对。单价法原则上简单易懂，但应用时相当繁琐。首先，整个施工过程要分解为若干个作业。一旦确定了这些作业，并且评定了其代表的工程量，每种作业的单价便确定下来，然后将每个作业发生的费用求和，就可确定总费用。分解作业的细目程度对于不同的估价项目有很大不同。

王先生：联合费用分摊过程中的基本成分种类是什么？

赵先生：在施工项目中，可根据劳动力、材料、施工设备、施工监理和普通的办公管理费对基本成本的账目进行分类。然后这些基本成分会按比例分摊到由一个施工项目分解的各项作业中。

MODULE 19 Claims of Construction Works(模块十九 工程索赔)

大卫：你能给我解释一下建筑领域的索赔吗？

史密斯：当然可以。首先，我们应该清楚索赔在建筑行业是一件很正常的事情。这就好比一个人总会不可避免地犯一些错误，然后在不断改进错误的进程中走向完美。

大卫：因此，索赔就是对纠正过失产生费用的索取，不是吗？

史密斯：对，你的理解基本正确。

大卫：索赔主要包括哪些项目呢？

史密斯：让我想一想。索赔主要包括技术问题、财务问题以及材料、机械、人工等方面的费用分歧问题。

大卫：你能给我举一个技术索赔的实例吗？

史密斯：当然可以。技术索赔主要是由延误颁发施工图纸、不及时回答技术核校单以及图纸与规范相互矛盾等问题引起。

大卫：那财务索赔呢？

史密斯：财务索赔是由于延误拨发工程进度款以及因美元与当地货币的汇率差浮动等问题而产生的。

大卫：索赔的程序是什么？

史密斯：索赔程序相当复杂，它一般包括三步。第一步是索赔的时间期限，也就是，在合同规定的14天内必须递交索赔通知书；第二步是索赔金额，也就是，在索赔通知书递交后的30天内应该递交索赔费用的账单；第三步是在14天内必须递交索赔更详细的分析资料。

大卫：现在我已经明白了索赔的程序和时限，多谢。

史密斯：不客气。但是我还有一点要指出，那就是所有的记录和报告都应该经双方人员验收签字。

大卫：我知道了。这一定是最后的结论，做出最终结论要花很长的时间，也许两三个月。

史密斯：是的，这是按照正常程序进行索赔的最长期限。

大卫：哦，多么复杂的索赔程序啊！什么时候才能收到索赔的总金额？

史密斯：根据合同条款，在收到索赔的进一步证明材料后的60天内，工程师同业主协商后将索赔的最终决定通知承包商。如果索赔是合理的，对于你们提出的要求，我们将予以解决。

大卫：我明白了。谢谢你给我讲了这么多关于索赔的知识。

史密斯：没什么！

MODULE 20　Acceptance of Construction Works(模块二十　工程验收)

乔丹：现在，整个工程按合同已经达到基本竣工。我们期盼着您尽早颁发移交证书。
林先生：真是个好消息！但是对于工程的检查验收与试验，我们需要制定一个详细的计划，包括验收时间表、竣工图纸以及要检查与试验的各部分的清单。
乔丹：是的，你说得对。这些资料不提交给你们，工程还不能被认为已基本竣工。
林先生：你们认为还有什么未完成的工作吗？
乔丹：是的，还有点，不过都是些扫尾工作，比如说恢复地表面等。
林先生：依照我个人的意见，验收过程可分为两个阶段：第一阶段，在你方技术人员的协助下，我们的专家组将检查完工的工程，看看他们是否满意。如果一切正常，我们将进入第二阶段，也就是对合同中规定的设备和仪器进行性能试验。
乔丹：我同意。什么时候我们可以开始验收检查？
林先生：我们需要大约三天的时间来做一些准备。本月的19号开始怎样？
乔丹：没问题。
(整个验收过程进展顺利，共持续5天。现在，他们正在讨论竣工报告和移交证书的有关事宜。)
林先生：祝贺你！整个工程已经通过全部试验，我们的工程师对试验结果非常满意。然而，验收中也发现了几处小缺陷和一些扫尾工作尚待完成。你打算怎样处理这些工作？
乔丹：的确，有几处小缺陷需要修补以及某些扫尾工作有待完成，但它们并不影响整个工程的正常运行。所以，根据合同，工程业已达到基本竣工，我们应该从你方获得工程的移交证书。
林先生：我们可以向你方签发移交证书，但是你方须交给我们一份保证书，承诺你方在保修期内迅速地完成扫尾工作和修复有关缺陷。
乔丹：没问题。
林先生：现在，我们可以向你方认可本工程已于2011年11月24日基本竣工。既然整个工程已验收，为什么不放松一下呢？
乔丹：我们仍然有两件事要做：第一，为这个项目申请一个优质竣工证书；第二，向你要提前竣工奖。
林先生：你们有权拥有这个(优质工程)证书和(提前竣工)奖金。

APPENDIX Ⅳ   Glossary
附录4   词汇表

1. Architectural Courses（一、建筑课程）

architectural engineering   建筑工程
architectural economics   建筑经济学
architectural design   建筑设计
conspectus of architecture   建筑学概论
basic architectural design   建筑设计基础
architectural graphing   建筑制图
architectural mechanics   建筑力学
theory of architectural design   建筑设计原理
history of architecture   建筑史
architectural psychology   建筑心理学
structural lectotype   结构体系与选型
structural mechanics   结构力学
mechanics of materials   材料力学
engineering mechanics   工程力学
building mechanics   建筑力学
building physics   建筑物理
building construction   建筑构造
building structure   建筑结构
surveying   测量学
building equipment   建筑设备
engineering mathematics   工程数学
hydraulic engineering   水利工程
engineering machinery   工程机械
municipal engineering   市政工程
construction technique   施工技术
construction overview   施工概论
construction organization   施工组织
construction budget   施工预算
electrical installation   电气安装
water supply and sewerage   给水排水
heating and ventilation   供暖与通风
electrical engineering of architecture   建筑电工

2. Architectural Majors（二、建筑专业）

architectural design technology   建筑设计技术
architectural decoration engineering technology   建筑装饰工程技术
Chinese ancient architectural engineering technology   中国古建筑工程技术
interior design technology   室内设计技术
environmental art design   环境艺术设计
garden engineering technology   园林工程技术
landscape architecture design   景观建筑设计
town planning   城镇规划
urban planning   城市规划
city management and supervision   城市管理与监察
town construction   城镇建设
building construction technology   建筑工程技术
underground and tunnel engineering technology   地下工程与隧道工程技术

foundation engineering technology 基础工程技术
civil engineering 土木工程
building equipment engineering technology 建筑设备工程技术
heating ventilation and air-conditioning engineering technology 供热通风与空调工程技术
building electrical engineering technology 建筑电气工程技术
building intellectualization engineering technology 楼宇智能化工程技术
industrial equipment installation engineering technology 工业设备安装工程技术
heating ventilation and sanitary engineering technology 供热通风与卫生工程技术
mechanical and electrical installation engineering 机电安装工程
architectural environment and equipment engineering 建筑环境与设备工程
architectural engineering management 建筑工程管理
engineering management 工程管理
engineering cost 工程造价
architectural economics and management 建筑经济管理
project supervision 工程监理
power engineering management 电力工程管理
engineering quality supervision and management 工程质量监督与管理
construction project management 建筑工程项目管理
municipal engineering technology 市政工程技术
city gas engineering technology 城市燃气工程技术
water supply and sewerage engineering technology 给排水工程技术
water industry technology 水工业技术
fire-fighting engineering technology 消防工程技术
building hydropower technology 建筑水电技术
real estate operation and valuation 房地产经营与估价
estate management 物业管理
estate facility management 物业设施管理

3. Architectural Institutes & Schools（三、建筑院校）

Institute of Architectural Engineering 建筑工程学院
Institute of Civil Engineering 土木工程学院
Vocational College of Architectural Engineering 建筑工程职业学院
Technical College of Construction 建筑技术学院
Workers and Staff College of Construction 建筑职工大学
Secondary Construction School for Workers and Staff 建筑职工中专
School of Architectural Engineering 建筑工程学校
Technical School of Building Installation 建筑安装技工学校
School of Urban and Rural Construction 城乡建设学校
Architectural University of Science & Technology 建筑科技大学
Academy of Building Research 建筑科学研究院

Architectural Design and Research Institute　建筑设计研究院
Institute of Architectural Designing　建筑设计院
National Institute of Building Science　国家建筑科学研究所
Research Institute of Housing Construction　房屋建筑研究所
Research Institute of Ecological Buildings　生态建筑研究院
Research Institute of Energy-saving Buildings　节能建筑研究院
Research Institute of Intelligent Buildings　智能建筑研究院

4. Architectural Workers（四、建筑工程人员）

civil construction worker　土建工	glazier　玻璃安装工
hoister　起重机司机	warehouse keeper　料工/库管员
bricklayer　瓦工	surveyor　测量工
road builder　筑路工	crane operator　吊车司机
carpenter　木工	bulldozer operator　推土机手
steel fixer　钢筋工	scraper operator　铲土机手
concrete worker　混凝土工	excavator operator　挖土机手
stone mason　石工	loader operator　装载机手
scaffolder　架子工	pneumatic drill operator　风钻工
building installer　建筑安装工	air-compressor operator　空压机工
plumber　水暖工	building decorator　建筑装饰工
electrician　电工	cost estimator/engineer　造价员/师
fitter　安装钳工	construction supervisor　监理员
welder　焊工	safety supervisor　安全员
riveter　铆工	contract administrator　合同员
ventilator　通风工	construction crew　施工员
turner　车工	quality inspector　质检员
assembler　装配工	engineering documenter　工程资料员
joiner　细木工	construction material administrator　材料员
plasterer　粉刷工	registered architect　注册建筑师
painter　油漆工	construction engineer　建筑工程师

5．Construction Enterprises（五、建筑施工企业）

CSCEC（China State Construction Engineering Corporation）　中国建筑工程总公司
CCEC（Civil Construction Engineering Corporation）　土木建筑工程总公司
CIEC（Construction Installation Engineering Corporation）　建筑安装工程总公司
RBECC（Road & Bridge Engineering Corporation of China）　中国路桥工程总公司
No．1 Construction Engineering Company　第一建筑工程公司
Construction Decoration Company　建筑装饰公司
Construction and Installation Engineering Co．，Ltd　建筑安装工程有限公司
Giant Building Machinery Inc．　巨人建筑机械公司

Construction Materials Supplying Company　建筑材料供应公司
Construction Transportation Company　建筑运输公司
Construction Engineering Branch　建筑工程分公司
Construction Engineering Brigade　建筑工程施工队
Construction Engineering Stock Company　建筑工程股份公司
Construction Engineering Limited Company　建筑工程有限公司
Jiangsu Nantong No. 3 Construction Group Co., Ltd　江苏南通三建集团有限公司
Nantong Construction Project Central Contracting Co., Ltd　南通建筑工程总承包有限公司
Nantong Construction Group Joint-Stock Co., Ltd　南通建工集团股份有限公司
Jiangsu Suzhong Construction Group Co., Ltd　江苏省苏中建设集团股份有限公司

6. Kinds of Buildings(六、建筑物类型)

modern architecture　现代建筑	teaching building　教学大楼
ancient buildings　古代建筑	business building　营业大楼
industrial architecture　工业建筑	married quarters　家属楼
civil architecture　民用建筑	apartment/flats　公寓
residential architecture　住宅建筑	mansion　豪华宅邸/大厦
commercial architecture　商业建筑	hotel-style apartments　酒店式公寓
public architecture　公共建筑	low-rent house　廉租房
agricultural architecture　农业建筑	box buildings　盒子房
pseudo-classic architecture　仿古建筑	tube-shaped apartment　筒子楼
energy-saving architecture　节能建筑	skyscraper　摩天大楼
ecological architecture　生态建筑	villa　别墅
vernacular building　乡土建筑	multi-storey building　多层建筑
western style architecture　西式建筑	high-rise building　高层建筑
Chinese style architecture　中式建筑	lower-rise building　低层建筑
European-style architecture　欧式建筑	bungalow　平房
Spanish-style architecture　西班牙式建筑	brick-and-timber building　砖木结构建筑
the English residence　英式住宅	steel building　钢结构建筑
the American residence　美式住宅	brick-and-concrete building　砖混结构建筑
office building　办公大楼	reinforced concrete building　钢混结构建筑

7. Building Materials(七、建筑材料)

installation materials　安装材料	explosive materials　爆破材料
decorative materials　装饰材料	insulating materials　绝缘材料
foreign materials　外来材料	fire-proof materials　耐火材料
artificial materials　人造材料	cementing materials　粘结材料
additional materials　附加材料	substitute materials　代用材料
defective materials　残次材料	roofing materials　屋面材料

rust-resisting materials　防锈材料
road materials　筑路材料
plastic materials　塑性材料
structural materials　结构材料
aluminum alloy factory　铝合金厂
steel tubing plant　钢管厂
enamel plant　搪瓷制品厂
plywood factory　胶合板厂
glass works　玻璃厂
ceramic factory　陶瓷厂
plastics factory　塑料厂
felt roofing factory　油毡厂
brick & tile works　砖瓦厂
cement plant　水泥厂
crushing stone mill　碎石厂
paint factory　油漆厂
asbestos tile works　石棉瓦厂
construction materials company　建材公司
fiber-board plant　纤维板厂
steel window factory　钢窗厂
glass-fiber factory　玻璃纤维厂
metal products plant　五金厂
metal-structure works　金属结构厂
electric bulbs factory　电灯泡厂
timber processing plant　木材加工厂
concrete parts factory　混凝土构件厂
red brick　红砖
clay brick　粘土砖
glazed brick (ceramic tile)　瓷砖
fire brick　防火砖
hollow brick　空心砖
facing brick　面砖
flooring tile　地板砖
clinker brick　缸砖
mosaic　马赛克
glazed tile　琉璃瓦
ridge tile　脊瓦
asbestos tile (shingle)　石棉瓦
gypsum　石膏

marble　大理石
white marble　汉白玉
rubble　毛石
granite　花岗岩
crushed stone　碎石
vermiculite　蛭石
gravel　砾石
terrazzo　水磨石
cobble　卵石
course sand　粗砂
fine sand　细砂
medium sand　中砂
asbestos fiber　石棉纤维
portland cement　波特兰水泥
silicate cement　硅酸盐水泥
white cement　白水泥
cement mortar　水泥砂浆
lime mortar　石灰砂浆
cement-lime mortar　水泥石灰砂浆
thermal mortar　保温砂浆
water-proof mortar　防水砂浆
acid-resistant mortar　耐酸砂浆
alkaline-resistant mortar　耐碱砂浆
bituminous mortar　沥青砂浆
plain concrete　素混凝土
reinforced concrete　钢筋混凝土
lightweight concrete　轻质混凝土
fine aggregate concrete　细石混凝土
asphalt concrete　沥青混凝土
foamed concrete　泡沫混凝土
cinder concrete　炉渣混凝土
asphalt felt　沥青卷材
asphalt filler　沥青填料
asphalt grout　沥青胶泥
asbestos sheet　石棉板
willow　榴木
elm　榆木
cedar　杉木
teak　柚木

camphor wood　樟木
preservative-treated lumber　防腐处理的木材
plywood　胶合板
laminated plank　层夹板
tongued and grooved board　企口板
fiber-board　纤维板
glue-laminated lumber　胶合层夹木材
log　原木
round timber　圆木
square timber　方木
plank　板材
batten　木条
lath　板条
board　木板
red pine　红松
white pine　白松
spruce　云杉
deciduous pine　落叶松
bamboo　竹子
alloy steel　合金钢
titanium alloy　钛合金
stainless steel　不锈钢
corrugated steel bar　竹节钢筋
deformed bar　变形钢筋
plain round bar　光圆钢筋
steel plate　钢板
thin steel plate　薄钢板
low carbon steel　低碳钢
cold bending　冷弯
steel pipe tube　钢管
seamless steel pipe　无缝钢管
welded steel pipe　焊接钢管
iron pipe　黑铁管
galvanized steel pipe　镀锌钢管
cast iron　铸铁
steel bar　圆钢
square steel　方钢
steel strap, flat steel　扁钢
steel section shape　型钢

channel　槽钢
angle steel　角钢
equal-leg angle　等边角钢
unequal-leg angle　不等边角钢
I-beam　工字钢
wide flange I-beam　宽翼缘工字钢
T-bar Z-bar　丁字钢
light gauge cold-formed　冷弯薄壁型钢
pig iron　生铁
wrought iron　熟铁
galvanized steel sheet　镀锌铁皮
galvanized steel wire　镀锌铁丝
steel wire mesh　钢丝网
manganese steel　锰钢
high strength alloy steel　高强度合金钢
nails　钉子
screws　螺丝
flat-head screw　平头螺丝
bolt　螺栓
spiral-threaded roofing nail　螺纹屋面钉
cinch bolt　胀锚螺栓
washer　垫片
annular-ring gypsum board nail　环纹石膏板钉
common bolt　普通螺栓
high strength bolt　高强螺栓
insert bolt　预埋螺栓
primer　底漆
rust-inhibitive primer　防锈底漆
varnish　透明漆
anti-corrosion paint　防腐漆
mixed paint　调和漆
flat paint　无光漆
aluminum paint　银粉漆
enamel paint　磁漆
drying oil　干性油
thinner　稀释剂
asphalt paint　沥青漆
Chinese wood oil　桐油
red lead　红丹

lead oil 铅油
putty 腻子
granitic plaster 水刷石
artificial stone 斩假石
lime wash 刷浆
casein 可赛银
white wash 大白浆
hemp cuts and lime as base 麻刀灰打底
lath and plaster 板条抹灰
polythene, polyethylene 聚乙烯
nylon 尼龙
pvc polyvinyl chloride 聚氯乙烯
polycarbonate 聚碳酸酯

polystyrene 聚苯乙烯
acrylic resin 丙烯酸树酯
vinyl ester 乙烯基酯
rubber lining 橡胶内衬
neoprene 氯丁橡胶
bitumen paint 沥青漆
epoxy resin paint 环氧树脂漆
anti-rust paint 防锈漆
acid-resistant paint 耐酸漆
alkali-resistant paint 耐碱漆
sodium silicate 水玻璃
resin-bonded mortar 树脂砂浆
epoxy resin 环氧树脂

8. Building Machinery（八、建筑机械）

starter 启动机
dumper 翻斗车
fork-lift 装载机
trailer 拖车，挂车
trolley 台车，手推车
semi-trailer 半挂车
electric dipper 电铲
mixer 搅拌机
pulley 滑车
loader-dozer 带式输送机
hydraulic pump 液压泵
tipper truck 自卸车
universal crane 万能起重机
electric crane 电动起重机
derrick crane 悬臂起重机
platform hoist 平台式起重机
travelling hoist 移动式卷扬机
builder's lift 施工用升降机
windlass 卷扬机，起锚机
bridge crane 桥式起重机
power capstan 动力绞盘
builder's winch 施工绞车
snatch block 辘轳紧线滑轮
overhanging pile driver 伸臂式打桩机

automatic ram pile driver 自动冲锤打桩机
pile frame 打桩架
pile drawer 拔桩机
jack bit 钻头
pile hoop/band 桩锤
hydraulic drill 液压钻机
electric rammer 电夯机
track-lift 叉式升降机，铲车
lane maker 车道画线机
stone breaker 碎石机
asphalt layer 沥青铺面机
road paver 铺路机
road roller 压路机
road ripper 松土机
road scraper 刮路机
tar sprayer 焦油浇注机
stabilized soil mixer 稳定土拌和机
road cutter 路面切割机
road-marking vehicle 划线车
snow remover 除雪机
asphalt distributor 沥青洒布车
asphalt dumping equipment 沥青脱桶设备
pavement repairing vehicle 路面修补车
mixture transfer vehicle 混合料转运车

groover　刻纹机
paving machine　摊铺机
milling machine　铣刨机
slurry seal machine　稀浆封层机
pavement maintenance vehicle　路面养护车
pavement breaker　路面破碎机
road block removal truck　道路清障车
garbage-treatment car　垃圾处理车
breakstone disperser　碎石撒布机
sweeping vehicle　清扫车
excavating loader　挖掘装载机
hydraulic excavator　液压挖掘机
trencher　挖沟机
crawler excavator　履带式挖掘机
concrete mixing truck　混凝土搅拌运输车
shotcrete machine　混凝土喷射机
concrete pump　混凝土输送泵
concrete breaker　混凝土粉碎机
concrete paver　混凝土摊铺机
concrete mixer　混凝土搅拌机
concrete pump truck　混凝土泵车
concrete trailer pump　混凝土拖泵
crawler crane　履带式起重机
elevator　升降机
lift car　升降车
pipe crane　吊管机
aerial platform vehicle　高空作业车
tower crane　塔式起重机
tyre crane　轮胎式起重机
towing machine　牵引机
gantry crane　门式起重机
transport vehicle　运输车
scraper　铲运机
grader　平地机
tyred loader　轮胎式装载机
crawler loader　履带式装载机
skid loader　滑移式装载机
bulldozer　推土机
vibrating tamper　振动夯实机

vibratory roller　振动压路机
static roller　静力式压路机
impact compactor　冲击夯实机
compactor　压实机
roller compactor　碾压机
tyre roller　轮胎压路机
heading machine　掘进机
multifunctional drillingrig　多功能钻机
rotary drilling rig　旋挖钻机
percussive drilling rig　冲击式钻机
construction drill　工程钻机
rotary-percussive drill　冲击回转钻机
water well rig　水井钻机
anchor drill　锚固钻机
opencast driller　潜孔钻机
electric nacelle　电动吊篮
mud pump　泥浆泵
mortar pump　砂浆泵
heater　加热器
edger　磨边机
spraying pump　喷涂泵
plastering machine　抹灰机
pile driver　桩机
hydraulic shear　液压剪
diaphragm-wall grab　连续墙抓斗
hydraulic tong　液压钳
steel adjusting cutter　钢筋调直切断机
jack　千斤顶
anchor device　锚具
steel bending machine　钢筋弯曲机
cold rolling mill　冷轧机
tube straightening machine　钢管矫直机
cutting machine　切割机
hydraulic machine　液压机
screw machine　滚丝机
roller　滚丝轮
steel sleeve　钢套筒
compressor　压缩机
ball mill　球磨机

magnetic separator　磁选机
hydraulic crusher　液压破碎机
breaking hammer　破碎锤
rock drill　凿岩机

9. Architectural Drawings(九、建筑图纸)

diagram　示意图
sketch　草图
topographical map　地形图
earth-work drawing　土方工程图
developed drawing　展开图
formwork drawing　模板图
standard drawing　标准图
plan　平面图
schematic plan　平面示意图
sectional plan　平剖面图
plan of provision of holes　留孔平面图
section　剖面
longitudinal section　纵剖面
cross (transverse) section　横剖面
elevation　立面
front elevation　正立面
side elevation　侧立面
perspective drawing　透视图
general layout　总图
building drawing　建筑图
roof/foundation plan　屋面/基础平面图
typical drawing　定型图
installation drawing　安装图
equipment drawing　设备图
process flow diagram　工艺流程图
reinforcement drawing　配筋图
dimensioned drawing　标有尺寸的图纸
make/read drawings　制/识图
legend　图例
scale of a drawing　图纸比例
copy of a drawing　图纸副本
drawing instruments　绘图仪器
drawing pen　绘图笔
drawing-compasses　绘图圆规
T-square　丁字尺
drawing scale　绘图比例尺
drawing paper　绘图纸
tracing paper　描图纸
French curve　曲线尺
drawing board　绘图板

10. Construction Tendering(十、建筑招投标)

tender document　标书文件
tender accepted　中标
lose a tender　未中标
tender quotation　报标
tender opening　开标
tender discussion　议标
tender decision　决标
tender submission　投标
tender invitation　招标
tender assessment　评标
tender board/committee　投标委员会
tender conditions　标书条件
tender in date　截标日期
tender out date　出标日期
tender validity period　标书有效期
tender period　投标期
tender deposit　投标按金
tender price index　投标价格指数
tender rate　标额
tender offers　投标开价
tender negotiation　投标协商
joint tender　联合招标
international tender　国际招标
advertised tender　公开招标
competitive tender　竞争招标
tender procedures　投标程序

Tender Selection Board　投标遴选委员会
tender selection criteria　选标准则
tenderer/ee　投标者/招标者
successful tenderer　中标人
tender guarantee　投标保证书
tender reference　招标编号
tender for construction　投标承建

tender for purchase　投标承购
tender notice　招标告示；招标公告
tender recommendation　标书举荐
tender referral　标书转介
tender schedule　标书附表
tender specifications　标书规格
base price limit on tender　标底

11．Construction Contract(十一、建筑合同)

construction contract　建筑合同
decoration contract　装饰合同
contract management　合同管理
contract provisions/stipulations　合同规定
contract clauses　合同条款
contract number　合同编号
contract period　合同期限
expiration of contract　合同期满
contract party　合同当事人
contractual obligations　合同义务
long-term contract　长期合同
short-term contract　短期合同
terminal/fixed term contract　定期合同
void contract　无效合同
negotiate a contract　洽谈合同
approve a contract　审批合同
tear up a contract　撕毁合同
complete a contract　完成合同
terminate a contract　终止合同
hold a contract　信守合同

make a contract　订立合同
revise a contract　修改合同
sign a contract　签署合同
cancel a contract　取消合同
infringe/break a contract　违反合同
execute/perform a contract　履行合同
prolong a contract　延长合同
countersign a contract　会签合同
originals of the contract　合同正本
copies of the contract　合同副本
renewal of contract　合同的续订
contract of employment　雇佣合同
contract of carriage　运输合同
contract of arbitration　仲裁合同
contract for goods　订货合同
contract for purchase　采购合同
contract for service　劳务合同
contract for future delivery　期货合同
contract of sale　销售合同
contract of insurance　保险合同

12．Construction Laws and Regulations(十二、建筑法律法规)

definition　定义
general provisions　总则
examination of premises　场地的检查
ordinance and regulation　法令和法规
building permit　建筑许可
permits and inspection fees　许可证和审查费
specifications and drawings　规格和图纸

reference specifications　参照规格
contract assignment　合同转让
contract subletting　合同分包
intellectual property　知识产权
fire protective measures　防火措施
liability and indemnification　责任和赔偿
indemnity bonds　赔偿担保

property insurance　财产保险
casualty insurance　伤亡保险
confidentiality　保密
surveys and project layout　勘察和项目布局
legal liability　法律责任
time of completion　竣工时间
delays and extension of time　延误和延期
suspension of operation　中止作业
completion of the work　竣工
as-built records　竣工记录
termination　终止
acceptance of equipment　设备验收

guarantee　担保
force majeure　不可抗力
jobsite safety　工地安全
title and risk of loss　所有权和损失风险
right to audit　审计权
no implied waiver　无暗示放弃
severability　可分割性
dispute resolution　争议的解决
entire agreement　全部协议
terms and pages　条款和页数
supplementary provisions　附则
regulations on administration　管理规定

13. Construction Testing(十三、建筑试验)

concrete test　混凝土试验
concrete design　混凝土设计
test cube　试块
test specimen　试样
test piece　试件
slump test　坍落度试验
vibratory test　振动试验
steel reinforcement test　钢筋试验
tensile test　拉力试验
welding test　焊接试验
extension test　拉伸试验
bending test　弯曲试验
destructive test　破坏性试验
non-destructive test　无损试验
pilling test　打桩测试
pile load test　桩荷载试验
pile pulling test　拔桩试验
penetration test　贯入度试验
standard penetration test　标准贯入试验
field density test　现场密度测试

pile redriving test　桩复打试验
cold test　冲击试验
magnetic particle inspection　磁粉检验
bending plastic inspection　弯曲塑性检验
penetrate inspection　渗透探伤
ultrasonic inspection　超声波探伤
field identification　现场鉴定
field moisture equivalent　现场含水等量
pressure testing record　试压记录
driving record　打桩记录
concrete stress　混凝土应力
steel bar strength　钢筋强度
pile capacity　单桩承载力
driving stress　打桩应力
pile driving resistance　打桩阻力
depth of penetration　贯入深度
specified penetration　指定贯入度
final penetration　最终贯入度
visual examination　外观检查
lateral pile load test　桩的侧向荷载试验

14. Construction Surveying(十四、建筑测量)

types of survey　测量种类
plane survey　平面测量
geodetic survey　大地测量

topographic survey　地形测量
route survey　路线测量
hydrographic survey　水文/河道测量

construction survey	施工测量
photogrammetric survey	摄影测量
surveying lines	测量线
straight line	直线
broken line	折线
solid/full line	实线
base line	基线
building line	建筑红线，房基线
datum line	基准线
datum point	基准点
axis	轴线
positioning line	定位线
central line	中心线
dimension line	尺寸线
perpendicular line	垂直线
line of level	水平线
surveying instruments	测量仪器
theodolite	经纬仪
high-precision theodolite	高精度经纬仪
repetition theodolite	复测经纬仪
direction theodolite	方向经纬仪
leveling instrument	水平仪
dumpy level	定镜水平仪
quickset level	速调水平仪
automatic level	自动水平仪
microwave ranger finder	微波测距仪
leveling rod	水准标尺
ranging pole	标尺测杆
readjust focusing	调整聚焦
leveler	水准测量员
surveyor	测量员
rod man	标杆员

15. Nouns of Engineering Surveying（十五、工程测绘学名词）

engineering survey	工程测量
surveying	测量学
elementary surveying	普通测量学
topography	地形测量学
surveying control network	测量控制网
horizontal control network	平面控制网
vertical control network	高程控制网
horizontal control point	平面控制点
vertical control point	高程控制点
horizontal coordinate	平面坐标
control survey	控制测量
topographic survey	地形测量
trilateration network	三边网
triangulateration network	边角网
traverse network	导线网
trilateration survey	三边测量
triangulateration survey	边角测量
traverse survey	导线测量
horizontal angle	水平角
vertical angle	垂直角
description of station	点之记
station	测站
station centring	测站归心
sighting centring	照准点归心
sighting point	照准点
closed traverse	闭合导线
connecting traverse	附合导线
open traverse	支导线
theodolite traverse	经纬仪导线
subtense traverse	视差导线
stadia traverse	视距导线
plane-table traverse	平板仪导线
distance measurement	距离测量
standard field of length	标准检定场
electro-magnetic distance survey	电磁波测距
EDM traverse	光电测距导线
minor triangulation	小三角测量
linear triangulation chain	线形锁
linear triangulation network	线形网
mapping control	图根控制
traverse leg	导线边
traverse angle	导线折角

junction point of traverses 导线结点
lateral error of traverse 导线横向误差
meandering coefficient of traverse 导线曲折系数
control point 控制点
linear-angular intersection 边角交会法
traverse point 导线点
vertical control survey 高程控制测量
mapping control point 图根点
longitudinal error of traverse 导线纵向误差
elevation point 高程点
detail point 碎部点
increment of coordinate 坐标增量
graphic mapping control point 图解图根点
[forward]intersection 前方交会
analytic mapping control point 解析图根点
side intersection 侧方交会
resection 后方交会
linear intersection 边交会法
Bessel method 贝塞尔法
Lehmann method 莱曼法
repetition method 复测法
leveling 水准测量
annexed leveling line 附合水准路线
closed leveling line 闭合水准路线
elevation of sight 视线高程
polygonal height traverse 多角高程导线
height traverse 高程导线
rigorous adjustment 严密平差
approximate adjustment 近似平差
engineering control network 工程控制网
construction control network 施工控制网
three-dimensional network 三维网
construction survey 施工测量
profile survey 纵断面测量
constructioncompletion survey 竣工测量
cross-section survey 横断面测量
profile [diagram] 纵断面图
cross-section profile 横断面图
detail survey 碎部测量

plane-table survey 平板仪测量
mapping method with transit 经纬仪测绘法
rectangular grid 直角坐标网
leveling network 水准网
spur leveling line 支水准路
small scale topographical map 小比例尺地形图
slope distance 斜距
rectangular map-subdivision 矩形分幅
square map-subdivision 正方形分幅
horizontal distance 平距
base map of topography 地形底图
arbitrary axis meridian 任意轴子午线
assumed coordinate system 假定坐标系
independent coordinate system 独立坐标系
deformation observation 变形观测
displacement observation 位移观测
settlement observation 沉降观测
deflection observation 挠度观测
oblique observation 倾斜观测
geological survey 地质测量
prospecting network layout 勘探网测设
prospecting line survey 勘探线测量
prospecting network survey 勘探网测量
prospecting baseline 勘探基线
geological point survey 地质点测量
point for shaft position 井口位置点
bore-hole position survey 钻孔位置测量
geological profile survey 地质剖面测量
fault displacement survey 断层位移测量
regional geological survey 区域地质测量
adit planimetric map 坑道平面图
prospecting line profile map 勘探线剖面图
geological section map 地质剖面图
map of mineral deposits 矿产图
geological scheme 地质略图
field geological map 野外地质图
geological sketch map 地质草图
geological photomap 影像地质图
regional geological map 区域地质图

title of survey area　测区名称
code of survey area　测区代号
coverage of survey area　测区范围
geostress survey　地应力测量
petroleum pipeline survey　输油管道测量
mine surveying　矿山测量学
underground oil depot survey　地下油库测量
mine survey　矿山测量
petroleum exploration survey　石油勘探测量
connection survey　联系测量
mine surface survey　矿山地面测量
geometric orientation　几何定向
control survey of mining area　矿区控制测量
physical orientation　物理定向
shaft orientation survey　立井定向测量
orientation projection　定向投影
connection point for orientation　定向连接点
laser plumbing　激光投点
projection by suspended plumbing　吊锤投影
sighting line method　瞄直法
damping-bob for shaft plumbing　稳定锤投影
straight triangle　直伸三角形
pendulous-bob for shaft plumbing　摆动锤投影
orientation error　定向误差
orientation connection survey　定向连接测量
rough orientation　粗略定向
connection triangle method　联系三角形法
precise orientation　精密定向
connection quadrangle method　联系四边形法
reversal points method　逆转点法
gyrostatic orientation survey　陀螺定向测量
gyro azimuth　陀螺方位角排
tape zero observation　悬挂带零位观测
gyro meridian　陀螺仪子午线
gyro orientation error　陀螺定向误差
induction height survey　导入高程测量
underground survey　井下测量
roof station　顶板测点
gyro EDM traverse　陀螺定向光电测距导线

floor station　底板测点
direction-annexed traverse　方向附合导线
centering under point　点下对中
underground height measurement　井下高程测量
mining panel survey　采区测量
connection survey in mining panel　采区联系测量
stop survey　采场测量
detail survey of workings　巷道碎部测量
opencast survey　露天矿测量
underground cavity survey　井下空洞测量
reclamation survey　垦复测量
setting-out of technical edge　技术境界标定
setting-out of mining yard　矿场标定
blasting survey of open pit
　　　　露天矿爆破工作测量
setting-out of shaft center　井筒中心标定
setting-out of side plumb-bob　边垂线标定
shaft-deepening survey　井筒延伸测量
laser guide of vertical shaft　竖井激光指向
closure plan of ice wall　冻结壁交圈图
construction survey for shaft drilling
　　　　钻井施工测量
mineral deposits geometry　矿床几何
setting-out of junction　交叉点放样
holing through survey　贯通测量
setting-out of workings slope
巷道坡度线标定
reserve management　储量管理
footage measurement of workings
　　　　巷道验收丈量
angle of critical deformation　移动角
geometrisation of ore body　矿体几何制图
boundary angle　边界角
geometrisation of mineral property
　　　　矿产几何制图
mining map　矿山测量图
underground prospecting survey
　　　　井下勘探测量
mining yard plan　矿场平面图

determination of seam elements 矿层要素测定
shaft bottom plan 井底车场平面图
mining subsidence observation 开采沉陷观测
main workings plan 主要巷道平面图
prediction of mining subsidence 开采沉陷预计
opencast mining plan 露天矿矿图
observation of slope stability 边坡稳定性观测
waste dump plan 排土场平面图
topographic map of mining area 井田区域地形图
urban survey 城市测量
mining engineering plan 采掘工程平面图
map of mining subsidence 开采沉陷图
plan of striping and mining 采剥工程平面图
urban control survey 城市控制测量
urban topographic survey 城市地形测量
urban planning survey 城市规划测量
public works survey 市政工程测量
building works survey 建筑工程测量
utility survey 公用事业工程测量
setting-out survey 放样测量
alignment survey 定线测量
pipe survey 管道测量
subway survey 地下铁道测量
surveying for site selection 选厂测量
airport survey 飞机场测量
airfield runway survey 机场跑道测量
square control network 施工方格网
setting-out of main axis 主轴线测设
point of square control network 方格网点
building axis survey 建筑轴线测量
property line survey 建筑红线测量
laser alignment 激光准直
optical alignment 光学准直
plan of a zone 带状平面图
topographic map of urban area 城市地形图
synthesis chart of pipelines 管道综合图
underground pipeline survey 地下管线测量
revision of topographic map 地形图更新
underground pipe-driving survey 顶管测量
checking datum mark 校核基点
data base for urban survey 城市测量数据库
starting datum mark 起测基点
exiguous triangle method 微三角形法
collimation line method 视准线法
method of tension wire alignment 引张线法
method of laser alignment 激光准直法
minor angle method 小角度法
direct plummet observation 正锤线观测
inverse plummet observation 倒锤线观测
reservoir survey 水库测量
dam site investigation 坝址勘查
dam construction survey 堤坝施工测量
reservoir storage survey 库容测量
monumental boundary peg 永久界柱
non-monumental boundary peg 临时界桩
catchment area survey 汇水面积测量
canal survey 渠道测量
drainage map 水系图
harbor engineering survey 港口工程测量
road engineering survey 道路工程测量
railroad engineering survey 铁路工程测量
reconnaissance survey 勘测
sketch survey 草测
preliminary survey 初测
location survey 定测
route plan 线路平面图
plane curve location 平面曲线测设
vertical curve location 竖曲线测设
circular curve location 圆曲线测设

spiral curve location　缓和曲线测设
hair-pin curve location　回头曲线测设
center line survey　线路中线测量
method of deflection angle　偏角法
tangent off-set method　切线支距法
chord off-set method　弦线支距法
area leveling　面水准测量
route leveling　路线水准测量
profile leveling　中桩水准测量
grade location　坡度测设
slope stake location　边坡桩测设
turnout survey　道岔测量
construction details　施工详图
construction plan　施工平面图
bridge survey　桥梁测量
tunnel survey　隧道测量
bridge axis location　桥梁轴线测设
location of pier　桥墩定位
bridge-culvert survey　桥涵洞测量
forest survey　林业测量
forest basic map　林业基本图
stock map，type map　林相图
forest distribution map　森林分布图
compartment survey　林班测量
compass survey　罗盘仪测量
magnetic declination　磁偏角
magnetic dip　磁倾角
magnetic meridian　磁子午线
true meridian　真子午线
magnetic azimuth　磁方位角
magnetic bearings　磁象限角
rural planning survey　乡村规划测量
survey for land smoothing　平整土地测量
land planning survey　土地规划测量
river improvement survey　河道整治测量
irrigation pumping station survey
　　　　　　　　　　　灌溉泵站测量
planimeter method　求积仪法
square method　方格法

grid-point method　网点板法
graphical method　图解法
irrigation layout plan　灌区平面布置图
cadastre　地籍
cadastral survey　地籍测量
cadastral survey system　地籍测量系统
cadastral map　地籍图
cadastral lists　地籍册
land register　地籍簿
cadastral management　地籍管理
cadastral survey manual　地籍测量细则
cadastral map series　地籍图册
tax cadastre　征税地籍
multipurpose cadastre　多用途地籍
photogrammetric cadastre　航测地籍
numerical cadastre　数值地籍
coordinate cadastre　坐标地籍
real estates cadastre　房地产地籍
cadastral revision　地籍修测
renewal of the cadastre　地籍更新
cadastral inventory　地籍调查
land consolidation　土地整理
subdivision of land　土地划分
land evaluation　土地评价
land registration　土地登记
statistics of land record　土地统计
land archives　土地档案
certificate of land　土地证
land use　土地利用
present land-use map　土地利用现状图
land boundary survey　地界测量
property boundary survey　地产界测量
natural boundary survey　自然边界测量
land boundary map　地类界图
parcel survey　地块测量
survey for marking of boundary　标界测量
boundary mark，boundary point　界址点
data base of parcel　地块数据库
clearance limit survey　净空区测量

military engineering survey　军事工程测量
military road survey　军用道路测量
military large scale mapping
　　　　　　　　　　军用大比例尺测图
military bridge survey　军用桥梁测量
military tunnel survey　军用坑道测量
precise alignment　精密准直
plane hole survey　飞机洞库测量
ship's hole survey　航艇洞库测量
quarter building survey　营房建筑测量
missile orientation survey　导弹定向测量

target road engineering survey
　　　　　　　　　　靶道工程测量
military base survey　军事基地测量
precise engineering survey　精密工程测量
precise ranging　精密测距
particle accelerator survey
　　　　　　　　　　粒子加速器测量
ring control network　环形控制网
precise survey at seismic station
　　　　　　　　　　地震台精密测量
precise plumbing　精密垂准

16. Construction Plan（十六、施工计划）

general description of construction
　　　　　　　　　　施工说明
construction permit　施工许可
construction specifications　施工规格
construction design　施工设计
construction phase　施工阶段
construction documents　施工文件
construction error　施工误差
construction worksite　施工现场
project under construction　施工项目
construction efficiency　施工效率
general conditions of construction
　　　　　　　　　　施工总则
construction plan　施工计划
detailed schedule　详细计划/进度表
schedule of construction　施工进度表
schedule of earthworks　土方工程进度表
schedule of material delivery
　　　　　　　　　　材料交付计划
schedule of decoration　装修进度

be ahead of schedule　超进度
maintain a schedule　保持进度
draw up a schedule　制定进度
revise a schedule　修订进度
run on schedule　按进度施工
compliance with a schedule　与计划一致
fulfilment of a schedule　完成计划
departure from a schedule　与计划不符
be behind of schedule　落后于原计划
construction steps　施工步骤
preparations for construction　施工准备
preconstruction stage　施工前阶段
construction management　施工组织
work acceptance　施工验收
inspection of construction　施工检查
supervision of construction　施工监督
construction progress　施工进度
construction period　施工工期
size of construction　施工规模

17. Construction Inspection（十七、施工检查）

safety precautions　安全预防措施
safety regulation　安全规则
total safety control　全面安全管理
safety education　安全教育

safety inspection　安全检查
safety apparatus　安全设施
safety measures　安全措施
safety code　安全操作规程

safety in operation   安全操作
labour safety   劳动安全
labour protection   劳动保护
labour insurance   劳动保险
site security   现场安全措施
construction sign   施工标志
safe and sound   安然无恙
labour protective supervision
　　　　　　　　　劳动保护监督
construction regulations   施工规则
labour protection appliances   劳动保护用品
safety helmet   安全帽
safety belt   安全带
safety lamp   安全灯
safety catch   安全档
safety chain   安全链

protective clothing   安全服
quality management   质量管理
engineering quality   工程质量
quality standard   质量标准
quality control   质量控制
quality inspection   质量检查
quality supervision   质量监督
site inspection   现场检验
site investigation   现场调查
limiting quality   极限质量
acceptable quality   合格质量
defective works   劣质工程
high quality project   优质工程
acceptance test   验收检验
quality certification system   质量保证制度

18．Building Installation(十八、建筑安装)

equipment arrangement   设备布置
installation drawing   安装图
sanitary fittings   卫生器具
pipes and fittings   管子与管件
water supply works   给水工程
water supply fittings   给水配件
water supply pipes   给水管道
riser water pipe   直立水管
water meter   水表
shower and bathtub   淋浴和浴盆
drainage works   排水工程
sewerage fittings   排水管件
floor drain   地漏
rain-water pipe   雨水管道
flange   法兰
heating works   采暖工程
heating installation   供暖安装
heating pipe   供暖管道
heating radiator   供暖散热器

plumber's tools   水暖工工具
ventilating works   通风工程
ventilation installation   通风安装
ventilation facilities   通风设施
dust keeper   除尘装置
air-conditioning equipment   空调设备
electrical installation   电气安装
electrical works   电气工程
electrical construction   电气施工
lighting engineering   电气照明工程
architectural lighting   建筑照明
circuit installation   线路安装
electrical materials   电气材料
electric welding works   电焊工程
welding technique   焊接技术
riveting works   铆接工程
fitter's works   设备安装工程
measuring tools   量具
steel structural works   钢结构工程

19. Building Decoration(十九、建筑装饰)

wall decoration　墙面装饰
decorative arts　装饰艺术
interior decoration　室内装饰
exterior decoration　室外装饰
folding screen　屏风
folding partition　折壁
mural　壁画
fiber board ceiling　纤维板顶棚
embossing　雕刻凸饰
carved figures　雕刻画像
decorative materials　装饰材料
white cement　白水泥
hemp cut　麻刀
lime putty　白灰膏
straw pulp　纸筋
granite　花岗石
aluminium alloy　铝合金
non-fading coloured paint　不褪色面漆
mosaic　马赛克
quarry tile　缸砖
ceramic ware　陶瓷制品
glazed brick　釉面砖
dolomite　白云石
brocatelle　彩色大理石
face brick　面砖
terrazzo tile　水磨石
adhesive　胶黏剂
plastic steel　塑钢
marble　大理石
stainless steel　不锈钢
glass cutter　玻璃刀
putty knife　油灰刀
working bench　工作台
wooden decoration materials　木装饰材料
plastering tools　粉刷工具
scratching board　刮板
chalk line case　粉线盒
wood-working machines　木工机械

20. Common Wood(二十、常见木材)

FIGURED ANEGRE　红影
FIGURED MAKORE　麦哥利
ASPEN　亚士宾
FIGURED AVIGA　亚米加虎影
PERO　美洲梨木
SWISS PEAR　瑞士梨木
BIRCH　桦木
MAPLE　枫木
TEAKWOOD　柚木
EBONY　乌木(黑檀木)
WENGE　乌班木
WHITE ASH　白栓木
ZEBRANO　斑马木
BLISSWOOD　碧灰木
BOXWOOD　盒木
BRASSWOOD　巴式木
BRONZEWOOD　铜木
BROWNWOOD　咖啡木
CHARCOALWOOD　炭木
GOLD TAU　金檀木
LAND TAU　地檀木
SKY TAU　天檀木
SUNTAU　太檀木
SEA TAU　海檀木
SILKYOAK　丝绸橡木
GRAYWOOD　灰栓木
GREENWOOD　格兰木
HAZELWOOD　紫粟木
LAND CROCODILE　灰鳄木
WHITE CROCODILE　白鳄木
CREAMYCROCODILE　乳鳄木
DARK CROCODILE　黑鳄木
LACEWOOD　尼丝木
FIGURED MAPLE　有影枫木

BIRCH BURL　桦木树根
BIRD'S EYE MAPLE　雀眼枫木
BUBINGA POMELE　花梨保美利
MAKORE POMELE　麦哥利保美利
MAPLEPOMELE　枫木保美利
FIGURED EUCALYPTUS　有影尤加利
XENON FRISE　式龙影木
COPPER FRISE　灰影木
COPPERACER　铜板影
SAPELE　沙比利
GOLDENACER　金枫影
SILVER FRISE　银影
SILVERACER　银枫影
MOUVINGUE　金影
SYCAMORE　白影（欧洲）
LEMON POPLAR　柠檬杨
DARKERABLE　黑雀眼
GREY ERABLE　灰雀眼
BUBINGA　花梨直纹

RED OAK　红橡直纹
LARCH　松木直纹
BEECH　红榉直纹
ASH　栓木直纹
WHITE OAK　白橡直纹
CHERRY　樱桃
FIGURED CURLY MAPLE　卷纹枫影
MAPPABURL　白杨树根
MAPLE BURL　枫木树根
LAUELBURL　月桂树根
MADRONA BURL　麦当娜树根
LACEWOODBURL　尼丝木树根
VAVONA BURL　苇云娜树根
SANTOSROSEWOOD　山度士酸枝
INDIAN ROSEWOOD　印度酸枝
KAYA　桃花芯
MAHOGANY POMELE　球纹桃花芯
LAUROPRETO　普利托月桂
WALNUT　黑胡桃

21．Building Cost（二十一、建筑造价）

estimate/cost estimate　估算/费用估算
types of estimate　估算类型
equipment estimate　设备估算
control estimate　控制估算
analysis estimate　分析估算
proposal estimate　报价估算
initial control estimate　初期控制估算
check estimate　核定估算
direct material cost　直接材料费用
equipment cost　设备费用
bulk material cost　散装材料费用
construction cost　施工费用
labor cost 施工人工费用
standard hours　标准工时
labor productivity　劳动生产率
manhours rate　人工时单价
cost of construction supervision
　　　　　　　　　施工监督费

indirect cost of construction　施工间接费用
subcontract cost　分包合同费用
non payroll　非工资费用
profit/expected profit　利润/预期利润
service gains　服务酬金
risk analysis　风险分析
risk memorandum　风险备忘录
contingency　未可预见费
client change　用户变更
approved client change　认可的用户变更
pending client change　待定的用户变更
project change　项目变更
contract change　合同变更
internal change　内部变更
authorised change　批准的变更
mandatory change　强制性变更
optional change　选择性变更
internal transfer　内部费用转换

escalation 涨价值
lump sum contract 总价合同

reimbursible contract 偿付合同

22. Claims of Construction Works(二十二、工程索赔)

abide by the contract 遵守合同
accept a claim 接受索赔
refuse a claim 拒绝索赔
waive a claim 放弃索赔
satisfy a claim 满足索赔
clear up a claim 清理索赔
act of god 天灾，不可抗力
amicable settlement 友好解决
amount of claim 索赔额
cause for claim 索赔原因
claim for quantity 数量索赔
claim for quality 质量索赔
claim for construction period 工期索赔
procedure for claims 索赔程序
claim sheet 索赔清单
claims agent 索赔代理
notice of claim 索赔通知
claim adjuster 索赔理算人
claimer 索赔人
compensator 赔偿人
blanket claim 一揽子索赔
claim right 索赔权

claim management 索赔管理
assessment of claims 索赔评定
detailed claim 详细索赔
interim claim 中间索赔
final claim 最终索赔
payment of claims 索赔的支付
unreasonable claim 不合理的索赔
valid period of claim 索赔时效
claim for additional payment 索赔额外费用
contractual claims 合同规定的索赔
arbitration agreement 仲裁协议
arbitration award 仲裁解决
place of arbitration 仲裁地点
rules for arbitration 仲裁规则
notice of default 违约通知
substantiation of claim 索赔证明
conflict of interest 利益冲突
potential dispute 潜在争议
defect liability 缺陷责任
default party 违约方

23. Acceptance of Construction Works(二十三、工程验收)

building appraisement 工程评价
judgement of quality 质量评定
acceptance check 验收检查
acceptance standard 验收标准
acceptance procedure 验收程序
acceptance certificate 验收证书
function of acceptance 验收函数
limit of acceptance 验收界限
acceptance lot 验收批量
acceptance code 验收规范
completion certificate 完工证书

QA/QC inspection forms 质保/质控文件
survey records 测量记录
execution-tracing files 隐蔽工程记录
construction tolerance 施工允许误差
refer to working drawing 参见施工图
inspection certificate 检验合格证
inspection of works progress 工序检查
construction plan 施工方案
quality management 质量管理
standardized works 标准化工程
technical sampling 抽样法

taking-over procedure   移交程序
as-built drawing   竣工图纸
minor items   细小项目
performance test   性能试验
completion report   竣工报告
written undertaking   书面承诺，书面保证

excellent execution certificate   优质竣工证书
bonus for early completion   提前竣工奖
substantial completion   实质性竣工
practical completion   基本竣工

APPENDIX Ⅴ   References
附录5　参考书目

[1] 姜海燕.建筑专业英语[M].北京：中国建材工业出版社，2003
[2] 盛根有.建筑技术与管理英语情景会话[M].北京：中国建筑工业出版社，2008
[3] 盛根有.建筑施工现场英语情景会话[M].北京：中国建筑工业出版社，2010
[4] 盛根有.建筑校园与国外生活英语情景会话[M].北京：中国建筑工业出版社，2011
[5] 夏行时，江景波.英汉土木建筑大词典[M].北京：中国建筑工业出版社，1999
[6] 俞戊孙.建筑施工实用英语会话[M].北京：中国建筑工业出版社，1999
[7] 张水波，刘英.国际工程管理实用英语口语[M].北京：中国建筑工业出版社，1997